INDEPENDENT AUDITOR'S GUIDE TO OPERATIONAL AUDITING

MODERN ACCOUNTING
PERSPECTIVES AND PRACTICE

Gary John Previts, Series Editor

PRACTICAL ACCOUNTING FOR LAWYERS
Robert O. Berger, Jr.

INDEPENDENT AUDITOR'S GUIDE TO OPERATIONAL AUDITING
Dale L. Flesher and Stewart Siewert

AN ACCOUNTANT'S GUIDE TO COMPUTER SYSTEMS
William E. Perry

INDEPENDENT AUDITOR'S GUIDE TO OPERATIONAL AUDITING

Dale L. Flesher
University of Mississippi

Stewart Siewert
Deloitte Haskins & Sells

A RONALD PRESS PUBLICATION

JOHN WILEY & SONS

New York · Chichester · Brisbane · Toronto · Singapore

Library of Congress Cataloging in Publication Data

Flesher, Dale L.
  Independent auditor's guide to operational auditing.

  (Modern accounting perspectives and practice)
  "A Ronald Press Publication."
  Includes index.
  1. Management audit.   I. Siewert, Stewart.
II. Title.

HD58.95.F55   658.4   81-19726
ISBN 0-471-09368-8   AACR2

Printed in the United States of America

10 9 8 7 6 5 4 3 2 1

*To our wives, Tonya K. Flesher
and Ann T. Siewert*

PREFACE

An operational audit is an organized search for ways of improving efficiency and effectiveness. Although popularized by internal auditors and the federal government's General Accounting Office, operational auditing is increasingly being performed by independent auditors and management consultants. Many industrial managers are performing self-audits. Since operational audits are undertaken to produce greater efficiency, effectiveness, and economy, the problems of inflation and energy use mean a greater number of audits are going to be conducted in future years. Some large CPA firms are specializing in operational audits of energy use called energy audits. In addition, CPA firms that perform audits for federal or other government agencies are required to perform an operational audit along with the traditional financial audit.

As more accounting firms, management consulting firms, and corporations have realized the potential of operational audits, the demand for practical guidelines has increased. This book is a "how-to-do-it" guide, which should probably be the constant companion of the operational auditor. The first two chapters give an overview of operational auditing. The third chapter deals with the procedural aspects of engagement letters, working papers, and audit reports. Chapter 4 discusses the implications of program evaluation audits for government agencies. Chapters 5 through 16 consist of individual programs (questionnaires) for auditing each department or function of a company. One chapter is devoted to energy use (although no company has a separate energy department or function, the subject of energy audits is worth separate mention because of the importance of energy conservation).

DALE L. FLESHER
STEWART SIEWERT

University, Mississippi
Memphis, Tennessee
March 1982

CONTENTS

INDEPENDENT AUDITOR'S GUIDE TO OPERATIONAL AUDITING

part one

BACKGROUND FOR AN OPERATIONAL AUDIT

one

OPERATIONAL AUDITING— A JOB FOR THE INDEPENDENT AUDITOR

An operational audit is a nonfinancial audit whose purpose is to appraise the managerial organization and efficiency of a company or part of a company. It can be considered a form of constructive criticism.

Known by many names, it appears in the literature as operations auditing, management auditing, performance auditing, systems auditing, efficiency auditing, expanded scope auditing among others. As might be expected of a concept bearing many different names, its purposes and objectives have been defined in a variety of ways. At one extreme, operational auditing is "characterized more by a state of mind than by distinctive methods."[1] At the other extreme, it "results in a statement of opinion by a CPA with regard to the performance of the management function."[2] The authors of one article even attempted to develop the underlying postulates of the theory of operational auditing as it might be performed as merely an extension of the annual financial audit.[3]

Perhaps the following "middle-of-the-road" definition is more appropriate and useful in explaining the scope of this book. Operational auditing is:

---

[1]Bradford Cadmus, *Operational Auditing Handbook* (New York: Institute of Internal Auditors, 1964), p. 51.

[2]Neil C. Churchill and Richard M. Cyert, "An Experiment in Management Auditing," *Journal of Accountancy* (February 1966), p. 39.

[3]Harold Q. Langenderfer and Jack C. Robertson, "A Theoretical Structure for Independent Audits of Management," *Accounting Review* (October 1969), p. 777.

3

A systematic review and evaluation of an organization, or subunit thereof, made with the purpose of determining whether the organization is operating efficiently. It is, in effect, an organized search for efficiency-related problems within the organization.[4]

There are two reasons for not accepting the definition that equates operational auditing with the CPA's opinion of the performance of management. First, there are no objective and generally accepted measurement standards for determining the efficiency of management. Second, CPA's would be exposed to an unprecedented degree of liability to third parties if they attempted to give opinions on various human qualities. The search for efficiency-related problems avoids these two pitfalls.

Other helpful published definitions of operational auditing include the following:

Operations auditing is a technique for regularly and systematically appraising unit or function effectiveness against corporate and industry standards by utilizing personnel who are not specialists in the area of study with the objectives of assuring a given management that its aims are being carried out and/or identifying conditions capable of being improved.[5]

Operations auditing is a review and appraisal of the efficiency and effectiveness of operations and operating procedures. It carries with it the responsibility to discover and inform top management of operating problems, but its chief purpose is assisting management to solve problems by recommending realistic courses of action.[6]

This last definition is not completely acceptable because it states that the auditor should include specific recommendations and courses of action. Although many authors have defined operational auditing as both a problem-finding and problem-solving tool, the most recent works on the topic have emphasized that the tool is useful only to determine what efficiency- and effectiveness-related problems exist. There is nothing new about trying to solve problems; it is the technique of trying to find problems that is more recent. The job of operational auditing is not necessarily to suggest how problems could be solved.[7] The job is usually

---

[4]Corinne T. Norgaard, "The Professional Accountant's View of Operational Auditing," *Journal of Accountancy* (December 1969), p. 46.
[5]Roy A. Lindberg and Theodore Cohn, *Operations Auditing* (New York: American Management Association, 1972), p. 16.
[6]Peter A. Phyrr, "Operational Auditing: A Run for Day-Light," *Financial Executive* (May 1969), p. 19.
[7]Lindberg and Cohn, *op. cit.*, p. 8.

considered finished when the problems have been located, identified, and defined. Developing solutions is the job of management, management consultants, or the management services department of a CPA firm.

Solving identified problems is not a new concept; the systematic search for problems and for opportunities to increase efficiency is new. However, this is not to say that the typical engagement for a CPA firm does not entail solving problems. Indeed, the client often wants the CPA to recommend solutions for problems that are uncovered. However, by definition, recommending solutions is not an auditing job, but a management services function. This book cannot tell how to solve a problem since the solution will depend on the company under audit. This book covers the basic field of operational auditing, defined as the problem-finding stage of the typical operational audit engagement. The problem-solving stage, if requested by the client, follows the audit and relies on the auditor's experience.

In the operational audit, the auditor tries to determine the extent to which company objectives have been achieved. One author defined the audit as follows:

> Operational auditing is using common sense, or logical audit techniques, with management perspective, and applying them to company objectives, operations, controls, communications and information systems. The auditor is more concerned with the who, what, when, where, why and how of running an efficient and profitable business than just the accounting and financial aspects of the business functions.[8]

Of course, not everyone supports the concept of operational auditing. One corporate finance director stated that the "management audit would seem to be the latest in the series of cure-all packages thrust upon unwary industrialists by well-meaning academics or more commercial profit-seekers."[9]

Despite a few critics, operational auditing does fill a need for a valuable management tool. As business and government grow increasingly large, management finds it increasingly difficult to keep informed in all areas under its responsibility. Traditional sources of managerial information do not meet all the needs of management in large organizations:

> Central to the whole concept of operations auditing is the idea that, if they are to operate incisively and creatively, managers need some kind of early

---

[8]Anton Steven, "Operational Audits of Construction Contracts," *The Internal Auditor,* XXX (May–June 1973), p. 10.

[9]J. Santocki, "Management Audit—Chance, Challenge, or Lost Opportunity," *The Accountant,* CLXX (January 3, 1974), p. 16.

warning system for the detection of potentially destructive problems and opportunities for improvement. That is, modern business has had to develop ways to anticipate and cope with the heightened risks and more sophisticated resources involved in reaching its objectives.

Operations auditing is one of those ways.[10] With the use of operational auditing, management can maintain its effectiveness despite the growing complexity of the company and the constantly increasing demands on management's time from inside and outside the office. Many managers could perform their operational auditing tasks themselves, but most managers are so busy implementing policy that they have little time to take adequate readings of department positions or directions.

THE ROOTS OF OPERATIONAL AUDITING

It is difficult to know exactly when operational auditing began. The Krupp Company in Germany apparently carried on some form of operational auditing as early as 1875, if the company audit manual is any indication:

> The auditors are to determine whether laws, contracts, policies and procedures have been properly observed and whether all business transactions were conducted in accordance with established policies and with success. In this connection, the auditors are to make suggestions for the improvement of existing facilities and procedures, criticisms of contracts with suggestions for improvement, etc.[11]

In the United States in about 1919 one leading railroad utilized its internal auditors to perform an operational audit of dining car service.[12] The auditors' report outlined a wide range of inefficiencies, extravagance, and dishonesty.

Perhaps one speaker summarized the history of operational auditing best with the following statement:

> It seems likely that the operational audit is even older than double-entry bookkeeping, inasmuch as it is purely the product of applied common sense.[13]

---

[10]Lindberg and Cohn, *op. cit.*, p. 6.
[11]Ronald S. Brown, "The Operational Audit," *Lester Witte Report*, V (No. 4, 1974), p. 1.
[12]Reginald H. Jones, "Audit of the Future" (Unpublished speech before the New York City Chapter, Institute of Internal Auditors, February 6, 1969), mimeographed.
[13]*Ibid.*

The development of modern operational auditing has followed two paths. Some aspects of operational auditing were developed by the internal auditing profession. Others came out of the management profession.

The development of operational auditing among internal auditors roughly parallels the history of internal auditing in general. Although the roots of internal auditing go back to the nineteenth century, real growth in the United States began in the early part of the twentieth century, with the rise of the large corporation. Tracing the history of internal auditing:

> The principal factor in its emergence was the extended span of control faced by management in conducting operations from widespread locations. Defalcations and improperly maintained accounting records were obvious problems under these circumstances, and the growth in the volume of transactions presaged a substantial bill for public accounting services for the business that endeavored to solve the problem by continuing the traditional form of audit by the public accountant.[14]

The link between large company size and the employment of internal auditors is demonstrated by a study that showed that in companies that employed internal auditors, there was an average of 769 other employees for each internal auditor.[15]

Early internal auditors focused primarily on the protection of company assets. The National Industrial Conference Board's study of internal auditing explained this early role as follows:

> Protection of company assets and detection of fraud were the principal objectives. Consequently, the auditors concentrated most of their attention on examinations of financial records and on the verification of assets that were most easily misappropriated. A popular idea among management people a generation ago was that the main purpose of an auditing program was to serve as a psychological deterrent against wrongdoing by other employees.[16]

There was little need for the pioneer internal auditor to perform the expanded functions handled by today's internal auditors:

> In less complicated times, of course, management frequently maintained control over company operations by personal supervision. There were not

---

[14]Howard F. Stettler, *Systems Based Independent Audits,* 2nd ed. (Englewood Cliffs, New Jersey: Prentice-Hall, 1974), p. 78.
[15]*Internal Auditing,* Studies in Business Policy, No. 111 (New York: National Industrial Conference Board, 1963), p. 9.
[16]*Ibid.,* p. 4.

so many levels of authority separating policy makers from production workers, and demands on senior executives' time were neither so numerous nor so urgent. The need had not yet arisen to adapt the internal auditing function to the requirements of an elaborate management control system.[17]

This old, defensive concept of internal auditing was really a form of insurance. Its major objective was to uncover fraud before it could be detected by a public accountant during the annual audit. The modern internal auditor, on the other hand, is an "arm of management." He is no longer strictly a policeman, but an integral part of the management process.

The year 1941 marked a major turning point in the development of internal and operational auditing. The first major book on the subject, Victor Z. Brink's *Internal Auditing*, was published and the Institute of Internal Auditors was formed by 24 individuals. The institute grew rapidly during the 1940s.

During the 1940s, internal auditors began to expand their audits to encompass much more than the traditional financial audit. The term "operations" or "operational" auditing was adopted to describe the expanded activity. The first article in *The Internal Auditor* to describe the expanded scope audit was in March 1948, when Arthur H. Kent's "Audits of Operations" appeared. In that article, Kent made frequent mention of an "operations audit." Earlier authors had discussed the subject, but had referred to "non-accounting matters," instead of "operational" subjects. The first technical paper to use the phrase "operational auditing" in the title was published in *The Internal Auditor* in June 1954. That article was written by Frederic E. Mints. Mints later recalled that the term "operational" evolved in a 1953 brainstorming session with Arthur Kent before Mints was to deliver a speech. The two men considered several labels and finally decided that "operational" had the most ear appeal. Mints has stated that he later had some regrets about using the term. Following the publication of Mints' article, there have been hundreds of publications in professional journals on the subject.

Perhaps the Institute of Internal Auditors best described the broad role of internal auditing in its 1957 *Statement of Responsibilites of the Internal Auditor*. According to that publication, the services that the internal auditor provides to management include such activities as:

1. Reviewing and appraising the soundness, adequacy and application of accounting, financial and operating controls.

[17]*Ibid.*, p. 4.

2. Ascertaining the extent of compliance with established policies, plans and procedures.

3. Ascertaining the extent to which company assets are accounted for, and safeguarded from, losses of all kinds.

4. Ascertaining the reliability of accounting and other data developed within the organization.

5. Appraising the quality of performance in carrying out assigned responsibilities.[18]

Note that three of the above categories (1, 2, and 5) are activities normally included in the duties of an operational auditor.

The author of a more recent book on the subject of internal auditing emphasized the management services and management auditing aspects of the profession.[19] An article by the same author tends to indicate that "operational auditing" and "modern internal auditing" are virtually synonymous.[20] Although this writer realizes that there has been a great change in the duties of the internal auditor during the past decade, there is some doubt that the two functions are as similar as many internal auditors believe.

The 1963 study by the National Industrial Conference Board surveyed 177 companies about the principal objectives of the companies' internal auditing programs. The five primary objectives were as follows:

1. Determine the adequacy of the system of internal control.

2. Investigate compliance with company policies and procedures.

3. Verify the existence of assets, see that proper safeguards for assets are maintained and prevent or discover fraud.

4. Check on the reliability of the accounting and reporting system.

5. Report findings to management and recommend corrective action where necessary.[21]

These primary objectives of internal auditing were followed by several secondary objectives:

Aid in promoting accounting efficiency

[18]*Statement of Responsibilities of the Internal Auditor* (Orlando, Florida: Institute of Internal Auditors, 1957).
[19]Lawrence B. Sawyer, *Modern Internal Auditing* (Orlando, Florida: Institute of Internal Auditors, 1973).
[20]Lawrence B. Sawyer, "Just What is Management Auditing?," *The Internal Auditor*, XXX (March–April, 1973), pp. 10–21.
[21]Internal Auditing, *op. cit.*, p. 5.

Provide a training ground for personnel

Supplement the work of the public accountants and cooperate with them on the annual audit

Appraise personnel performance

Investigate compliance with rules of regulatory agencies

Assist in profit improvement activities

Provide general assistance to management

Assist in instituting new procedures[22]

It is interesting to note that the objectives of "appraise personnel performance," "assist in profit improvement activities," "provide general assistance to management," and "assist in instituting new procedures" were included in the list of secondary objectives. Yet all these would be considered an aspect of operational auditing. Perhaps another study of the principal objectives of internal auditing is needed to determine whether the objectives have really changed during the past decade or whether internal auditors are only fooling themselves.

Various governmental audit agencies have led in the development of operational auditing procedures. The General Accounting Office (GAO), particularly, has played a major role in broadening the scope of the auditor. That organization's publication, *Standards for Audit of Governmental Organizations, Programs, Activities and Functions*, explains the metamorphosis in the following manner:

> This demand for information has widened the scope of governmental auditing so that such auditing no longer is a function concerned primarily with financial operations. Instead, governmental auditing now is also concerned with whether governmental organizations are achieving the purposes for which programs are authorized and funds are made available, are doing so economically and efficiently, and are complying with applicable laws and regulations.[23]

The auditing standards laid down in that publication apply to all audits relating to government activities whether performed by internal auditors of federal, state, or local governments, or by independent public accountants.

The GAO standards include all of the standards adopted by the AICPA

[22]*Ibid.*, p.5.
[23]*Standards for Audit of Governmental Organizations, Programs, Activities and Functions* (Washington, D.C.: U.S. Government Printing Office, 1974), p. i.

for use in audits to express an opinion of the fairness of financial statements. The governmental audit standards, however, go a step further:

> The interests of many users of reports on government audits are broader than those that can be satisfied by audits performed to establish the credibility of financial reports. To provide for audits that will fulfill these broader interests, the standards in this statement include the essence of those prescribed by the American Institute of Certified Public Accountants and additional standards for audits of a broader scope as will be explained subsequently.[24]

The scope of a governmental audit (i.e., an audit of or for a government agency) is composed of three elements. These are:

1. *Financial and compliance*—determines (a) whether financial operations are properly conducted, (b) whether the financial reports of an audited entity are presented fairly, and (c) whether the entity has complied with applicable laws and regulations.

2. *Economy and efficiency*—determines whether the entity is managing or utilizing its resources (personnel, property, space, and so forth) in an economical and efficient manner and the causes of any inefficiencies or uneconomical practices, including inadequacies in management information systems, administrative procedures, or organizational structure.

3. *Program results*—determines whether the desired results or benefits are being achieved, whether the objectives established by the legislature or other authorizing body are being met, and whether the agency has considered alternatives which might yield desired results at a lower cost.[25]

The typical financial audit would not include elements 2 and 3, which are operational auditing techniques.

Not only was the GAO innovative in defining the scope of its audits, but it has also been quite successful in performing the broadened audits. The successes of the GAO auditors have been reported in newspapers and in accounting journals such as *The Internal Auditor*. As a result, internal auditors in private industry have taken steps to broaden the scope of their audits. Thus the concept of operational auditing is becoming more and more common among internal audit staffs everywhere. A 1971 edition of one leading auditing textbook states:

[24]*Ibid.*, p. 1.
[25]*Ibid.*, p. 2.

Internal auditing activities fall into two major categories: (1) financial and (2) operational or management auditing.[26]

The work of the GAO has led the AICPA to get more actively involved in the subject of operational auditing. The AICPA has recently published a small book entitled *Guidelines for CPA Participation in Government Audit Engagements to Evaluate Economy, Efficiency, and Program Results*.[27] Earlier, an AICPA committee acknowledged the contributions of the GAO in this area:

> The members of the Committee agree with the philosophy and objectives advocated by the GAO in its standards and believe that the GAO's broadened definition of auditing is a logical and worthwhile continuation of the evolution and growth of the auditing discipline.[28]

At the same time that internal auditors were developing the concept of operational auditing, a similar practice called "management auditing" was being developed by the management profession. The first book on the subject, *The Management Audit*, by T. G. Ross, was published in 1932 in London.[29] The book recommended a questionnaire-type interview which was designed to analyze departmental activities. In 1940 the Metropolitan Life Insurance Company published a similar guide entitled *Outline for a Management Audit*. The Metropolitan Life publication expanded on the work of Ross, but was not nearly as sophisticated as Howard G. Benedict's *Yardsticks of Management*,[30] published in 1948. Benedict's questionnaire had nine major divisions and attempted to evaluate management by means of factorial analysis. These works represented the earliest attempts to develop the interview type of management audit, but none of them generated much interest among management professionals. In the 1950s the subject of management auditing received a great deal of attention in management literature. Throughout the 1950s, the American Institute of Management published books and case studies on the subject of management audits. The institute even published a periodical for a

---

[26]Arthur W. Holmes and Wayne S. Overmyer, *Auditing Principles and Procedures* (Homewood, Illinois: Richard D. Irwin, 1971), p. 133.
[27]*Guidelines for CPA Participation in Government Audit Engagements to Evaluate Economy, Efficiency, and Program Results* (New York: AICPA, 1977).
[28]*Auditing Standards Established by the GAO—Their Meaning and Significance to CPAs* (New York: AICPA, 1973), p. 12.
[29]T. G. Ross, *The Management Audit* (London: Gee & Co., 1932).
[30]Howard G. Benedict, *Yardsticks of Management* (Los Angeles: Management Book Company, 1948).

short while entitled *The Management Audit*. By the early 1960s, the fields of management auditing and operational auditing began to merge, as internal auditors saw the merits of the management literature. Today the two terms are considered to be synonymous.

The Scope of the Engagement

The biggest difference between the traditional financial audit and the operational audit is in the scope of the engagement. The traditional financial audit has the objective of determining the fairness of financial statements, placing great emphasis on the internal controls of the company. The operational audit includes a review of the objectives of the company, the environment in which the company operates, its operating policies, personnel, and even its physical facilities. The operational auditor uses a great variety of tools to obtain the information necessary to fulfill the objectives of the audit.

The evaluation aspects of an operational audit require the auditor to utilize several procedures that are not usually part of the financial audit. The similarity of the two types of audits is that the auditor measures against certain standards in performing both audits.

The standards used in an operational audit come from two basic sources. These two sources are the individual company and the industry of which the company is a part. Company standards include lists of objectives, goals, plans, budgets, records of past performance, policies, procedures, and directives. Industry sources include industry averages and common business practices. These are not always objective standards, so the auditor should not accept an engagement to render an opinion to a third party, but subjective judgments can be used to identify possible problem areas. Remember, the objective of an operational audit is to point out situations where efficiency and effectiveness can be improved.

In the overall approach to an operational audit, the auditor:

1. Seeks out and identifies company objectives.
2. Determines the pertinent facts and conditions.
3. Defines problem areas or opportunities for improved efficiency, effectiveness, and economy.
4. Presents the findings to management.

Since operational auditing standards can never be precisely defined, it is the responsibility of the auditor to use good judgment in all phases of the work. Because of the judgmental nature of the work, operational auditing can provide its practitioners an outstanding opportunity for professional fulfillment.

SOURCES OF DATA

The sources of the operational auditor's data include a physical tour of the plant or department, interviews in each functional area with the use of management and operational control questionnaires, and financial analysis work.

An operational audit normally begins with an orientation meeting with high-level management to discuss the scope of the audit, the reason for the audit, and the broad policies, goals, and objectives of the company. This orientation meeting is followed by a preliminary audit of the company. The preliminary audit usually includes a physical tour of all facilities and interviews in each functional area (or at least those areas that might economically gain from an intensive operational audit effort). Occasionally the preliminary audit can be eliminated because management already knows what departments it wishes to have audited in depth. A company might want an audit of a production department, for example, where frequent slowdowns occur or a purchasing department where there have been costly delays in obtaining key materials. Energy use is another area that has been subject to audit quite often in recent years; some large CPA firms and management consultants now even specialize in energy audits. In practice, the one or two departments that are audited are those where an audit will yield the greatest savings to the company. It should be remembered that operational audits are not mandatory and such audits must be justified to management on the basis of their cost/benefit ratio. Therefore the auditor must limit his study to the areas where he can do the most good.

Financial analysis plays a key role in the preliminary part of the operational audit. Various financial ratios for the company for the current year, for previous years, and for the industry as a whole can be useful tools to help the auditor spot trends of increasing efficiency or patterns of decreasing efficiency. It is often argued that, because these ratios are already available to management, the operational auditor is not performing a unique service. The question is, though, does management have time to find out what the ratios are and does management know what the ratios really mean? The auditor's first recommendation might just be that management start utilizing the ratios that are available to them.

Once the preliminary audit has been completed, the auditor should prepare an audit report (often called a survey memorandum), but this is only for personal use. The survey memorandum should not be submitted to anyone, because it is based on inconclusive evidence. The only reason for a survey memorandum is to enable the auditor to collect his thoughts prior to selecting a particular department or functional area for further audit. Although the preliminary audit may indeed indicate inefficiency in a particular area, the auditor normally has not done sufficient work to be certain of that fact, nor does he know the causes of the inefficiency.

After the preliminary audit and survey memorandum have been completed, the auditor selects the department for the in-depth audit. There are three broad sources of information that the auditor should utilize during the in-depth state of the audit: (1) people, (2) internal documents, and (3) direct observation.

The people working in the department being audited are the primary source of audit data. The use of a well-conducted interview and a good questionnaire are essential. The time invested in developing a good questionnaire is the most rewarding part of the operational auditing process. The use of a thorough questionnaire ensures that audit coverage is complete and that all audits are uniform in scope. The questionnaires should be used with different respondents to obtain several answers to each question. This is not a wasteful step, because the auditor is more likely to unearth the truth about a situation when he obtains several different viewpoints.

The internal documents of a department that an operational auditor should obtain include such items as procedures manuals, organization charts, flow charts, recruiting brochures, advertisements, financial statements, budgets, and variance reports.

Finally, direct observation is a powerful tool that can uncover otherwise hidden problems of inefficiency or ineffectiveness and problems that employees are trying to hide or of which they are not aware. Observation also provides a source of examples which will be useful later in illustrating general conclusions. In fact, some auditors carry a camera so that they can buttress their recommendations with pictures.

Once the in-depth audit of a department has been completed, it should be followed by an exit interview with personnel from the department. A discussion of the audit results will benefit both the auditor and the department employees. The employees can get a head start on solving the problems that have been identified and the auditor can get another opportunity to test the findings before filing the final audit report. In fact, a rough draft of the final audit report should be available for discussion. As an example, the auditor may have overlooked the fact that a particular inefficiency is unavoidable owing to regulatory requirements. Explaining this to the auditor before the final report is complete, the department head can save the auditor from embarrassment. Although there will often be disagreement about how important some problems are, the conflicting views may add insight into the problem.

The end product of an operational audit is a formal, written report to the management of the company. The report should detail the problems that have been found. The purpose of the report is to advise management how the company can become more efficient and more effective; therefore, the report should include plenty of examples, photographs, charts, graphs, and schedules. It might even be advisable to include some of the comments made by the managers in the units audited (usually those obtained during the exit interview).

LIMITATIONS OF OPERATIONAL AUDITING

Operational auditing will not solve all of the world's problems. Like anything else, operational auditing has its limitations. The principal constraints on the operational auditor are time, knowledge, and cost. Time is a limiting factor, because the auditor must inform management about problems quickly enough for it to attack them. Therefore, it is imperative that operational audits be performed with sufficient regularity to ensure that major problems do not become entrenched in the company.

A lack of knowledge is the most common complaint about operational auditors. It would be impossible for the operational auditor to be expert in every area of business. As a rule, operational auditors are better trained in auditing than in the client's business. It is precisely this factor that has brought CPAs into operational auditing. Because departments are audited by individuals who are not technically qualified in the field being audited, the audit must necessarily be limited to major deficiencies.

The operational auditor must always remember that cost is a limitation of the job. The operational auditor is trying to save money for a client. Therefore, the cost of the audit must be less than the problem being solved. This means that the auditor must often overlook smaller problem situations which would be expensive to isolate. In order to weigh costs, some companies require the operational auditor to put a dollar value on each problem he identifies.

Although the definition of operational auditing still varies among accountants (a limitation in itself), the concept is a useful tool. In fact, operational auditing can be called the intelligence system of management.

Why an Independent Public Accountant?

There is some question about who should perform operational audits. The first problem is whether audits should be performed by personnel within the company or by outsiders. Second, should operational audits be performed by accountants or by some other professional group?

The question of internal auditor/external auditor is related to the size of the company. Many companies cannot afford to hire a full-time in-house operational auditor. Therefore, these companies must rely on outsiders to perform operational audits. Even a large company which could afford to have a full-time operational audit staff,—some authorities apparently believe—might be better off retaining outside auditors:

> I have known many instances where internal auditors have made truly excellent suggestions for achieving improvements. For any one of several practical obstacles—possibly personal politics or the general unwillingness to change on the part of other company officials—such suggestions may not have been implemented. The outside auditors, by virtue of their independence and objectivity, can repeat and reinforce these suggestions.[31]

The publisher of *Forbes* magazine discussed the problem in the "Fact and Comment" section:

> Why do corporate managers tell all to outside management consultants and clam up with inhouse talent trying to do the same sort of analysis? Principally because the outside experts are not seeking to replace all the vice presidents and managers to whom they talk. A called-in management consultant usually settles only for the CEO's job.[32]

Whatever the reason, an outsider often seems to be able to accomplish something an equally talented employee cannot. The American Institute of Certified Public Accountants has finally recognized the role of the independent CPA in performing operational audits with the publication of a special report, *Operational Auditing by CPA Firms.*[33]

The other major question with respect to who should perform the operational audit is whether these audits belong in the realm of the accountant. Historically, operational audits have been performed by internal auditors. Because internal auditors usually have an accounting background, the performance of operational audits has been associated with the accounting profession. The term "audit" connotes accounting, which in itself prompts many calls to accountants. For their part, most accounting firms with management services departments feel that opera-

---

[31]William B. Haase, "Cooperation Makes the Difference," *Internal Auditor* (July–August 1973), p. 43.
[32]Malcolm S. Forbes, "Fact and Comment," *Forbes* CXIV, (October 1, 1974), p. 18.
[33]*Operational Auditing by CPA Firms* (New York: AICPA, 1980).

tional audit engagements can eventually lead to profitable management services jobs.

The performance of operational audits, however, does not necessarily require an accounting background. Some management lenting consulting firms also undertake such engagements, although most do not, because they feel that their real strength lies in problem-solving, not problem-locating.[34]

Some accountants accept such engagements only out of fear that otherwise someone else will take the engagement and use it to get a foot in the door to obtain the annual financial audit engagement. It should be noted that a partial operational audit is usually performed in connection with the financial audit. This mini-operational audit culminates in the management letter that is (supposedly)[35] given to management annually at the completion of the audit. Although the CPA is required only to discuss the more material internal control weaknesses in this letter, most firms usually include a discussion of any inefficiencies uncovered during the course of the financial audit.

Most national CPA firms perform a large number of operational audits and many regional firms have also recognized the potential of such engagements. CPA firms should be willing to provide operational audit services at a nominal charge for two reasons. First, the work can be scheduled during slack periods of the year. Second, it can be an adjunct to the firm's management services division, which can help the client implement the recommendations. In fact, the firm may find it advisable to place knowledgeable members of the management service staff on the audit team. The audit would benefit from their expertise, and the firm would gain from their working relationship with the client. There is no consensus among CPA firms as to which of their staff members should perform operational audits. Some firms use only their auditing personnel, some use only management services staff members, and others use a group of both types of employees.

Perhaps another definition of operational auditing can help explain why accountants can perform operational audits as well, or better than, other professional groups:

> The most important thing to appreciate is that there is no such thing as an operational audit. It is a question of approach and scope—the audit techniques are the same.[36]

[34]Lindberg and Cohn, *op. cit.*, p. 15.
[35]Neil Doppelt, "Operational Auditing and the Management Letter," *Journal of Accountancy*, CXXXIII (August, 1971), p. 80.
[36]E. R. Evans, "Some Benefits of Operational Auditing," *Internal Auditor* (March/April 1969), p. 47.

Accountants are qualified to perform operational audits because of their training and experience as auditors, even when the subject is not financial. Furthermore, accountants usually are in a position to have a broad overview of the entire company. This gives them at least some competence in all aspects of the business. Despite the lack of technical skills in a particular business, the accountant can utilize previous audit training and general business sense to capably perform an operational audit.

Both accountants (internal and external) and management consultants perform operational audits. The question of who performs such audits is not important. What is important is the improved efficiency that results from an operational audit. Companies should also consider the possibility of performing self-audits. If certain management-level employees are less busy during some seasons of the year, it might be economical to assign these individuals to the task of performing an operational audit.

Applicable CPA Professional Standards

There are several standards that have been adopted by the accounting profession that apply to operational audit engagements. Both the rules of conduct (ethics code) and several practice and technical standards should be followed by the independent practitioner. Under the category of rules of conduct, the following rules are most applicable to an operational audit engagement:

Rule 102—Integrity and Objectivity. A member shall not knowingly misrepresent facts, and when engaged in the practice of public accounting, including the rendering of tax and management advisory services, shall not subordinate his judgment to others.

Rule 201—General Standards. A member shall comply with the following general standards as interpreted by bodies designated by Council, and must justify any departures therefrom.
A.   Professional competence. A member shall undertake only those engagements which he or his firm can reasonably expect to complete with professional competence.
B.   Due professional care. A member shall exercise due professional care in the performance of an engagement.
C.   Planning and supervision. A member shall adequately plan and supervise an engagement.
D.   Sufficient relevant data. A member shall obtain sufficient relevant data to afford a reasonable basis for conclusions or recommendations in relation to an engagement.

E.   Forecasts. A member shall not permit his name to be used in conjunction with any forecast of future transactions in a manner which may lead to the belief that the member vouches for the achievability of the forecast.

Rule 301—Confidential client information. A member shall not disclose any confidential information obtained in the course of a professional engagement except with the consent of the client.

Rule 302—Contingent fees. Professional services shall not be offered or rendered under an arrangement whereby no fee will be charged unless a specified finding or result is attained, or where the fee is otherwise contingent upon the findings or results of such services. However, a member's fees may vary depending, for example, on the complexity of the service rendered.

Fees are not regarded as being contingent if fixed by courts or other public authorities or, in tax matters, if determined based on the results of judicial proceedings or the findings of governmental agencies.

Rule 501—Acts discreditable. A member shall not commit an act discreditable to the profession.

Rule 502—Advertising and Other Forms of Solicitation. A member shall not seek to obtain clients by advertising or other forms of solicitation in a manner that is false, misleading, or deceptive.

Rule 503—Commission. A member shall not pay a commission to obtain a client, nor shall he accept a commission for a referral to a client of products or services of others. This rule shall not prohibit payments to individuals formerly engaged in the practice of public accounting or payments to their heirs or estates.[37]

All of the above rules are rather self-explanatory, and compliance with them should place no great burden on any firms with respect to their operational audit engagements, particularly since the requirements also apply to financial audit engagements.

The specific technical and practice standards for financial audits do not normally apply to operational audits. However, a few of the Statements on Auditing Standards (SASs) may be applicable in specific situations. Relevant SASs include (1) reviews of and reports on internal control and (2) using the work of a specialist.

Some of the practice standards that apply to management advisory services engagements apply also to operational audits. For example, the following authoritative publications from the AICPA Management Services Guideline Series may provide useful information:

[37]*AICPA Professional Standards,* Vol. 2 (New York: AICPA, 1978).

No. 2. *Documentation Guides for Administration of MAS Engagements.*

No. 5. *Guidelines for Cooperative Management Advisory Services Engagements.*

No. 6. *Guidelines for CPA Participation in Government Audit Engagements to Evaluate Economy, Efficiency, and Program Results.*

For audits of federal agencies and programs, the GAO publication *Standards for Audit of Governmental Organizations, Programs, Activities, and Functions* should be considered the authoritative guide. An AICPA report, *Operational Auditing by CPA Firms,* provides additional insight into the concept of operational audits.

Operational audits by independent accountants are a relatively new concept, as evidenced by the lack of specific, authoritative guidelines. Hence the independent auditor must utilize concepts developed in financial audits and in other fields to complete an operational audit engagement. Subsequent chapters serve as a guide which operational auditors can use in developing this new area of practice.

SUMMARY

The role of the auditor has broadened in recent years. Management has become more aware that the size of big business and the increasing squeeze on management time have caused a need for an outsider who will advise on various aspects of an organization. This need has been filled by operational auditors, who search out inefficiency and ineffectiveness. Operational auditing can be viewed as a control technique that provides management with a method for evaluating the effectiveness of operating procedures and internal controls.

Traditionally, operational audits have been performed by internal auditors. The U.S. General Accounting Office has been a major advocate of the technique. Independent CPA firms began offering operational audit services to fill the needs of companies that did not have an internal audit staff. The CPA firms' annual financial audits were thereby extended and a link provided with their management services departments.

Starting with detailed questionnaires that are used as a basis for interviewing company personnel and adding subsequent financial analysis, the auditor can find problem areas or areas of inefficiency within the company. The auditor attempts to measure what is actually happening against ideal or typical performance standards and then communicates these findings to management. The audit report recommends areas where improvements might be made or notes examples of inefficiencies. It is up to management to determine the solution to the problem. The goal of operational auditing is not to solve problems; the operational auditing job is finished when the problem has been located and communicated to management. However, the typical engagement by independent auditors usually involves solving problems as well as locating them. Thus it is important to differentiate between pure operational auditing as it is defined, and the typical operational auditing engagement in practice. If the client wants the auditor to recommend and implement problem-solving ideas, the auditor should clarify in the original engagement letter what is to be done during this extended engagement.

Operational audits are much broader than financial audits and often more complex. Operational auditing can help management maintain and enhance its effectiveness despite the increased complexity of business. Most managers are too busy implementing policies to take an adequate reading of each department's position or direction.

The operational audit can be a valuable tool in the management information system of an organization. Efficient management is a key to any company's success. Checking and improving the management can be accomplished through the operational audit. As an outsider, the operational auditor does not have to worry about the day-to-day problems of a department but can assess the efficiency and effectiveness of the entire operation. The operational auditor can distinguish between the forest and the trees. Most independent CPAs and management consulting firms are well qualified to perform these audits.

two

A STANDARDIZED FRAMEWORK FOR AN OPERATIONAL AUDIT

An operational audit is a nonfinancial audit of all aspects of an operation. An operational audit is a thorough examination with the objective of appraising managerial organization, performance, and techniques. It might be considered as a type of constructive criticism. The auditor attempts to determine the extent to which company objectives have been achieved.

Operational auditing is a control technique that provides management with a method for evaluating the effectiveness of operating procedures and internal controls. The reduction of waste and inefficiency is a primary goal of an operational auditor. The operational audit is the broadest type of audit and examines all functions of the business. Depending on the scope of the engagement, an operational audit may result in some or all of the following benefits:

1. Identification of previously undefined organization objectives, policies, goals, and procedures.
2. Identification of criteria for measuring the achievement of organization objectives and assessing management performance.
3. An independent, objective evaluation of specified operations (the assessment of performance).
4. Determination of whether the organization is in compliance with objectives, policies, directives, and procedures.
5. Determination of the effectiveness and efficiency of management control systems.

6. Determination of the reliability and usefulness of various management reports.
7. Identification of problem areas and (perhaps) the underlying causes.
8. Identification of opportunities for potential profit improvement, revenue enhancement, and cost reduction or containment within the organization.
9. Identification of alternative courses of action in numerous areas.

As with any type of audit, there are standards against which the auditor compares the performance of the audit client. In a financial audit the auditor uses generally accepted accounting principles as the standard. In an operational audit, the standards are various criteria established by the individual company and the industry of which the company is a part. Examples of operational audit standards include budgets, goals, job descriptions, common business sense, industry averages, and various internal directives.

The audit report resulting from an operational audit consists primarily of recommendations of areas where improvements might be made or emphasizes the absence of problems, where appropriate. The auditor does not necessarily recommend in the audit report what the improvements should be; the objective is only to point out the problems.

Any qualified auditor can perform an operational audit. Traditionally, operational audits have been performed primarily by internal auditors and government audit agencies. The General Accounting Office (GAO) has been particularly effective in this area. A small company without an internal audit staff would find it more economical to (1) use outside auditors for performance of operational audits or (2) to make self audits periodically by administrative personnel. Most large CPA firms place a great amount of emphasis on operational auditing and many regional firms have also recognized the possibilities of such engagements.

THE NEED FOR A MODEL

An operational audit is a large undertaking, no matter who performs the audit. Most businesses are integrated structures consisting of hundreds of functions performed by hundreds of employees. Such is the diversity of the operation that very few employees have identical job descriptions. Thus, the operational auditor needs a framework in which to work. A format, combined with a detailed audit program, provides the necessary groundwork for an operational audit.

Although operational audits have been performed for years by the GAO and numerous private firms, there has never been a comprehensive model developed that was general enough for an outside auditor to use on all companies. This is partly because most operational audits are performed by internal auditors within a single entity. When multiple entities are involved, there is sufficient difference among the entities to limit the possibility of generalizing some parts of the audit. Secondly, the previous lack of a standardized framework for an operational audit may be attributable to a lack of interest in the topic by academicians and researchers, as evidenced by the fact that no major auditing textbook offers more than a couple of paragraphs on the topic and few universities offer a course on the subject.

An audit model is not a new idea. Mautz and Sharaf in their study, *The Philosophy of Auditing*,[1] developed a generalized model for a financial audit. This chapter begins where Mautz and Sharaf stopped, by developing a comprehensive operational audit model. Although there have been many journal articles on the topic of operational auditing, most have been of the definitional type. The most comprehensive work, *Operations Auditing* by Lindberg and Cohn,[2] discusses the topic from the point of view of an internal auditor working in a manufacturing firm. The two-stage aspect of the audit (preliminary and in-depth) advocated in these earlier works is used also in this book. This chapter is primarily concerned with the preliminary stage of the audit.

There are four basic steps in the preliminary stage of the operational audit. These are: (1) a physical walking tour of the facility, (2) acquisition of written data, (3) interviews with management personnel, and (4) certain financial analysis work. The results of these four steps are summarized in a preliminary audit report that is commonly called a survey memorandum. The survey memorandum is not given to anyone; it is used by the auditor to determine which department will require an in-depth audit. An in-depth examination is performed only for those departments which appear to have the most serious problems and which would yield material benefit after their solution. Chapters 5 through 16 cover the in-depth audit for several departments and functions.

---

[1] R. K. Mautz and Hussein A. Sharaf, *The Philosophy of Auditing* (Evanston, Illinois: American Accounting Association, 1961).
[2] Roy A. Lindberg and Theodore Cohn, *Operations Auditing* (New York: American Management Association, 1972), p. 16.

PRELIMINARY STAGE

The preliminary survey stage of the audit permits an orderly approach to planning and carrying out the audit work. Thus the preliminary survey can be an effective guideline for applying scarce auditing resources where they will do the most good. In an audit concerned with economy and efficiency, the preliminary survey efforts will be directed toward locating areas where the most time, money, and other valuable resources can be saved. In an audit concerned with effectiveness or program results, the preliminary survey efforts may be devoted primarily toward identifying program goals and determining whether information necessary for evaluating the results is available.

The scope of the preliminary survey and the time allotted to it will depend on the auditor's training and experience and his or her knowledge of the areas being examined, the type of audit being performed, the size and complexity of the activities or programs being examined, and the geographic range of an organization's operations. Whether the audit is a first-time engagement or a follow-up will also affect the amount of time the auditor spends on the job.

By means of the preliminary survey, the auditor gains enough knowledge to identify important issues and problem areas and to decide whether and where further investigation is needed. At the completion of the preliminary survey, enough information should have been gathered to prepare a systematic plan for conducting the in-depth audit—the "audit program" outlined in Chapters 5 through 16.

Physical Tour

In this first phase of the preliminary audit, direct observation provides an excellent source of information about the company and its subdivisions. The operational auditor must conduct a physical tour of the facilities:

> The auditor who consciously observes will become aware of many problems that are not recorded or are incapable of analysis through data. Feelings of openness, communication freedom, respect for subordinates, manner in which supervision is performed, neatness, housekeeping, and so forth tell a good deal about conditions in the unit being audited. Observation is also a rich source of specific examples that are useful in illustrating general conclusions.[3]

[3]*Ibid.*, p. 36.

Another author explained the physical walk-through as follows:

> Every operations audit includes a survey of physical facilities. One of the purposes of this survey is the identification of areas which appear to merit special attention—the approach follows the "management by exception" philosophy. . . . During this tour the auditor could observe conditions which—perhaps because of their very obviousness—may have escaped the attention of local management.[4]

In the physical tour stage of the operational audit, like all the stages of the audit, the auditor is searching for indications of problems. The criteria and objectives are the same in the physical tour stage for example, as in the interview with management. In effect, the auditor could take the questionnaire used for interviewing management and apply it to the physical tour stage.

A discovery that might be made during a physical walkthrough of an operation might be the existence of idle equipment. This indicates that the company is not earning the maximum return on its investment and perhaps should transfer these idle assets to departments which have a shortage of equipment.

A physical tour of all departments provides the auditor with the opportunity to view the entire operation and obtain an overall impression of the organization. The auditor will usually be accompanied on the tour by a higher-level management official. In a smaller company, this official may be the president, vice president, or controller.

Either prior to, or simultaneous with, the physical tour, the auditor should ask the tour director whether the audit was prompted by a specific problem or intended as a preventive measure. The administrator or controller should acquaint employees with the reasons for the audit and the benefits that are expected. Employees should be made to understand that the audit does not imply criticism of their efforts, but is an effort to make them more effective in their work.

The auditor must keep in mind at all times that the main purpose of the physical tour is to orient the auditor to the company. However, the physical tour is also an integral part of the preliminary stage of the audit, which selects departments for in-depth audit. Thus the physical tour, although often called an orientation tour, is oriented in part toward the discovery of potential cost-saving situations.

---

[4]Felix Pomeranz, "Communications—Raw Material of the Operational Audit," *The Internal Auditor*, XVIII (Winter 1961), p. 23.

Exhibit 2-1 lists the questions that an operational auditor should be thinking about as he or she proceeds through the physical tour of the company. The questions in Exhibit 2-1 have been selected on the basis of discussion with department heads as important criteria for efficient management. All the questions in the questionnaire in Exhibit 2-1 can be answered by observation without explanation from the tour director. The questions have been categorized by department when specific questions apply only to certain departments. Most of the questions are applicable to all departments.

It must be pointed out that no evidence gathered in the preliminary stage of the audit should be considered positive proof of the existence of problems or inefficiency. Although the questions in Exhibit 2-1 have been designed so that a "no" answer indicates a possible problem, this should be considered as prima facie evidence only, because such a small amount of time is spent in each department during the physical tour. Even though the results of the physical tour may give a strong indication that a particular department is having problems, further audit steps (such as the finanacial analysis stage) may indicate otherwise. The objective of the preliminary stage is to make several rather quick analyses and try to pinpoint one or more departments that have more problems than the others. At no time should a department be branded as inefficient during the preliminary stage of the audit; those departments which receive bad scores should be considered "in need of further study."

The operational auditor must remain aware of the fact that the questionnaire for the physical tour is intended to serve only as a basic guide; it is not intended to be all-inclusive. Thus the auditor must remain alert for any other indication of inefficiency. At the same time, not all questions can be answered during the physical tour. For example, Question 13, "does the company have a suggestion box?" may not be answerable simply because the auditor does not see a suggestion box during the tour. This does not mean that a suggestion box does not exist. Question 15, "is copying machine use controlled?" would be another example of a situation where the auditor would not always be sure through observation alone that an undesirable practice existed. It could be that an authorization sheet was in a drawer, where the auditor would not be likely to see it. Conversely, if the auditor observed an employee making copies of a personal tax return or a cookbook and then leaving without recording the nature of the work copied or who authorized such copying, this could indicate an undesirable and costly problem.

Some questions will always be easily answered as a result of the tour. For instance, Questions 28 ("is there a centralized personnel function . . . ?"), 29 ("is Personnel a separate department from Payroll?"), 40 ("is

EXHIBIT 2-1 Physical Tour Questionnaire

The auditor should place a check mark in the columns at the left to indicate a possible undesirable situation that is observed in a particular department.

Accounting	EDP	Energy Usage	Mail Room	Marketing	Payroll	Personnel	Production	Purchasing	Quality Control	Recvg. & Matls. Handlg.	Treasury	*All Departments*
												1. Are the physical facilities of the department adequate?
												2. Is there an adequate amount of office equipment available in the department?
												3. Are machines and equipment being used to maximum capacity?
												4. Is the number of telephones adequate but not excessive?
												5. Does office layout facilitate the normal flow of operations?
												6. Are physical conditions (smell, heat, etc.) of the department satisfactory?
												7. Are all employees working diligently?
												8. Does the proper amount of floor space exist in the department?
												9. Are aisles and doorways wide enough for traffic?
												10. Is storage space adequate?
												11. Is the department overstocked with supplies that it may not use in the near future or may never use?
												12. Is there an adequate supply of fire extinguishers?

Accounting
EDP
Energy Usage
Mail Room
Marketing
Payroll
Personnel
Production
Purchasing
Quality Control
Recvg. & Matls. Handlg.
Treasury

EXHIBIT 2-1 (Continued)

13. Does the company have a suggestion box?

14. Is all filing of records kept up to date?

15. Is copying machine use controlled?

16. Is a record kept of reasons for long distance calls?

17. Is the department staff large enough?

18. Are employees in view of supervision?

19. Are all tasks necessary?

20. Are windows closed when heat or air conditioner is on?

21. Is lighting adequate but not excessive?

Accounting and Payroll

22. Are employee time cards used?

23. Does anyone oversee the clocking-in process?

24. Are checks locked up when not being used?

25. Is a check protector used?

26. Are accounting and payroll separate functions?

27. Has the feasibility of accepting charge cards (Master Charge, Bank Americard) been examined?

Personnel

Purchasing

Recvg. & Matls. Handlg.

Mail Room

EXHIBIT 2-1 (Continued)

Personnel

28. Is there a centralized personnel function through which all applicants must pass?

29. Is personnel a separate department from payroll?

30. Is a nondiscrimination policy clearly stated and posted?

31. Does the personnel department maintain an open door policy to all employees?

32. Do interviewers have their own private offices?

33. Is the department easy to reach by the public?

34. Is the department easy to reach by employees?

35. Is there a bulletin board available for communication of information to company employees?

36. Is there an internal newspaper or magazine for employees?

Purchasing

37. Are quantities purchased consistent with actual requirements?

38. Do purchase orders normally include prices?

39. Is there an adequate library of catalogs and current price lists?

Receiving and Materials Handling

40. Is there a centralized receiving function?

41. Do all received goods come through the receiving department?

42. Is the department kept in neat order?

43. Are all materials easily accessible when needed?

44. Are all items counted as they are unloaded?

45. Are the storerooms conveniently close to the receiving dock?

46. Is access to storeroom restricted to specific employees?

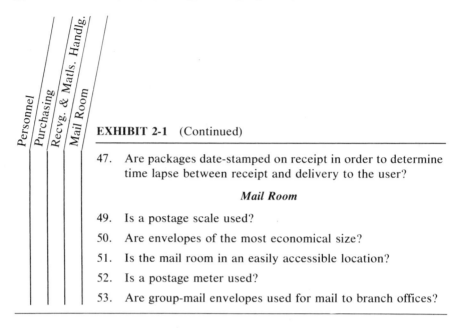

Personnel / Purchasing / Recvg. & Matls. Handlg. / Mail Room

EXHIBIT 2-1 (Continued)

47. Are packages date-stamped on receipt in order to determine time lapse between receipt and delivery to the user?

Mail Room

49. Is a postage scale used?

50. Are envelopes of the most economical size?

51. Is the mail room in an easily accessible location?

52. Is a postage meter used?

53. Are group-mail envelopes used for mail to branch offices?

there a centralized receiving function?''), and 45 (''are the storerooms conveniently close to the receiving dock?'') will always be answered during the physical tour. (If these questions are not answered, the tour was incomplete and should be repeated.)

It is the opinion of this writer that the questionnaire sheet should not be carried along on the physical tour, but instead filled out from memory after the tour. This does not mean that the auditor should not take notes during the tour if there are so many unusual situations that the auditor might tend to forget some of them. Some operational auditors even recommend carrying a camera on the tour to snap pictures of areas that need drastic improvement.[5] The pictures would not only serve to refresh the auditor's memory at a later time, but might also provide material that could be used in the final audit report.

The physical tour stage can make the best use of the auditor's inventiveness. The tour can be used not only as orientation, but also for an initial glimpse into both good and bad situations. The auditor must use the questionnaire as a guideline, but it should not be used as the only source of information on the physical tour. The benefits to the auditor (and ultimately the client) from the physical tour will be related to the auditor's initiative and ability to observe the forest as well as the trees.

---

[5]Robert R. Ringwood, ''Operational Auditing for Government Programs,'' *International Journal of Government Auditing,* I (January 1974), p. 13.

Acquisition of Written Data

In this second phase of the preliminary audit, the objective of the operational auditor is to determine whether the company enjoys consistent management practices. Consequently, it is imperative that the auditor obtain documentation with which departmental data can be compared. Types of written documents that the auditor should acquire would include the following:

Written goals and objectives

Policies and procedures manuals

Job descriptions

Organization charts

Budgets

Internal departmental reports

Financial statements

Catalogs

Flow charts

Forms

Management letter rendered by external financial auditors

Government or other regulatory requirements

Minutes of the board of directors meetings (in some cases, this would not always be needed)

It is usually possible to obtain much of the above data during the physical tour stage of the audit or in the interviews-with-management stage. Therefore, the acquisition of written data is not really a separate stage in time. However, it should be considered a separate stage, at least for planning purposes. Just because it may take place at the same time as other stages does not mean that the acquisition of written documentation is not a separate step.

The objective of the acquisition-of-data stage of the audit is different from that of the other stages in that the auditor is not necessarily trying to reach a conclusion. Instead the auditor's major emphasis is on obtaining raw material for future stages of the audit. This is not to say that the auditor will never obtain important information from the data-acquisition stage itself. For example, if some of the documents were not readily available, or never existed, this might indicate a problem.

It must be remembered that the operational auditor has two sources for standards of measurement: the individual company and its industry. In order to learn the individual company's standards, the auditor must rely on the data accumulated during this stage of the audit, particularly the company goals, objectives, policies, and procedures.

Written goals and objectives are important for both a company as a whole and its individual departments. Without goals and objectives that are known to all employees, there is a danger that all the departments will not be oriented toward the same final objectives. Written goals and objectives help ensure that there is unity, continuity, and consistency within a company. The auditor must also assure himself that there has been communication of these goals and objectives to all individuals in the organization.

There should also be a periodic follow-up to determine whether established goals and objectives are being met. Not only can goals and objectives take all elements of a company along the same path, but they can also serve as a tool in evaluating segments of the organization.

Policies and procedures manuals can help to ensure adherence to stated goals and objectives. The manuals can serve as a reference source when no precedent for a particular action exists, so all employees can tend to react similarly in a given situation and lend consistency to their actions. The auditor will want to ascertain whether written policies and procedures are being properly carried out. If not, the organization is either acting incorrectly or the manual should be changed to reflect a new procedure.

Written job descriptions permit management and the operational auditor to effectively determine whether each employee is meeting the obligations of his or her job. Without a job description the employee could explain a less-than-adequate performance by claiming "That's not my job."

Job descriptions are valuable also when a position is being filled with a new employee. A written job description gives the personnel director a guideline that could be used in measuring the qualifications of applicants. Without a written job description, she or he might hire under- or over-qualified employees. This would reduce departmental efficiency, because extra training costs would be required and the progress of work past the new employee would be slow or even bottlenecked.

A clear organization chart should be available. An employee should know where he or she stands in relation to other employees:

> An organization chart . . . serves as an authoritative source of information. Official answers to organization questions are provided. Allocation of activities by specific positions is direct and clear cut. Disputes involving jurisdiction over activities can be settled, and information as to who handles a specific task can be readily ascertained.[6]

[6]George R. Terry, *Principles of Management,* 4th ed. (Homewood, Illinois: Richard D. Irwin, 1964), p. 454.

Organization systems are sometimes quite complicated and the written charts are often erroneous. The auditors will want to determine whether the written organization chart corresponds to the de facto organization.

Written budgets in most companies are prepared at least a year in advance. The auditor should obtain a copy of the master budget for use in the subsequent financial analysis stage of the audit. In addition, the auditor will want to be assured that the budget is actually used, not merely prepared. The budget should be both a planning tool and a control tool. The budget can also serve as a motivating device for employees, particularly if the employees play a part in the preparation of the budget. The preparation of a budget serves the purpose of forcing personnel to think in terms of overall company objectives rather than the day-to-day problems that are normally their prime consideration. In a sense, a budget is a communications tool in that it outlines company goals. Without a budget, department goals might be misunderstood. For instance, the sales manager may want to keep as much inventory on hand as possible so that no sales will be lost. On the other hand, the finance department may want to keep the inventory as low as possible. If the company has a budget that specifies how much inventory should be on hand, all employees can work to reach the same goal.

There is one additional reason why the budget is so important to the operational auditor. The budget shows the auditor which departments are expected to spend the most money. In general, these departments offer the greatest potential for cost savings. Since operational audits must be justified on the basis of a cost/benefit ratio, the auditors must allot their time to the areas offering the greatest opportunity for savings. At the same time, however, many small departments, taken collectively, can be quite large, and the auditor may sometimes find that the elimination of one or more departments is the most effective means of combatting unnecessary costs.

Examples of all internal reports should be obtained by the auditor. Some of the reports will prove valuable for financial analysis work. Others should be examined for usefulness or overlap: there is little point, for example, in continuing to prepare reports that were required for defense purposes during World War II (as was done by one company audited by the author).

Both interim and annual financial statements should be obtained by the auditor for use in performing financial analysis work. Prior years' statements should also be assembled, because they would be required for trend analysis.

Company catalogs and price lists should be obtained for use in auditing the Marketing department. The dates and publication schedule of each catalog should be ascertained.

Flow charts can help employees of the company and the operational auditor understand how an operation is supposed to be run. If written flow charts are not available, the auditors may want to sketch their own for purposes of understanding a particular problem. Flow charting is discussed in the appendix to this chapter.

The auditor will want to obtain copies of all forms used by the departments under study. This will enable the auditor to determine such things as whether the size of the forms is conducive to easy filing and whether the spacing allows for easy typing. The auditor may also observe whether several departments might be able to utilize the same form if certain modifications were made in it. The necessity for the information recorded on the forms is another factor the auditor should include in the examination.

If a CPA firm has made an evaluation of the company's internal control system, it has usually given management a letter with recommendations for improvements in the system. These management letters may include other recommendations regarding levels of efficiency and effectiveness. The operational auditor should obtain the most recent management letter to help determine what the major problem areas are and whether management has acted on earlier recommendations to resolve the problems.

Government regulation is a nemesis that in some way affects all forms of business. The operational auditor should become familiar with the regulations affecting the client's industry, because not only may the company be in violation of the law for not complying with certain regulatory requirements, but also many regulatory requirements can introduce inefficiencies into a company's operations. The auditor must realize that these inefficiencies cannot legally be corrected; thus there is no need to make recommendations to increase efficiency. To make a recommendation with which management cannot comply may be the auditor's downfall; if the company considers that the auditor is not knowledgeable about specific regulatory requirements, it might assume that the auditor lacks knowledge in other areas as well.

Finally, the minutes of the board of directors meetings are sometimes useful in acquainting the auditor with company goals and objectives and the degree of agreement on goals and objectives. The minutes can help the auditor uncover particular problem situations. However, an auditor may not always be able to obtain board minutes. Because the minutes often contain confidential salary data, the directors will sometimes forbid access to outsiders (and even to internal auditors).

Like the listed elements of the physical tour, the above list of written data should not be considered all-inclusive. If any other data is observed or offered that might be useful in other stages of the audit, the auditor should obtain copies. The auditor should also be alert for internal reports that have been thrown in the waste basket. In many companies, employees receive reports they do not need and do not want. The printing of these excess reports can be eliminated.

Interviews with Management

Interviews with individual managers are the third part of the preliminary phase of the operational audit. Operational auditing relies on what people perceive and feel as much as it does on recorded data and statistics. The operational auditor learns from people. The experts in a particular company are the people that run the company. Therefore the auditor can obtain the best information by asking managers to identify the problems. Naturally, this is not always as easy as it sounds. It is up to the auditor to ferret out the problem situations by asking the proper questions. Often a manager is not aware of a problem, because the immediate problems of day-to-day work have caused the overall company objectives and goals to be subordinated to the task of keeping the top of a desk clear of papers. In other cases, a manager may be aware of a problem but may be unable to convince top management that the problem exists. The support of the outside auditor can add weight to a manager's suggestions.

The questionnaire in Exhibit 2-2 was designed for use in interviewing management personnel. The questions in the Exhibit 2-2 questionnaire were drawn from the questionnaires in subsequent chapters on the basis of their importance. For convenience, the questions on the Management questionnaire are grouped by department. This categorization has no significance during the interview; it is only for the auditor's benefit when analyzing the questionnaires. All questions on the Management questionnaire should be asked of all managers who might have information regarding other departments.

The individuals to be questioned are those who have, or should have, some knowledge of departments besides their own. Normally, this would include the following:

Top management (president, vice-presidents, plant manager, treasurer)
Controller
Marketing department head
Payroll supervisor
Accounting supervisor
Production supervisor

EXHIBIT 2-2   Management Questionnaire

Personnel

1. Is there an up-to-date published statement of personnel policies and procedures available to all company employees?

2. Is there an established wage and salary scale to ensure equitable rates of pay?

3. Are accurate and complete personnel records kept for each employee?

4. Is there a system for immediate notification of the Personnel department when an employee is terminated?

5. Do you feel that Personnel employees are knowledgeable about personnel policies and employee benefits?

6. Do you feel that company employees understand the personnel policies?

7. Does the personnel department have an open line of communication with all other department heads and managers?

Payroll

8. Is an employee's initial salary authorized in writing by someone designated to do so?

9. Are salary changes authorized in writing?

10. Are employees paid by check?

11. Is payroll always completed on time?

12. Are time cards kept long enough to meet legal requirements?

13. Are quarterly tax reports always filed on time?

14. Are withholding tax deposits always made on time?

15. How often are errors made in the preparation of payroll?

Purchasing

16. Does the company utilize a centralized purchasing system?

17. Is there an inventory control system?

18. Does the Purchasing department have good relations with other departments?

19. Does the Purchasing department try to buy products that meet the needs of several departments rather than stocking several brands of nearly identical items?

Receiving

20. Is there a centralized receiving function?

21. Do all goods that are received come through the Receiving department?

22. Does the Receiving department check shipments for damage?

23. Are items which are radioactive, perishable, or require controlled temperatures always delivered immediately to the user?

24. Is there an adequate supply of fire extinguishers?

Accounting

25. Does the Accounting department provide pertinent historical and projected financial data accurately, speedily, and in a meaningful form?

26. Is it company policy to have receipts deposited in the bank and recorded in the Cash Receipts Journal daily?

27. Is the bank statement reconciled monthly?

28. Are financial statements and internal reports prepared monthly?

29. Are all revenues and expenses always posted to the proper department?

30. Are all charges posted promptly to the proper accounts?

31. Are statements mailed out regularly to former customers who still owe a portion of their bill?

Mail Room

32. Is the Mail Room conveniently located?

33. Are you satisfied with the service offered by the Mail Room?

34. Is the mailing schedule the best for your needs?

35. Do you feel that there is too much intracompany paper pollution?

36. Does incoming first class mail receive priority over other classes of mail?

Marketing

37. Do you feel the company's marketing efforts are adequate?

38. Are catalogs comparable to (or better than) those of competitors?

39. Does Marketing management compare sales forecasts to actual performance?

40. Does the marketing department perform any market research?

41. Is the advertising program coordinated with other company efforts?

42. Is the company catalog kept up to date?

43. Are analyses made of sales returns and allowances to determine causes?

44. Does Marketing coordinate its efforts with production capabilities?

Electronic Data Processing

45. Does EDP provide you with all of the computer service you need?

46. Are computer facilities up-to-date?

47. Is there a long-range plan for computer utilization?

48. Are EDP personnel sufficiently qualified?

49. Are EDP personnel being properly utilized?

50. Is access to EDP facilities restricted to specified personnel?

51. Are EDP facilities adequately protected from fire and other disasters?

52. Are priority policies clearly stated, and suitable for your needs?

53. Is EDP output relatively accurate on the first run?

54. Is EDP work completed without undue overtime?

55. Is the EDP workload being handled without undue delay?

Quality Control (Inspection)

56. Are inspection facilities adequate?

57. Are inspection records maintained and kept up to date?

58. Is there follow-up on substandard work?

59. Do Inspection personnel work cooperatively with Production personnel?

Accounting	EDP	Energy Usage	Mail Room	Marketing	Payroll	Personnel	Production	Purchasing	Quality Control	Receiving	Treasury
Yes				No							

EXHIBIT 2-2 (Continued)

All Departments

60. Are problems that affect work discussed with the department heads of the area that is at fault?

61. Are the employees in your department and the other departments with which you are familiar well qualified to perform the duties that are required of them?

62. Do you feel that all employees within your department, and other departments with which you are familiar, keep the information that they come in contact with confidential?

63. Is there an open line of communication between your department and the individuals to whom you report?

64. Do you feel that all departments treat customers with warmth and courtesy?

65. Do all of the forms that you come in contact with have enough space for all needed information?

66. Is lighting adequate in all offices?

67. Are sufficient machines and equipment available to those who need them?

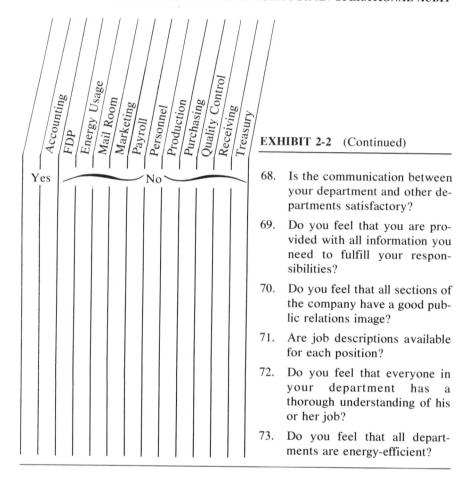

EXHIBIT 2-2 (Continued)

68. Is the communication between your department and other departments satisfactory?

69. Do you feel that you are provided with all information you need to fulfill your responsibilities?

70. Do you feel that all sections of the company have a good public relations image?

71. Are job descriptions available for each position?

72. Do you feel that everyone in your department has a thorough understanding of his or her job?

73. Do you feel that all departments are energy-efficient?

Purchasing agent
Receiving supervisor
Chief inspector in quality control
Personnel director

The same questionnaires should be used for each respondent. It might seem that several individuals' responses to the same question would be redundant, but:

This is not a wasteful suggestion because "facts" are seldom presented in the same way or equally emphasized by all the people who observe them.

The objective truth—which is inherently difficult to find—is more likely to be unearthed if the auditor obtains multiple answers to the same question.[7]

The operational auditor should be constantly alert for unique problem situations that may not be covered in the questionnaire. The questionnaire should never become a crutch which causes the auditor to restrict his judgment. The questionnaire is usually the most important part of an audit, but it cannot be all-inclusive.

Analysis Work

The final segment of the preliminary audit is the analysis work performed by the auditor. The documentation necessary for the analysis work should have been obtained in the data-accumulation stage.

The first step in the analysis stage involves an analysis of financial statements and other internal management reports. The operational auditor should compute the more traditional ratios such as current ratio, quick ratio, receivables turnover, inventory turnover, and asset turnover. Like any ratio, these must be compared with similar ratios of other companies that are considered to be operating efficiently. Financial ratios should be computed for several time periods in order to observe trends. The analysis work should include a review of budget and variance reports. Ratios and analyses of departmental financial statements are particularly important in determining which departments need an in-depth audit.

Also included in the analysis stage of the audit is a thorough review of all the internal documents collected during the acquisition-of-data stage. The auditor should also review the internal control systems and the flow of transaction data through the accounting system. The collected data should be compared with performance measurement criteria when appropriate. In addition, the auditor will want to assess business risks and inefficiencies to determine areas and activities where performance might be improved. Once the auditor has completed the financial analysis portion of the operational audit, the preliminary stage is complete.

Survey Memorandum

The auditor should now be ready to organize all of the data and recommend one or more departments for further study. This is accomplished by preparing a survey memorandum. In effect, a survey memorandum is sort of an audit report covering the findings made during

---

[7]Lindberg and Cohn, *op cit.*, p. 39.

the preliminary stage of the operational audit. However, this audit report is usually not seen by anyone other than the operational auditor. Occasionally, the auditor may want to show the survey memorandum to a high level official, particularly if it could quickly solve a costly problem. A potential lawsuit against the client would be an example of a situation in which the auditor would tend to share the contents of the survey memorandum with the client.

The reason for preparing a survey memorandum is to force the auditor to organize his findings and thoughts. The operational auditor has made a physical walkthrough of the company's facilities, has talked to numerous department heads concerning their opinions, obtained numerous internal documents, and computed several ratios. The sheer quantity of the data would exceed the auditor's ability to comprehend the situation if he did not organize the findings systematically.

The survey memorandum is the document that the auditor uses to help decide what department will be selected for the in-depth stage of the audit. Later, the survey memorandum can be referred to if there is any question about why that particular department was selected.

Even if the auditor feels strongly that he knows where the problems lie, his opinion should not be voiced at this stage of the audit. Following the in-depth stage of the audit the operational auditor will be given an opportunity to voice an opinion. By that time all of the evidence will have been analyzed. Therefore, the operational auditor must use due care to see that the survey memorandum is used only as an audit tool and not as an official report of the audit.

THE IN-DEPTH AUDIT

The in-depth audit consists of an extensive search for the facts. Because this is a time-consuming process, only a limited number of departments—often only one—are initially audited during the in-depth stage of an operational audit. The results of the preliminary stage revealed the department where it is most obvious that problems exist. During the in-depth stage, the auditor's objective is to uncover the causes of these problems.

During the in-depth stage, the operational auditor assembles views, suggestions, comments, and trends in a questionnaire interview of the problem department's employees. The auditor will usually utilize one questionnaire for most or all of the employees in the department. A questionnaire designed especially for the department to be audited (see

Part Two of this book) is the operational auditor's most valuable tool during the in-depth stage of the audit.

Although the use of a questionnaire accomplishes a major portion of the work of the in-depth stage of the operational audit, observation is also important. Consequently, it is imperative that the operational auditor remain alert for problems of inefficiency.

The Audit Report

Once the in-depth stage of the audit has been completed, the auditor is ready to prepare a formal audit report. The audit report consists of a written summary of the audit's scope and the findings of the audit. The report should define the exact nature of the problems that have been uncovered. Normally, the audit report will give examples of specific areas where changes in management practices that could result in greater efficiency might be most easily implemented.

Even though the audit report is the final step of the in-depth audit, it is best to not wait until the audit is completed to begin the task of preparing the report. The operational auditor would be well advised to start writing the report on the first day of the audit; the surest way to drag it out is to wait until the study is completed. Chapter 3 will cover the subject of the report in more detail.

The Recommended Operational Audit Model

A complete operational audit structure has been described in this chapter. Exhibit 2-3 illustrates the complete framework in a format that shows all of its interrelationships.

The audit framework begins with the industry averages and the individual company's goals, objectives, and budgets. These provide the standards against which the auditor measures the company being audited. The auditor obtains the data for his measurements by taking a physical tour, acquiring written documents, interviewing managers and department heads, and analyzing several financial ratios and statistics. On the basis of this data, the auditor compiles a survey memorandum which isolates the object (usually one department) for an in-depth audit. The auditor then probes that department in an extensive research effort. This search for facts relies primarily on the questionnaire interviews of the individuals working in the department. Once the auditor has completed his in-depth audit of the department, he prepares a report of his findings.

Copies of this audit report go to top management and to the management of the department that was audited.

Exhibit 2-4 provides an internal viewpoint of the steps listed in the left-hand column of Exhibit 2-3. A submodel of Exhibit 2-3, Exhibit 2-4 gives a more detailed look at the generalized preliminary steps shown in Exhibit 2-3.

With the operational audit model described in this chapter as a guide, a qualified operational auditor (whether internal auditor, external auditor,

EXHIBIT 2-3   Operational Audit Model

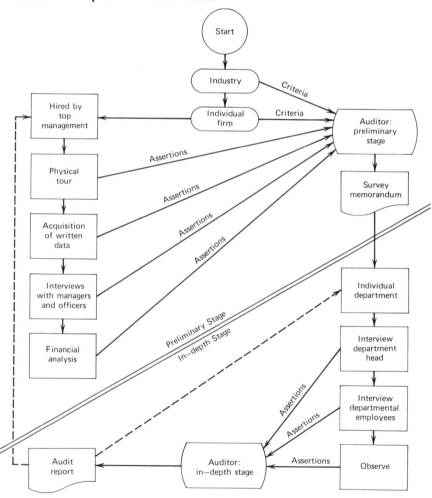

EXHIBIT 2-4   Operational Audit Model—Specific Sources

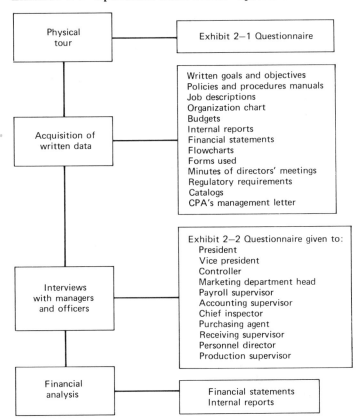

or company manager) should have no difficulty in performing a thorough audit. Using the framework that the model provides, plus the accompanying questionnaires, permits a systematic study of problems in all types of companies.

Although operational auditing has been defined as the application of common sense to a business situation, the auditor does need some type of format to follow when performing an operational audit. Until now, a lack of interest among researchers has left the area of the operational audit model largely undeveloped. The model sketched in this chapter, however, demonstrates that there is enough uniformity among client companies to warrant the expenditure of time and effort to prepare an operational audit model for most types of businesses.

APPENDIX—FLOWCHARTING

A flowchart is a graphic representation of a management information system. The flowchart illustrates the flow of data and the operations to be performed at each step in the system. The use of a flowchart offers several benefits. First, the visual picture of a system produced by a flowchart is easier to comprehend than a narrative description, particularly in a large or complex system. Second, flowcharts provide an easy means of spotting weaknesses or discrepancies in a system. Third, the use of a flowchart

EXHIBIT 2-5   Standard Flowcharting Symbols

Process	Flow
Input/output	Magnetic tape
Document	Punched card
Manual operation	Punched tape
Auxiliary operation	Display unit
Comment or annotation	On—line storage

makes it easier to project the effect of a proposed change in the system. Finally, the use of standardized flowchart symbols and format can increase auditor and reviewer efficiency.

Complex computer systems have led to the widespread use of flow-charts, but flowcharts are useful for describing both manual and electronic systems. The acceptance of flowcharting as a systems analyst's tool has led to agreement on a standard set of flowcharting symbols. Some of these standard symbols are illustrated in Exhibit 2-5. The operational auditor should be familiar with all of them.

Two types of flowcharts are often used with automated systems: a systems flowchart and a program flowchart. The systems flowchart describes the flow of data through a system. (The manner in which the computer processes the data is not considered.) A program flowchart illustrates the sequence of operations performed within the computer. The same symbols are used for program flowcharting as for systems flowcharting.

A flowchart is an important documentation and analytical tool for operational auditors. Although both the systems flowchart and the program flowchart are important, the systems flowchart is more useful during an operational audit.

Flowcharts can often be used to help spot internal control deficiencies. An overview of the system can reveal any internal control weaknesses much more easily than a narrative description of the system can. Since flowcharting requires such a modest amount of expertise and is such a valuable tool, it is a skill that should be mastered by every operational auditor.

three

ENGAGEMENT LETTER, WORKING PAPERS AND AUDIT REPORTS

In many respects, operational auditing is similar to financial auditing. For example, the following activities are common to both types of audits:

Planning, control, and supervision
Fact-finding, analysis, and documentation
Recommending
Reporting

Because of the similarity between a financial audit and an operational audit, many of the same procedural details are used in both types of audits. This chapter deals with the procedural aspects of an operational audit: (1) the engagement letter, (2) the working papers, and (3) the final report.

THE ENGAGEMENT LETTER

A company may engage an operational auditor for various purposes, including (1) assessment of operating performance, (2) identification of opportunities for improvement, and (3) development of recommendations for improved efficiency, effectiveness, and economy. Because a client may be expecting any or all of these objectives to be accomplished as a result of the engagement, it is important that there be a solid engagement understanding before the job is begun. Thus, a clear engagement letter is a prerequisite for an operational audit, just as it is for any auditing job.

At one extreme, a client may desire only an assessment of performance, probably because the assessment is required by a regulatory agency. Thus the audit report should be concerned solely with this task. At the other extreme, an organization which may be experiencing severe operating problems undertakes an audit to identify its problem areas and obtain recommendations for improvements. As a third example, the CPA is hired to assess operational performance and to report any weaknesses discovered, but the client does not want to pay the CPA to make recommendations for correction; instead the client wants to know only where the problems lie, and client personnel can then solve them. Because of this broad range of possible services in an operational audit engagement, the CPA should use extreme care in preparing the engagement letter. A thorough understanding of the terms of the letter will prevent any future disagreement about the exact purposes and objectives of the engagement.

Also, the nature of the engagement can affect the CPA firm's choice of personnel assigned to the job. For example, if the client wants only an assessment of performance, this can be handled by the auditors. On the other hand, if the client wants recommendations for improvement, it would be wise to include some management-services staffers in the engagement.

The engagement document for an operational audit may take the form of a proposal letter, contract, or confirmation letter. The document serves to establish an understanding of the engagement between the auditor and the engaging party. Subjects to be considered in the document include:

1. Purposes and objectives of the operational audit and the background of the engagement.
2. Scope of the auditor's work, defining what is to be included and excluded in:
   Departments or activities studied
   Sources of relevant data
   Other areas
3. Approach or work plan to be followed by the auditors.
4. Evaluative criteria to be used.
5. Course of action to be followed in the absence of specific company/industry/departmental criteria.
6. Nature of end products and reports to be expected from the operational audit, particularly with respect to whether, and to what extent, recommendations for corrective actions are to be included (as mentioned previously, this is a common source of misunderstanding).

7. Any special understandings, for example, that the CPA firm will not express an opinion on the overall level of efficiency and effectiveness of the organization.

8. Staffing of the audit team, including any subcontractor(s) or other professionals (such as pharmacists, engineers, or other specialists) to be used and the scope of their work.

9. Extent of client involvement, for example, assistance by client employees.

10. Estimated time, fee, and billing arrangements.

11. Nature of any progress reports to be submitted to the client prior to the final report.

12. Distribution of reports.

13. Any follow-up arrangements.

WORKING PAPERS

One of the activities performed during any audit involves the planning, control, and supervision of the engagement. These activities include the development of a complete audit program, the scheduling of the work to be performed, the selection of appropriate staff members (from both the auditing staff and the management services staff), the involvement of the client's personnel, the actual performance of the various aspects of the audit work, and provision for a final review of the work papers and reports. Thus, for any operational audit engagement, the working papers must include a description of how these functions were handled.

Among the auditor's working papers are the various questionnaires, analyses, and memoranda prepared during an engagement. Also included are documents obtained from the client such as catalogs, job descriptions, and organization charts. Working papers are the documents that describe and explain the audit work. As the basis for the final audit report, the working papers should substantiate its conclusions.

The audit program should be developed in accordance with the special circumstances and objectives of each engagement and should be tailored to the organization being audited. In the development of the program, consideration must be given to the sequence of specific tasks and it should list the client personnel to be interviewed. Chapter 2 elaborated on the overall work program for an operational audit, presenting the general outline. The auditor will need to apply the concepts from the general model to specific clients. In other words, the auditor should use Chapter 2 as a guide in preparing the audit program.

Once the audit has been properly planned, the auditor must undertake a process of fact-finding, analysis, and documentation. This requires the auditor to become familiar with the organization being audited. This includes learning about the nature of the company, its products, and services. The auditor needs to learn also the organization's objectives, policies, systems, procedures, and the operating results of each department and activity being audited—if only one department or segment of the client's business is being audited, that department's relationship to other parts of the organization needs to be ascertained. This background aspect of the audit is normally accomplished as part of the orientation tour and the acquisition-of-data stage of the audit (Chapter 2).

Interviewing client personnel is usually a necessary part of any operational audit engagement. Employee interviews are often essential because manuals, reports, and other written data may not reflect actual practice at the time of the audit. In addition, interviews give insight into problems as they are seen by people who work with the problems every day. Subsequent chapters are designed for use as interview tools in specific activity areas. The appendix to this chapter provides some hints on general interviewing techniques.

Audit documentation involves compiling and recording sufficient data to arrive at conclusions and make recommendations. The type of documentation will differ from one engagement to the next, but in general will include charts, schedules, interview notes, forms, manuals, financial analyses, internal reports, and various memoranda that the auditor has filled out during the course of the audit (such as the results of the physical tour).

The auditor's working papers will usually consist of the following documents:

The audit work program

Documents obtained during the acquisition-of-data stage

Physical tour questionnaire

Questionnaires from the interviews-with-management stage

Memoranda prepared by the auditor during the analysis stage

The survey memorandum

Questionnaires from the in-depth interview of departmental employees

Memoranda prepared during the analysis stage of the in-depth audit

Although the first five items on the above list pertain to the preliminary survey phase of an audit, they would, with the exception of the survey memorandum, also be necessary even if a preliminary survey were not

being conducted. Thus, all of the work papers (except the fifth) are necessary for an in-depth audit.

The organization of working papers can be handled in a variety of ways, but the most common method is to use an indexing plan that follows the sequence of steps in the audit: that is, the papers from the preliminary survey should precede those from the in-depth audit. Keep documents from each section of the audit (such as physical tour, management interviews) separate. All working papers should have headings that have been prepared in a uniform manner and should be neat and legible (neatness and legibility not only foster efficiency, but also show the painstaking care involved in the preparation of the papers and the conduct of the audit as a whole).

Perhaps the federal guidelines for compliance audits of government programs by independent auditors best describe the reason for good working papers:

> Sufficient, competent, and relevant evidence is to be obtained to afford a reasonable basis for the auditor's opinions, judgments, conclusions, and recommendations. This standard places upon the auditor the responsibility for accumulating sufficient evidence to provide an appropriate factual basis for opinions, conclusions, judgments and recommendations.[1]

Whether an operational audit is for regulatory purposes or strictly for management use, the working papers should support the audit report. In essence, the working papers should be such that another auditor, one who did not work on the engagement, would arrive at the same conclusions on the basis of the papers. The working papers are the legs that support the audit report; without legs, the report cannot stand.

AUDIT REPORTS

The nature of the report issued by the operational auditor depends on the needs of the engaging party. Typically, the report will include a description of the work performed, list those areas where there is potential for improvement, and make specific recommendations. The report should provide a rationale for the conclusions and recommendations. The report should be addressed to the person or persons who made the arrangements to have the audit performed. This could include a senior officer, the board

---

[1]*Guidelines for Financial and Compliance Audits of Federally Assisted Programs* (Washington, D.C.: U.S. General Accounting Office, 1978).

of directors, or even a third party. Normally, the report would be distributed only to the addressee, although there would be no reason for the practitioner to veto a client's instructions to distribute the report more widely.

An operational audit report should be thoroughly discussed with officials of the client company before it is finalized. Such discussion is accomplished in an exit interview with the manager of the department that was audited in depth. The exit interview will help to ensure the accuracy of facts and will facilitate acceptance of the report by those who will be affected by it. An account of management's response to the report may be included in the report or presented in a separate report. Some audit reports even include photographs in order to illustrate what may be described as ''ugly'' situations.

Content of The Report

The contents of an operational audit report will vary with the nature of the client company and the types of problems uncovered. In general, the report should contain the following elements:

Objectives and scope of the engagement

General procedures utilized by the auditor

Specific findings

Recommendations, where appropriate

In addition, the report may contain an overall auditor's summary, especially if it is a longer report. The report may also include the comments of management made during the exit interview.

The section of the audit report covering the audit objectives and scope is important, because most audits are designed to cover only certain activities of the company. Thus, a brief summary of the objectives and scope agreed upon in the engagement letter is a useful reminder to the recipients of the report.

The section on Procedures performed is particularly important because each operational audit differs so much. A general description of the procedures used is sufficient. Any limitations imposed by the client should be mentioned. The Procedures section of the report should also include a rationale for selecting the procedures. In addition, the auditor's measurement criteria should be described. The report usually contains a caveat that says that the findings are based upon an enterprise's operations for a particular period of time. Many auditors conclude the Procedures section of the report with the observation that the usual purpose of an operational audit is to find problems and areas for improvement, rather than the organization's many strengths.

The sections of the report covering the auditor's Findings and recommendations are not highly standardized and one report will differ materially from another report in this respect. Basically, the auditor presents the findings and recommendations in the most understandable way possible.

If the operational audit engagement did not involve making recommendations, the meat of the audit report will be a list of problem areas without suggestions for improving performance. More often specific recommendations are listed in the audit report. Some recommendations may simply suggest the need for further study of a particular problem.

Summarizing the elements of a typical audit report, all reports should:

1. Clearly explain the scope and objectives of the audit.

2. Be as concise as possible but, at the same time, clear and complete enough to be understood.

3. Present factual matter accurately, completely, and fairly.

4. Explain findings and conclusions objectively and in language as clear and simple as the subject matter permits.

5. Include only factual information, findings, and conclusions that are supported by enough evidence in the auditor's working papers to demonstrate or prove, when called on, the basis for the matters reported and their correctness and reasonableness. Detailed supporting information should be included in the report to the extent necessary to make a convincing presentation.

6. Include, when possible, the auditor's recommendations for actions to effect improvements in problem areas noted and to make other improvements in operations. Information on underlying causes of problems reported should be included to assist in implementing or devising corrective actions.

7. Place primary emphasis on future improvement rather than on criticism of the past; negative comments should be presented in a balanced perspective, recognizing any unusual difficulties or mitigating circumstances faced by the operating officials.

8. Identify and explain issues and questions needing further study and consideration by the auditor or others.

9. Include recognition of noteworthy accomplishments, particularly when management improvements made in one program or activity might be extended elsewhere.

10. Report the views of responsible internal officials on the auditor's findings, conclusions, and recommendations. Except where the

possibility of fraud or some other compelling reason dictates otherwise, these officials should review the auditor's tentative findings and conclusions.

Exhibit 3-1 gives a sample audit report. Note that the report does not include a section of recommendations.

In summary, professional standards define the elements of a report of a financial audit. However, no such standards exist for an operational audit report. Thus, the auditor should use logic in producing a report that communicates the necessary information. Normally, an operational audit report does not express an overall opinion; instead, the auditor comments on specific problem areas. These specific findings and recommendations should follow a general discussion of the audit objectives, scope, and procedures used.

EXHIBIT 3-1.   Sample Operational Audit Report
_____

To the Plant Manager
Client Company
Oxford, Mississippi 38655

In December 1981, we concluded an operational audit of the accounting department at Client Company.

Objectives and Scope

The general objectives of this engagement, which were more specifically outlined in our letter dated October 30, 1981, were to:

Document, analyze, and report on the status of current operations at the Oxford plant

Identify areas which require attention

Make recommendations for corrective action or improvements

Our operational audit initially encompassed the 12 following functional areas at the Oxford plant: accounting, EDP, energy, mail room, marketing, payroll, personnel, production, purchasing, quality control, receiving, and the treasurer's office. Our evaluations included the operating conditions of the units. Based on our preliminary survey, we selected the accounting department as the one function in need of a more in-depth study. Consequently, this report is limited to the problem areas encountered in the accounting department. It must be remembered that an operational audit generally focuses on weaknesses and areas for improvement. Consequently, this report does not enumerate the many strengths of the accounting department and other departments in the organization.

The operational audit involved interviews with management personnel and

EXHIBIT 3-1 (Continued)

---

selected operations personnel in each of the units studied. We also reviewed and evaluated appropriate documents, files, reports, systems, procedures, and policies. After analyzing the data obtained, we developed recommendations with the appropriate accounting management personnel and with you, which are submitted in this report.

Findings and Recommendations

The recommendations in this report represent, in our judgment, those most likely to bring about improvements in the operation of the organization. However, all of our significant findings are included in this report for your consideration. It should be noted that the recommendations vary in such respects as difficulty of implementation, urgency, visibility of benefits, impact, and investment in facilities, equipment, and additional personnel entailed. These differences should be weighed in deciding on your course of action.

Specific Findings

1. The accounting department does not have a procedures manual. The availability of a procedures manual, including job descriptions, organization chart, and internal control system, could improve department operations.

2. Monthly financial statements are not prepared. The availability of monthly statements, coupled with a budget system, might encourage all department heads within the organization to perform better.

3. Bank statements are reconciled quarterly by an outside audit firm. By eliminating the bank reconciliation from the duties of the audit firm and returning it to the accounting department, the controller would be more aware of the financial pulse of the organization.

4. The company does not take advantage of discounts available for early payment of invoices, nor does it know the amount of discounts lost this way each year. The use of the "net method" of recording invoices would accentuate the actual costs of not taking discounts.

5. Control accounts are not regularly reconciled with the subsidiary ledgers. Regular reconciliation would uncover errors as they were committed rather than allowing a problem situation to develop. This condition is true for receivables, payables, and plant equipment.

6. A few of the questionnaire responses indicated that there is a problem with employee morale.

7. Some control should be placed over the use of the copying machine. A monthly tabulation of machine use would help determine whether a problem exists.

8. There are fewer electronic calculators in the office than there are accountants. This occasionally presents a problem, since some employees are forced to wait until a machine is available.

EXHIBIT 3-1   (Continued)

9. No record is kept of the reason for long distance telephone calls. If a permanent record were required, the number of unnecessary and personal calls might be reduced.

The accounting department is fortunate to have a group of highly talented personnel, who for the most part are performing their jobs capably. However, the department could be of even more service to the organization. If management can solve the problems cited above, the contributions of the accounting function will be enhanced significantly.

Although the audit report is basically one of constructive criticism, the auditor should attempt to avoid making the report sound too negative. This can be accomplished by expressing comments in a positive way and by using such words as "enhancing," "strengthening," "improving," and "increasing." The operating managers will be more receptive to these terms, which are less threatening. At the same time, these terms do not conceal a negative situation.

The Objectives and Scope section of the report should be based on the contents of the engagement letter. The engagement letter should spell out the exact details of the audit, including the departments or functions to be audited. The engagement letter is probably even more important for an operational audit than it is for a financial audit because operational audits are less standardized than financial audits.

The audit report should be based on the audit work performed by the practitioner. This work should be documented in the auditor's working papers. In an operational audit, working papers are generally questionnaires, analyses, and memoranda. The working papers have to substantiate all findings listed in the audit report.

As in any audit, the engagement letter, working papers, and audit report are mandatory. In this way, an operational audit is very much like a traditional financial audit. The two types of audits may have different objectives, but follow the similar steps in reaching their objectives.

APPENDIX—INTERVIEWING TECHNIQUES

Since an operational audit is so dependent on questionnaire interviews, it is imperative that an auditor know how to conduct an interview. A good interview should first establish rapport with the interviewee, then result in the collection of information. Interviewing is not an easy skill; however, through proper preparation and practice, it is possible for an auditor to become a good interviewer.

The beginning of an interview is the most critical time for establishing rapport with the interviewee. The auditor should begin by explaining the purpose and objective of the audit, and then inform the person being interviewed that he or she forms an integral part of the operational audit. The operational auditor needs to impress on the interviewee the important part his or her knowledge plays in determining the success of the audit.

One of the first rules an interviewer should keep in mind is to not talk down to the person being interviewed. The interviewee will be more responsive if the interviewer is perceived as an equal. Unfortunately, middle-level management personnel are often the hardest to interview. Middle managers often feel threatened by operational auditors. Because, this is the group that may have the best information, the auditor must work particularly hard to create rapport with them. One comment that an auditor might make to a less-than-cooperative interviewee might note the fine job the manager is doing, for example: "We want to do a complete review of your department in order to learn why you are so effective. We hope your successes can be passed along to other departments."

Sometimes a manager will be defensive because the interviewer has no operating experience in a similar department. The comment may be: "Where do you expect to get the knowledge to do this audit?" Such a question is a perfect opening for the auditor since an appropriate response would be: "You are the only expert in this operation; the success of the audit is dependent upon what you tell me."

Thus an auditor must be prepared to "sell" the advantages of an operational audit to lower-level employees, who will usually be initially reluctant to help. The way to gain rapport with the reluctant interviewee is to plan the interview and be able to discuss the industry. Although the auditor must avoid interrupting the person being interviewed and injecting his own ideas in the middle of a conversation, the auditor should speak in a manner to stimulate the respondent into conversation.

Interviews of the lowest-level operating personnel are usually the trickiest of all. Interviews with line workers should be positive, friendly, and reassuring. The auditor should probably avoid using words such as "efficient," "economical," or "fast" when interviewing line workers. Words like these can diminish rapport, because workers will assume the auditor is an efficiency expert who is trying to eliminate their jobs. Instead, the auditor should emphasize the opportunity for making work easier and increasing their chances of advancement.

Subsequent chapters of this book contain detailed questionnaires to be used in interviewing employees from various functional areas. Although this detailed list of questions is necessary, the auditor should never rely exclusively on the list. Instead, the auditor should add questions that arise during the course of the interview and should allow the interviewee to expand on topics raised by the questionnaire that are of particular interest to the respondent. A skilled interviewer goes into an interview well prepared, but is always willing to stray from the prescribed list of questions when spontaneous discussion may prove productive.

Basic Interview Techniques

Most interviewers believe they are problem-solvers and fact-finders who are objective, analytical, helpful, independent, persistent, tactful, cooperative, and understanding. Unfortunately, some interviewees may view the auditor as a policeman, spy, troublemaker, and nit picker. Since these attitudes hurt the auditor's chances for a successful interview, it is important that the interview be approached systematically. The following steps are recommended to avoid as many of the negative connotations as possible and make the interview more productive:

Schedule the Interview in Advance.   This will enhance the possibility that the auditor will be received in a positive way. Also, the interviewee will have sufficient time to gather records and forms that might be discussed during the interview. When scheduling the interview, the auditor should state the purpose of the interview and tell the interviewee whether any records or forms will be needed. A time should be selected that is mutually convenient. Interviews should be of the person-to-person type: the interviewee's supervisor, for instance, should not be present, since he or she might inhibit some of the responses. The interview is best held at the interviewee's office or desk, because people are normally more comfortable in their own territory. It is best to avoid hours immediately before or after lunch, and on Friday afternoons.

Do Advance Preparation.   The auditor should not go into an interview cold. Manuals, organization charts, and reports should be examined prior to the interview. The auditor should find out ahead of time about the interviewee's knowledge, experience, and personality (but the auditor should view this information objectively and not let it cause bias or prejudice).

Some of the techniques discussed in this section were developed by the Continuing Education division of the CPA firm Deloitte, Haskins & Sells, and are contained in the booklet, *Fact Finding Interviews for Internal Auditors,* published by that firm.

The Opening of the Interview Sets the Mood.   Naturally, the auditor should always arrive on time. Since interviewees are sometimes uncomfortable because they do not know what they are going to be asked, the opening should be very informal. The auditor can put the interviewee at ease by creating a pleasant atmosphere and getting the person to talk casually. For example, it might be possible to discuss a family portrait on the interviewee's desk or an interesting work of art in the office. In order to make the transition from small talk to the main purpose of the meeting, the auditor can restate the basic objectives of the interview.

Watch and Listen.   During the course of the interview, the operational auditor should not only listen closely to the interviewee's answers, but should also watch for facial gestures and use of body language. The interviewee should be asked to repeat or restate any point that the auditor does not thoroughly understand. The auditor should never correct a person who gives an obviously incorrect answer or ever quiz, ''Are you sure about that?'' and the like. Such comments can destroy all rapport between the auditor and the client's employee.

Close on a Positive Note.   One way to indicate to the interviewee that the meeting is almost over is to ask whether there is any additional information that the auditor should know. Once the interviewee has responded to this question, the auditor should ask something like, ''May I call you if I need any additional information about your department?'' The answer to this question will always be ''yes,'' because the person being interviewed will be glad the auditor is leaving. Also, the interviewee would not be too surprised in any case if the auditor did return for additional information.

Document the Interview.   Finally, the results of an interview should be well documented. The interviewer should jot down as many notes as possible during the course of the interview. Immediately after the interview is over, the auditor should write up a meaningful memorandum that covers all the points in the interview. Some auditors carry a pocket dictating machine to record their notes on the interview. Even so, it is essential to prepare this memorandum as soon as possible after the interview.

In summary, a good interview is more difficult than it seems on the surface. An operational auditor must prepare for the interview. The auditor must persuade the respondent of the advantages of the interview and then gain rapport with that person. Although the auditor should follow a prepared list of questions, he should never be limited to the list.

Instead, the interviewer must be willing to "go with the flow" of the questioning. Once the interview has been completed, the auditor should use his notes to prepare a complete memorandum of the respondent's answers.

Although interviewing is not a skill inborn in all auditors, it is the only way to carry out an operational audit. Consequently, the good operational auditor will practice and perfect the skill of interviewing.

four

REVIEW OF PROGRAM RESULTS— AUDITING A GOVERNMENT AGENCY

Operational audits of nongovernmental organizations are generally undertaken for purposes of evaluating efficiency and economy, and such audits are the primary subject of most of this book. Many practitioners, however, may be using this book as a guide to the performance of audits of government agencies. An audit of a government agency must be concerned with program results, in addition to the traditional aspects of financial and operational auditing. Therefore, this chapter highlights some of the approaches to evaluating program results. Reviewing program effectiveness is usually not an easy task. The difficulty arises in determining both how to conduct the review and what types of performance information will satisfy the review objectives. Since program result reviews are conducted in an uncertain environment, there can be no authoritative step-by-step guideline for the auditor. Consequently, this section describes the general process.

A government program consists of a group of activities that attempt to accomplish one or more objectives. A program result is the desired change or accomplishment that occurs as an outcome of a program. Effectiveness is a measure of the extent to which a program achieves a desired level of program results. Effectiveness, then, involves a comparison between what a program actually accomplishes and what it was intended to accomplish. Measurement of program effectiveness is usually not easy for the auditor because precise standards of expected accomplishments are often unavailable. Thus, the auditor must develop acceptable-performance standards before beginning the audit.

The following example illustrates the concept of effectiveness and its relationship to the performance standard used:

One objective for a fire department is to contain fires to the building in which the fire originates. During a program results review, a small town's professional fire department was found to have a containment rate of 80 percent. Since the fire department's charter did not cite a specific measurable goal, an acceptable performance standard had to be developed. Inquiries of other comparable fire departments were made. They reported containment rates between 85 and 90 percent.

Based on the above facts, it appears that the fire department's containment program was slightly less effective than similar programs in other localities.

A program results review has three overall objectives:

1. Assessing the adequacy of management's system for measuring effectiveness.
2. Determining whether a program satisfactorily achieves a desired level of program results.
3. Identifying causes that inhibit satisfactory performance.

These objectives determine both the planning and conduct of the audit. To satisfy these objectives, the GAO recommends that auditors follow a systematic process consisting of six major activities. The flow, interrelationship, and purpose of these activities are illustrated in Exhibit 4-1.

The format of Exhibit 4-1 is not intended to suggest that all program results review activities are the same. The amount of time and staff needed to accomplish each step will be based on the nature of the organization being audited. For instance, an auditor's prior exposure to a program may affect the amount of time needed for planning and familiarization. Or, if the program has already developed its own reliable effectiveness measurement system, the auditor will not need to design a system on the spot.

The first step in a program results review is for the auditor to become familiar with the agency to be audited. This would be accomplished during the physical tour of facilities. Following the physical tour, the auditor will assess the adequacy of any existing system for measuring effectiveness.

Good management practice requires a system to measure effectiveness, and such systems are common throughout the private sector. When profit is the primary objective, measurement systems can be fairly easily designed. Unfortunately, such measurement systems are not common and often not easy to design in the public sector.

EXHIBIT 4-1

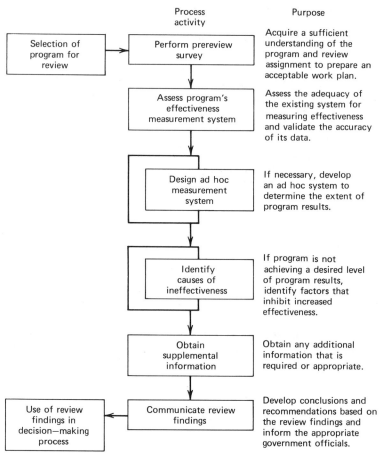

	Process activity	Purpose
Selection of program for review →	Perform prereview survey	Acquire a sufficient understanding of the program and review assignment to prepare an acceptable work plan.
	Assess program's effectiveness measurement system	Assess the adequacy of the existing system for measuring effectiveness and validate the accuracy of its data.
	Design ad hoc measurement system	If necessary, develop an ad hoc system to determine the extent of program results.
	Identify causes of ineffectiveness	If program is not achieving a desired level of program results, identify factors that inhibit increased effectiveness.
	Obtain supplemental information	Obtain any additional information that is required or appropriate.
Use of review findings in decision—making process ←	Communicate review findings	Develop conclusions and recommendations based on the review findings and inform the appropriate government officials.

EFFECTIVENESS MEASUREMENT SYSTEMS

Like all systems, an effectiveness measurement system has a structure. The structure describes what the system is. Effectiveness measurement systems consist of two structural components.

1. *Performance Indicators.* Quantifiable expressions of program objectives.
2. *Performance Standards.* Desired level of achievement for a performance indicator.

Performance Indicators

Program objectives are usually not expressed in detail, and meaningful surrogates of performance indicators need to be developed. Often multiple performance indicators are needed to capture the full intent of a program objective. For instance, a highway construction program may have as one of its objectives "the improvement of highway safety." Although safety is not directly measurable, several meaningful surrogates exist that measure several aspects of the magnitude and seriousness of unsafe conditions. For example, frequency of accidents, number of injuries, number of fatalities, and dollar value of property damage could be used as performance indicators to provide a reasonable approximation of the otherwise unmeasurable "safety" objective.

Performance indicators must always reflect the desired social change or result intended by the program objectives. Generally, the measurement of work or program outputs is not an acceptable substitute for a program objective. For example, a reduction in the number of traffic citations does not necessarily mean a reduction in unsafe driving. Similarly, an increase in the number of courses available through a vocational training program does not always imply an increase in the number of jobs of program participants.

When performance indicators are used as surrogates for program objectives they should possess the following qualities:

1. *Validity.*   The indicators reasonably represent the program objective.
2. *Sufficiency.*   The number of indicators used adequately reflects the intent of the program objective.

Performance Standards

A performance standard represents the desired level of achievement for a performance indicator. Selecting performance standards is the most elusive aspect of the design of an effectiveness measurement system. Although every program is expected to achieve a certain level of performance, the legal authorities that establish programs seldom designate what level or standard of performance is acceptable. Instead, program objectives are often stated in such general terms as "increasing" a particular service or benefit.

The scope of a program results audit is determined largely by the adequacy of management's effectiveness measurement system. Managers are generally free to determine effectiveness by whatever means they think appropriate. Systems range from those that are formal and well designed to those that are informal and rely heavily on management intuition. The resulting variation creates an uncertain environment for the program results audit.

Unfortunately, a well-defined and universally accepted body of principles and standards does not govern the design and use of effectiveness measurement systems. The variation in design and related uncertainty place a greater burden on the program results audit. In addition, if a measurement system is found to be inadequate, the auditor must not only propose recommendations to correct the deficiency but also expand the scope of the audit. This expansion may entail either modifying management's system for measuring effectiveness or developing an *ad hoc* system to generate the required performance data. As long as this uncertain environment exists, an auditor planning and conducting a program results audit will have to consider the possible variations in effectiveness measurement systems.

When management uses a system to measure program effectiveness, both the adequacy of the system and the accuracy of the data must be examined. From this examination the auditor can establish the reliability of management's performance reports.

The process of examining management's system can be summarized in terms of the following general activities:

Identifying and documenting management's system for measuring effectiveness

Assessing the validity and sufficiency of the performance indicators

Assessing the accuracy of the performance indicator data

Assessing the appropriateness of the performance standards

Determining effectiveness based on management's system

At this point, it should be noted that there are some circumstances under which a program results audit should not be undertaken at all. Exhibit 4-2 lists five situations in which the GAO doubts the desirability of an evaluative audit.

Using an Auditor-Created Measurement System

When management does not have an acceptable effectiveness measurement system, an *ad hoc* system may need to be developed to determine whether a program is achieving a desired level of results.

An *ad hoc* system is used in lieu of a permanent effectiveness measurement system to satisfy the program results review objective.

EXHIBIT 4-2. **Situations That Diminish the Desirability of a Comprehensive Program Results Review**

Situation	Example
Program is too immature to be reviewed.	A three-year training program is in its second year of operation.
Past performance data does not reflect current operations.	Having recently recognized its own weaknesses, program management implemented major new changes in operating policies and practices. (Note: A limited-scope review concentrating solely on the identification of causes of ineffectiveness and validation of management's changes may be appropriate.)
Program objectives are too imprecise or controversial.	A program objective "to improve the quality of life" is too general and hence precludes use of universally acceptable indicators.
Lack of measurable performance data.	Pure research and development programs with the objective of advancing the state of the art cannot generally be measured.
Inability to demonstrate causal relationship between the program and social change.	A general tax rebate program may have as one of its objectives a decrease in the unemployment rate. Such a change would be impossible to attribute directly to this program on a per-dollar basis since variables such as other monetary and fiscal strategies, the demand for new employees, the supply of trained workers, and various social programs with employment objectives would also effect changes in national employment statistics.

Generally, the measurements obtained from an *ad hoc* system cannot be as refined or comprehensive as those from a permanently established and well-designed effectiveness measurement system. Nonetheless, an *ad hoc* system provides the users of the program results audit findings with more reliable effectiveness data than they had previously and shifts the burden for fine-tuning the performance data back to program management. Regardless of the findings of the *ad hoc* system, program management should design and implement an acceptable effectiveness measurement system to continue to monitor program performance.

The scope of an *ad hoc* system depends on the circumstance that necessitates its use. The most extensive system is required when management has failed to establish a system or its system proves to be totally inadequate. Under these circumstances, the scope should include all program objectives that are subject to review.

THE AUDIT REPORT

The content of a program results audit report depends on the scope of the assignment. The types of findings, conclusions, and recommendations that might result from a comprehensive program results review involve:

1. A determination of whether the desired results are being achieved and how this determination was made.
2. An assessment of the adequacy of management's system for measuring effectiveness and general recommendations for improving the measurement system, if appropriate.
3. The identification of causes that inhibit the intended level of program effectiveness together with recommendations for appropriate corrective action.

The level of program effectiveness is based on the findings generated by either management's effectiveness measurement system or an *ad hoc* system. Regardless of the system used, the review team should report whether the program is achieving its desired results.

The auditor is not required to express an opinion as to the absolute effectiveness of a program. Such a definitive opinion would be possible only if program objectives were directly quantifiable and the program was charged with achieving specific results. In the absence of such precision, the auditor must qualify the effectiveness determination based on the system used. Thus a complete description of the effectiveness measurement system, including the performance indicators, performance standard, data sources, and data-collection techniques, should be included in the final report.

If effectiveness cannot be determined, the review agency should discuss the factors that obviate measurement. Some of the problems that diminish the ability or desirability of measuring effectiveness are presented in Exhibit 4-2.

The last major evaluative audit activity involves communicating the review findings to the appropriate government officials. Written reports are the normal method for communicating findings. Oral briefings, however, may also be required or appropriate.

SUMMARY

A program results audit of a government agency is a process by which qualified individuals determine the level of a program's effectiveness and, if necessary, identify areas for improved program performance. Although some might consider such an audit to be completely different from an operational audit, it is actually a part of the traditional operational audit. An operational audit deals with efficiency, economy, and effectiveness, the subject of this chapter deals only with effectiveness.

A program results audit of a government agency has three objectives:

1. Assessing the adequacy of management's system for measuring program effectiveness.
2. Determining whether a program achieves a desired level of results.
3. Identifying causes that inhibit satisfactory results.

A program results audit is defined as an expanded scope audit, because it involves more than the traditional financial audit. It is performed only for government agencies and programs and is not as inclusive as a complete operational audit engagement.

IN-DEPTH AUDIT PROGRAMS

The people working in a department are the real experts in how the department should be run. Thus the people working in the department being audited are the primary source of operational auditing data. A well-conducted interview and the construction of a good questionnaire are therefore mandatory. The time invested in developing questionnaires is probably the most important aspect of operational auditing. The use of a questionnaire ensures that audit coverage is complete and that all audits are similar in scope. The questionnaires should be used with several respondents, since individuals may view things differently and the auditor will often receive conflicting answers. The operational auditor is more likely to unearth the true facts about a potential problem when several viewpoints are obtained.

Direct observation is also a useful tool; problems that could not be determined in any other manner and problems that employees are trying to hide or of which they are not aware can be brought to light. Additionally, observation provides a source of examples that are useful in illustrating general conclusions.

The following chapters are built around the in-depth audit questionnaires for particular departments. The questionnaires have been generalized and apply to virtually every type of business (profit and not-for-profit). Most questions have been designed so that a ''yes'' answer indicates a good situation and a ''no'' answer suggests a possible problem.

The operational auditor must realize that these general questionnaires may not always cover each situation completely. The questionnaires should be subject to on-the-job revisions by the auditor.

While asking questions, the auditor should listen not only for the answers, but also for voice inflections, while watching for facial expressions that might add insight into the true nature of a problem. Interviews with employees should always be conducted on an informal basis. The auditor should follow the proper channels of authority before tying up an employee's time with an interview. The person being interviewed should be assured that the auditor is not looking for mistakes or errors on the part of the interviewee. Instead, the employee should be persuaded that the operational audit is designed to help, not to be critical. During the interview, the auditor should avoid taking sides on a particular issue or judging a particular policy. Many employees have a definite opinion about how their department should be run and seek the auditor's confirmation; the auditor should give due consideration to all these recommendations, but refrain from committing himself to any viewpoint before he has assembled and analyzed all the facts.

five

ACCOUNTING

In the past, the accounting department of many organizations was a luxury rather than a necessity. The past decade, however, has witnessed a change in the role of the accounting department. New laws mandate greater accuracy in business reporting, while new sources of financing put more emphasis on the preparation of financial statements.

The additional work this has created for the accountant has, in some cases, led to poor management practices. Accountants have had to contend with so much more paperwork that they have had little time to meet overall goals and objectives. Meanwhile, the field of accounting has expanded to cover a broad range of functions. At one extreme, accounting can embrace the formulation of major company policies. At the other extreme, accounting can be a record-keeping function that involves a great burden of paper shuffling. This range of activities and the fact that the accounting function impinges on the work of every other department in a company make the accounting department a likely candidate for an operational audit.

The operational audit's accounting department questionnaire (illustrated in Exhibit 5-1) is divided into five sections:

General
Budgets
Internal control
Procedures
Departmental staff

GENERAL

The General section begins with two questions pertaining to operating procedures: Are they codified in a procedures manual? (A lack of established procedures would be a real hindrance to a new employee, for

EXHIBIT 5-1   Accounting Questionnaire

Yes / No / DNA

General

1. Is there a procedures manual for the department?

2. Have steps been taken to provide assurance that the established procedures are being followed?

3. Are the reports that you prepare used by anyone?

4. Is there a "How to Use" manual for the reports you prepare?

5. Is there an organization chart defining where job positions in the department fit into the department and where the department stands in relation to the rest of the organization?

6. Is pertinent historical and projected financial data provided accurately, speedily, and in meaningful form?

7. Is financial and statistical data sufficient for use in performance evaluation and appraisal?

8. Is the accrual system of accounting used (as opposed to a cash basis system)?

9. Is there an open line of communication with all other departments?

10. Is the accounting system complex and detailed enough to give accurate cost figures for all items in each department?

11. Are the books of account adequate for an organization of this size?

12. Is the equipment in the department adequate?

13. Are the physical facilities of the office adequate?

14. Is the lighting sufficient?

15. Is the department telephone bill checked to be certain that each long distance call is necessary and made in the cheapest way possible?

16. Has the advisability of acquiring a WATS line been investigated?

17. Are there ever financial audits of the organization?

18. How many days of revenue are in Accounts Receivable?

19. What percentage of total Accounts Receivable is allowance for bad debts? Of Notes Receivable? Of Receivables from employees?

EXHIBIT 5-1 (Continued)

Yes / No / DNA

Budgets

20. Does the department prepare an annual budget?

21. Is the structure of the budget the same as that of the accounting system?

22. Has anyone questioned the cost of developing the budget in relation to its estimated value?

23. Are budgets the result of challenged calculations as opposed to prior figures developed without analysis from experience?

24. Are budgets prepared by the people responsible for meeting them?

25. Do budgets include cushions or fat that diminish their effectiveness as control instruments?

26. Are written budgets changed when future plans are changed?

27. Do you utilize cash flow budgets?

28. Are cash flow budgets updated periodically?

29. Is Accounting aware of the budgets of all departments?

30. Are actual-versus-budget reports prepared?

31. Is the Accounting department budget adequate?

32. Are capital budgeting techniques used for planning large capital expenditures?

Internal Control

33. Is there a written internal control policy?

34. Do you feel that there is a separation of duties among employees which fosters good internal control?

35. Are employees required to take a vacation at least annually?

36. Are duties periodically rotated among the employees?

37. Are journal entries supported by substantiating data?

38. Are assets adequately insured by an outside insurance company?

39. Are employees bonded?

40. Are allowances for discounts to appropriate customers authorized by a responsible official?

41. Is it company policy to require approval by a responsible official before writing off a bad debt?

42. Is it company policy to have receipts deposited in the bank and recorded in the cash receipts journal daily?

43. Are receipts deposited in the bank intact without first subtracting small payments in cash?

44. Is a For Deposit Only endorsement stamp applied immediately to all checks received?

45. Is it company policy to have vouchers and supporting documents presented simultaneously with checks for signature?

46. Are vouchers and supporting invoices effectively canceled (marked Paid) after the related check has been signed, in order to prevent duplicate payment?

47. Are checks prenumbered?

48. Is a check protector used?

49. Are unused checks stored in a safe or vault?

50. Are vault combinations and keys restricted to the minimum number of individuals?

51. Is the vault locked at all times when unattended?

52. Are miscellaneous cash receipts, such as from scrap sales, adequately controlled?

53. Are checks signed by someone other than the preparer?

54. Is there a distinction between individuals who are authorized to sign checks and employees who have access to accounting records, cash receipts, and petty cash funds?

55. Is the bank statement reconciled monthly?

56. Does someone other than the preparer of checks perform the bank reconciliation?

57. Are signed checks mailed without returning them to the individual who prepared them?

58. Does the person who prepares the bank deposits also have anything to do with customers ledgers?

59. Have instructions been issued to the bank not to cash checks payable to the company but to accept them for deposit only?

60. Is each petty cash fund in the sole custody of one person?

EXHIBIT 5-1 (Continued)

Yes / *No* / *DNA*

Procedures

61. How long after the close of the month are financial reports generated?

62. Are financial statements prepared monthly?

63. Are reports correct as issued or do they contain errors?

64. Are there any bottlenecks in the paper flow?

65. Are all tasks that are performed necessary?

66. Have you investigated the advisability of computerizing some or some more functions, possibly through timesharing?

67. For small organizations, has the feasibility of using a one-write system been examined?

68. Are internal reports to management prepared in a manner to highlight any unusual variations in figures?

69. Have you examined the possibility of reducing posting time by doing more summary posting?

70. Do you take advantage of all possible cash discounts?

71. Does the accounting system show the amount of any cash discounts not taken?

72. Are receivables, payables and other subsidiary ledger totals compared to the control account balances at monthly intervals?

73. Are errors ever uncovered in comparing receivables and payables ledger totals to the control account balances?

74. Are there ledgers for items of property and equipment?

75. Are property, plant, and equipment ledgers balanced periodically with general ledger control accounts?

76. Is a periodic inventory of plant and equipment items taken?

77. Is depreciation of plant and equipment recorded in the accounts?

78. Are all revenues and expenses always posted to the proper departments?

79. Do all charges get posted promptly to the proper customer accounts?

80. Are insurance claims filed promptly and is there any follow-up if payment is delayed?

EXHIBIT 5-1 (Continued)

Yes / No / DNA

81. Are accounts receivables aged regularly?

82. Are statements mailed out regularly?

83. Is the organization's price list kept up to date?

84. Is the size of the checking account balance appropriate to current cash needs?

85. Is excess cash ever used for short-term investment?

86. Is copying machine use controlled?

Department Staff

87. Is there a job description for each position in the department?

88. Is there any program—formal or informal—of new-employee orientation and training? Any manual?

89. Are employees competent to perform the duties they are supposed to be performing?

90. Do you feel that all employees in the department are loyal to the organization?

91. Do you feel that all employees in the department take pride in their work?

92. Do employees have a favorable attitude toward the department and the organization?

93. Do you feel that employees are knowledgeable in all areas of accounting, rather than in just the small area in which they work?

94. What is the employee turnover rate?

95. What is the employee absence rate?

96. Do all employees in the department have training in accounting?

97. Are accountants paid at approximately the same rate as other accountants in the surrounding area?

98. Do you have quantified standards of performance to measure each accounting employee's performance?

99. Does the Accounting department ever work overtime at a premium pay rate?

100. Has the possibility been considered of hiring temporary employees to assist in performing the month-end work?

EXHIBIT 5-1 (Continued)

101. Is the workload arranged so that one person is not idle while another is overloaded?

102. Do you feel any employees in the department are overburdened with work?

103. Is continuing education encouraged?

104. Is membership in professional organizations encouraged?

105. Does the company have an internal auditor?

instance) and Are the established procedures being followed? The organization chart, inquired about in Question 5, would similarly help new employees, as well as old employees.

Questions 3 and 4 relate to the quality and timeliness of the reports prepared by the accounting department. Financial reports must be user-oriented. Reports must provide usable information and provide it quickly. Financial data is nearly worthless unless it is provided soon after the end of the period. Too often, reports are thrown into the wastebasket on receipt because they are unclear, out of date, or simply misdirected. Both historical and projected data should be provided accurately and quickly (Question 6)—especially accurately. Sometimes a company issues reports so fast that some information is missing or erroneous. If report users begin to notice chronic revisions in subsequent reports, they will tend to doubt the initial reports.

Also relating to the usefulness of the statements, the adequacy of reports for use in performance evaluation and appraisal is examined by Question 7. Question 10 asks whether the accounting system is complex enough to provide accurate cost figures for each item in a department.

Question 8 asks whether the accrual system of accounting is used. This ordinarily will not be a problem area except for a few very small clients (generally, too small to retain an operational auditor) and for not-for-profit enterprises.

Communication with other departments (Question 9) includes use of nontechnical terms: not everyone "speaks accounting." Closely related are Questions 3 and 4 ("are reports used?" "is there a how-to-use manual?"). A layman's manual (an accounting dictionary, so to speak) helps realize the full value of financial reports.

Questions 11 through 14 examine the adequacy of the department's physical facilities, including the account books, general equipment, and lighting. Since the value of a modern accounting department has only recently been recognized, some departments have been slighted when facilities were provided. In addition to asking the appropriate questions, the auditor should use his own powers of observation to assess the adequacy and quality of facilities. For example, question 14, asking whether lighting is sufficient, can be difficult for a person to answer if they have never worked in another office. The respondent may say the lighting is excellent without realizing he may be making mistakes or ruining his eyes because of the dimness. Regardless of what the employees think, the auditor should use his or her own judgment on this question.

Questions 15 and 16 are concerned with proper use of telephone facilities. Accounting employees have frequent occasion to make long distance telephone calls (for example, trying to collect receivables, straighten out payables, and arrange financing). There should be some type of log of long distance calls and the reason for each call, in order to permit periodic review. A WATS line can reduce long distance costs for frequent users. Although it is not suitable for all companies, a well-managed company will at least have investigated the possibility of acquiring a WATS line, or similar service.

Question 16 asks whether the company is subject to an annual audit. A regular financial audit often goes hand in hand with a good accounting department. The accountants realize that their work will be scrutinized at year end. Also, the CPA firm makes annual recommendations for improving accounting department procedures.

The last two questions in the General section examine the amount of Receivables and Uncollectable accounts. Once the auditor learns the number of days of revenue represented by receivables, he should ascertain the client's credit terms and the prevailing credit terms in the industry. If the number of days of revenue in Receivables is above average, or if the volume of Receivables is on an uptrend, perhaps the accounting department is devoting insufficient time to pressuring customers for payment. The auditor should check also the nonroutine types of receivables such as notes and amounts owed by employees.

BUDGETS

The section of the questionnaire concerning budgets should be informative in a general way. The mere existence of a budget is indicative of some planning and looking ahead. In some organizations, the budgeting staff constitutes a separate department. Whether budgeting and accounting are in the same department, the budget system should be identical to the accounting system. This not only makes budgets easier to prepare, but also facilitates comparison between actual results and budgeted figures. Without identical systems, it would be very costly, if not impossible, to make these comparisons. Thus Question 21, asking whether the two systems are comparable, is probably the most important question in this section, after Number 20 ("do you prepare an annual budget?"). Question 22 inquires whether a budget is fully utilized. A well-prepared budget is a helpful tool, but in some organizations the budget is not used to its maximum potential.

Ideally, each year's budget should be based on reasoned expectations for the future (Question 23). Too often, unfortunately, the budget is prepared simply by modifying the prior year's budget by the indicated rate of inflation. It is preferable that managers be forced to justify each budget item. Such concepts as zero base budgeting are steps in this direction.

Employees should have the opportunity to participate in the preparation of the budget (Question 24). However, the final budget should represent a consensus of opinion of all levels of management, with some contribution from both the top of the organization and the grassroots level. Negotiating a budget which takes into consideration both top-level objectives and bottom-level capabilities can help cut down on the number of "cushions" in the final product (Question 25).

A negative answer to Question 26 ("is the budget rewritten or revised when company plans are changed?") may indicate that budgets are prepared but rarely used. The question is usually answered affirmatively at companies which really use their budgets.

Questions 27 and 28 ask about the use of the cash flow budget, which is probably the most useful and most widely used segment of the company budget. Even the smallest companies usually have a cash budget. Unfortunately, many organizations prepare a cash budget at the beginning of a year, but never update it during the year (Question 28). The cash budget should be periodically revised to prevent cash flow problems later in the year.

Question 29 (is Accounting aware of the budgets of all departments?) is usually a natural outgrowth of the budgeting process, but is occasionally ignored. A budget is really two tools; a control tool, as well as a planning tool. Little additional effort is necessary to utilize the control tool after the planning tool has been carefully developed. Thus, the Accounting department should have access to all departmental budgets in order to prepare the most useful reports.

This subject is continued in Question 30, which asks whether actual-versus-budget reports are prepared. Using the budget as a control tool, weekly or monthly budget reports can be prepared. These periodic budget reports also make the budget a motivation tool by giving employees a budget goal.

Question 31 relates to the adequacy of the Accounting department budget allocation. Experience indicates that few department heads ever feel that their budget is large enough, but the question may provide a welcome change of pace for both the auditor and the employees answering the questions.

The final question in the budget section concerns capital budgeting. All capital expenditures should be evaluated using capital budgeting techniques such as the internal rate of return method, net present value, or payback. Because of the large sums of cash required, capital expenditures should be carefully planned and prepared for as far in advance as possible. Some companies budget their capital expenditures at least five years ahead.

INTERNAL CONTROL

Internal control is usually covered in the course of the company's annual financial audit; the CPA firm that performs the annual financial audit is supposed to verify the existence of internal control. However, the financial auditor may not always insist that a problem of internal control be corrected. Instead, he may simply take steps to assure himself that the problem has not caused any other problem. For this reason, internal control should be investigated as part of the operational audit. If the CPA firm that performs the annual financial audit also does the operational audit, the auditors may already be familiar with the internal control system.

It should be noted that the purpose of an internal control system is not only to prevent employee fraud. It is designed also to catch errors as they happen (rather than waiting until year end for the auditor to make the correction) and to ascertain whether the goals and objectives of management are reached.

The first question (33) in the Internal Control section asks whether a stated internal control policy exists. If an organization is devoting adequate attention to internal control, it will have a written policy statement.

Question 34 deals with a primary principle of good internal control: is there a separation of duties among personnel? The cash handling and the cash recording functions, for example, should be separate, as should the cash receipts and cash disbursements functions. The same principle dictates that each employee be required to take an annual vacation, and that there should be a periodic rotation of duties (Questions 35 and 36). Vacation and rotation policies can nip an embezzlement scheme in the bud.

Question 37 inquires whether all journal entries are supported by adequate documentation. Every entry should be backed up by corresponding invoices and approvals in the files. Approvals of authorized officials for discounts and writeoffs (Questions 40, 41) are another form of documentation to support journal entries.

Regarding insurance coverage (Question 38), unless an organization has an explicit self-insurance policy, it should have adequate coverage on all its tangible assets. A lack of coverage may indicate that the company is mismanaged or that the assets do not exist. The bonding of company employees (Question 39) offers several advantages. First, the company will be reimbursed if a loss does occur. Second, employees may be less likely to steal because they will realize that they will be hounded and prosecuted by the bonding agency. Finally, the bonding agency screens employees, thus reducing the company's risk of unwittingly employing a convicted felon.

All cash receipts (the subject of Questions 42 to 44) should be stamped For Deposit Only upon receipt. The immediate deposit accompanied by duplicate record (the company's and the bank's) will result in less temptation for employees.

Questions 45 and 46 ask about the documentation to support cash disbursements. Required documentation should include the vendor invoice, receiving report, purchase order, purchase requisition, and an invoice approval form. The substantiating papers should be stamped Paid in order to avoid double payment. More than one embezzlement scheme could have been averted simply by stamping all copies of invoices and receiving reports Paid. Otherwise, a dishonest accountant can pull an old invoice from the files, change the date, and process it for a second payment. He can then intercept the signed check and cash it for his personal use.

The control of checks is examined in Questions 47 through 49. Checks should be prenumbered and stored in a locked vault. A check protector will prevent fraudulent raising of the amount on the check. In general, the fewer individuals who have access to the locked vault (Question 50), the better the internal control.

Some miscellaneous cash receipts might not be covered by the regular internal control system (Question 52). For example, sales of scrap may occur so infrequently that there is no routine for handling the proceeds. This author discovered, for example, a meat-cutter in a supermarket who was guilelessly pocketing the proceeds from the sale of bones. The meat-cutter did not intend to cheat the supermarket, which formerly paid to have the bones hauled away. The meat-cutter felt he was saving the company money by selling the bones. This procedure had gone on for several years, because the company had no policy for handling the sale of scrap items.

Questions 53 and 54 are devoted to the separation of duties connected with company checks. Those individuals who are permitted to sign checks should have no other responsibilities with respect to the process of check preparation and recording. The reconciliation of the monthly bank statement (Questions 55 and 56) should be performed each month by an individual who has no connection with the check preparation process.

Questions 57 through 60 concern miscellaneous principles of internal control. First, signed checks should be mailed without being returned to the preparer (this principle helps stop an embezzlement scheme based on payment of fraudulent invoices as discussed in a previous paragraph). The company's bank should be instructed not to cash checks payable to the company; these checks should be accepted for deposit only. Finally, petty cash funds should be in the sole custody of one individual in order to fix responsibility.

PROCEDURES

The section of the questionnaire relating to procedures attempts to detect problems within the department which can cause problems in other departments. For example (Questions 61 through 63), if the accounting department does not prepare financial statements frequently and quickly, other departments could be adversely affected by a lack of information. Question 63 examines the quality of internal reports as they are presented to the user. The existence of bottlenecks in paperflow is examined by Question 64.

Sometimes a department can do too much work. For example, the company may at one time have been required to prepare reports to comply with government-dictated price controls or other laws that are no longer in effect. When the law is revoked, the dogged accountants may in some instances continue to prepare the customary reports. Thus Question 65 asks whether all work performed is necessary. Similarly, the department can cut its work load through use of computers, one-write systems, and summary posting (Questions 66, 67, and 69).

Internal reports should be prepared in a manner that highlights any unusual variations in figures (Question 68). The preparation of comparative statements (covering two time periods) and common size statements will help guide the user to these anomalies. Showing the period-to-period changes in both percentages and absolute dollars will also be helpful.

Questions 70 and 71 ask about purchase discounts. An organization that does not take advantage of all cash discounts is effectively paying a high interest rate. The auditor may want to recommend that the company begin using the net method of recording purchases rather than the more common gross method; the net method requires that a loss account be debited whenever a discount is not taken. This account, usually called Discounts Lost, is a red flag that indicates inefficiency.

Questions 72 through 78 bear on internal control. Many companies neglect the periodic reconciliation of subsidary ledgers to the corresponding control account balances (Questions 72 and 73). These reconciliations are made so rarely that when an attempt to catch up is finally made, the resulting work is many times greater. Subsidiary ledgers for plant and equipment (Questions 74 through 77) are important controls. Although most companies have subsidiary records for receivables and payables, such is not always the case for plant and equipment (and some companies that do have property ledgers do not always keep them up to date). The final internal control type question listed under Procedures inquires whether revenues and expenses are always posted to the proper department. These errors go undetected in the overall financial compilation, but misreport individual departmental performance.

Questions 79 through 85 relate primarily to the management of cash flows. With the exception of Questions 84 and 85, all of these questions pertain to speeding the inflows. For example, if charges are promptly posted to customer accounts (Question 79), then up-to-date statements can be mailed to customers right away. Similarly, periodic aging of receivables (Question 81) will show which accounts need to be given special attention. Also, the faster insurance claims are filed (Question 80) and statements are mailed, the sooner payments will be received. Finally, are the prices being charged the current rates (Question 83)? New price lists sometimes get mailed to everyone except the Billing department.

The final question in this section relates to the pesky problem of excess use of the copying machine. With all of the documents that are either prepared or used in the accounting department, there is a real problem of copying machine costs. The most controllable part of this cost is the personal use of the machine by employees. A log requiring the signature of the person making copies might help to cut down on personal copying. Wasteful nonpersonal use can be reduced by periodic reminders by managers of the need to reduce copying costs.

DEPARTMENT STAFF

The last section of the Accounting questionnaire concerns department staffing. Job descriptions (Question 87) are necessary when positions are filled and when questions arise about the scope of jobs. A job description should also include standards of performance for each position (Question 98).

Questions 88 through 90 and 96 relate to the qualifications of the Accounting staff. Accountants in the organization being audited need the same type of knowledge as accountants in other firms. The department should have an orientation program for new employees and either a training program or manual. It is necessary to pay competitive wages to hire and hold good people (Question 97). Employees should have a favorable attitude toward their department and the organization for which they work (Questions 90 and 92). Pride in one's work (Question 91) is very important in this department, because the accountant's job involves so many opportunities to make mistakes. Thus the desire for personal accomplishment fosters quality control.

The rates of employee turnover and absence are examined in Questions 94 and 95. The auditor will want to compare these figures with those of other departments and other companies in the community. The ability to provide the figures for the department is in itself a positive sign; a problem recognized is a problem half solved.

Questions 99 through 102 are concerned with department workload. Overtime is expensive. Ideally a company should manage its employees' time in such a manner that overtime work is unnecessary. However, because an accounting department often has month-end deadlines, it may have to incur some overtime, hire temporary personnel (Question 100), or arrange a flexible working schedule.

Continuing education should be encouraged (Questions 103 and 104). Periodic refresher courses are essential for accountants, who have to keep abreast of changing laws and regulations. The company should encourage them to continue their training. Those accountants who are CPAs should be encouraged to join the American Institute of Certified Public Accountants or the American Woman's Society of CPAs. Both CPAs and non-CPAs should participate in the activities of the National Association of Accountants, the Financial Executives Institute, the Institute of Internal Auditors, or the American Society of Women Accountants. These groups have local chapters throughout the nation.

The final question (105) is "does the organization have an internal auditor?" The cost/benefit ratio of a staff internal auditor may not be favorable in a small company. However, if an organization is large enough, the net result may be greater economy and efficiency.

The Accounting department is the core of the business office. If Accounting performs its job well, all other departments will benefit. The operational auditor is naturally concerned that the Accounting department, like all departments, should operate efficiently and effectively. The auditor also realizes that the Accounting department is closely related to all other departments; no matter what department is being examined during the operational audit, the auditor will utilize the output of the Accounting department. Thus the activities of the Accounting department affect the auditor in all phases of an operational audit.

Finally, the auditor should keep in mind that the questionnaires in this book do not have to be used exclusively for operational audit engagements. The questionnaires can also be used by a practitioner who wishes to conduct a mini-operational audit as part of the annual financial audit. The practitioner might want to consider conducting one mini-operational audit each year in order to give the client a little extra for his money. The recommendations resulting from a mini-audit can help to maintain good client relations.

six

ELECTRONIC DATA PROCESSING

The purpose of this chapter is to present an approach to the operational audit of an electronic data processing (EDP) department and, in the process, to review some of the key principles of control and approaches to EDP effectiveness and efficiency that arise in most EDP operational audits. Operational auditing of EDP is complicated by the rapid growth of EDP technology and the corresponding growth in the ways companies use the technology. Although the principles of EDP control that were developed very early are still valid and are unlikely to be discarded, the techniques necessary for achieving those controls have had to change. For example, approaches to authorization control that depend heavily on obtaining signatures and filing all source documents are simply inappropriate in new communications-based systems where computer terminals have replaced input forms.

The auditor's appreciation of the extent to which the company has good controls, his ability to judge the efficiency and effectiveness of the systems he reviews, and his ability to make comprehensive and complete recommending control techniques, and he must be flexible in applying software, and related system designs encountered. He may be an expert in one EDP situation and an amateur in the next.

The EDP operational auditor must be open-minded in evaluating and recommendating control techniques, and he must be flexible in applying control principles. An audit program that is wholly appropriate for one installation may require modification for another.

The guidelines in this chapter are presented as a base on which to tailor a specific audit program. The questionnaire and forms were designed primarily for use in a medium-size in-house EDP department. They would probably need modifying to be suitable for a very small or very large installation, or for a service bureau, for example.

The following sections will cover (1) the collection of data prior to the on-site interview phase, (2) the EDP operational audit questionnaire and its objectives, and (3) some suggestions for the presentation of recommendations.

Collection of Data Prior to the Interview Phase

The EDP operational auditor can facilitate the planning and scheduling of interviews, prepare better for the on-site administration of the questionnaire, and facilitate the client's completion of necessary data collection tasks by requesting certain information in advance of the interviews. The auditor should prepare lists of required data and forms to assist in the data collection process and should present them to the client in person, if possible. On subsequently receiving and studying the data, the auditor may then amend the audit program as necessary to cover any new areas of inquiry suggested by the data, and then develop and propose an interview schedule to client management. The lists and forms illustrated in Exhibits 6-1 through 6-4 have been used to advantage by the author.

The Information Checklist. The forms of Exhibits 6-1 (Information Checklist 1) and 6-2 (Information Checklist 2) list basic information needed by the EDP operational auditor both in planning the interview phase and during the interviews. Checklist 1 data are essential to pre-interview planning. Checklist 2 requests copies of forms and emergency plans, none of which is essential to preparation for the interviews, but whose presence and quality give some indication of the department's use of standards. If the auditor is reluctant to disclose his interest in standards before the interviews, Checklist 2 could be sought during the administering of the questionnaire and not requested in advance. The Operations section of Checklist 1 is completed through the use of the two additional forms discussed below.

Applications Data. The auditor needs to know what applications are being processed on the computer, what departments are served, and whom to contact in each case. The Applications List (Exhibit 6-3) can usually be completed easily by an operator or a data control clerk.

A really clear picture of the scope of operations will be obtained only through descriptions of some of the important characteristics of each application. The Applications Brief Description (Exhibit 6-4) is suggested for collecting this data. One of these forms should be completed for each application on the Applications List.

Looking at all these forms gives the auditor a feeling for the total

EXHIBIT 6-1   Information Checklist 1

Organization

_____ Organization Chart

_____ EDP Job Descriptions

_____ Physical Plant Layout

Plans

_____ Corporate Objectives

_____ EDP Objectives

_____ EDP Plans and Budgets
Prior Year _____
This Year _____
Long Term _____

_____ Current Status/Progress Report

Equipment and Software

_____ Hardware List

_____ Software List

Project Control

_____ Current Task List

_____ Current Task Control Forms

Operations

_____ List of Applications (see form)

_____ Application Brief Descriptions (see form)

EXHIBIT 6-2   Information Checklist 2

System Development and Maintenance

_____ Job Request Form

_____ System Request Form

_____ System Change Form

_____ Approval Forms

Data Entry

_____ Sample Forms (by system)

_____ Sample Log

Data Control

_____ Sample Control Forms

_____ Sample Log

Operations

_____ Current Schedule of Operations

_____ Sample of Operator Instructions

_____ Sample Logs

Contingency Planning

_____ Copy of Emergency Plans

EXHIBIT 6-3 Applications List

Application Name	User Department	Contact Name

EXHIBIT 6-4   Application Brief Description

Name _____

Purpose _____

Data Entry:

Through Data Entry Department _____;
Online by user _____;
Other _____
Describe _____

	Batch	On-Line
System Characteristics:		
Approximate Number of Programs and Sorts	_____	_____
Principal Programming Language(s)	_____	_____
Stable (S) or Undergoing Change (C) or Developmental (D)	_____	_____
Operations Characteristics:		
Approximate Run Frequency (daily, weekly, etc.)	_____	_____
Requested (R) or Regularly Scheduled (S)	_____	_____
Approximate Run Time (Batch)	_____	_____
Approximate "Up" Time (On Line)	_____	_____

processing load, the number of languages being used, the approximate split in the EDP workload between maintenance and development activities, and a general idea of the systems approaches being used. Looked at individually, the brief descriptions indicate what kinds of system documentation and user instructions one should look for, where terminals are being used, what kinds of operator instructions to look for, and where to look for the application of specific controls forms.

The EDP Operational Audit Questionnaire

The EDP operational audit questionnaire (Exhibit 6-5) presented here is designed to be completed during or shortly after each interview in a series progressing (in Question order) from top management to members of the data control group. Questions are designed to disclose any weaknesses in overall controls, planning, communications, management practices, and various aspects of EDP systems development. Some of the Questionnaire sections end with queries about opinions and perceptions. These are especially useful in identifying communications problems.

A Yes response generally connotes good control and a No response generally indicates a potential problem. The response should be amplified by marginal notes, interview notes, and pertinent materials when a simple Yes or No is insufficient. When a question is inapplicable, it should be so designated in the DNA box.

Of course the questionnaire is only a device for recording the auditor's conclusions. He should verify all the responses except those in the perceptions sections. All other responses should be double-checked through observation, tests, and any other means available and appropriate. He should study the data gathered before the interviews before addressing the related section of the questionnaire so that he will be ready to discuss any inconsistencies. The questionnaire can and should be modified to the extent necessary to cover unanticipated questions that may arise when examining documentation or interviewing another functional area.

The following section-by-section discussion of the questionnaire highlights the principal objectives of the questions and, where appropriate, expands on the control problems being addressed. Each section defines the individuals who should have the answers to the section's questions.

EDP AND THE ORGANIZATION

Questions 1 through 11 are probably best answered by the person to whom the EDP head reports. For the perceptions group (Questions 12

Yes / No / DNA

EXHIBIT 6-5   EDP Operational Audit Questionnaire

EDP and the Organization

Position of EDP

1. Does the EDP manager report to a senior executive with authority sufficient to ensure that there is proper participation by users in determining EDP direction and adequate support of EDP for its responsibilities?

2. Is the EDP department completely independent of other operational units?

Planning and Budgeting

3. Is EDP required to prepare plans for management approval?
   short-term plans (one year or less)?
   long-term plans (more than one year)?

4. Is EDP required to prepare a budget?
   short-term budget (one year or less)?
   long-term budget (more than one year)?

5. Are there written procedures for planning and budgeting?

Control

6. Is there a steering committee for EDP?

7. Does top management require regular meetings of user representatives and EDP to review progress, requirements, problems, and plans?

8. Does the EDP manager regularly report performance compared with plans and budget to senior management?

9. Are there written procedures for the assessment and presentation of costs and benefits of proposed purchases. Such as:
   hardware
   software
   applications systems
   outside EDP services

10. Does top management review and approve all major EDP expenditures, including those for new applications?

11. Does top management review and approve all proposed EDP contracts?

Perceptions of EDP

12. Are EDP costs reasonable?

97

EXHIBIT 6-5 (Continued)

13. Is EDP staff performance wholly satisfactory?

14. Are all urgent systems needs being addressed?

15. Are systems performing to specifications?

16. Is the EDP department able to keep up with corporate requirements?

17. Is turnover of EDP personnel satisfactory?

18. Is the EDP department up-to-date?

19. Does it compare favorably with competitors' departments?

EDP Management

Organization and Staffing

20. Are there up-to-date job descriptions for all EDP department positions?

21. Are the functions of programming, operations, data control, and data entry separated?

22. Are all available positions filled?

23. Are all staff well qualified for their positions?

24. Is staff turnover at a reasonable rate?

25. Are salaries and other benefits adequate?

26. The company's attitude toward employee participation in educational and professional development programs is one of:
    encouragement
    financial support

27. Are there written procedures for the review and evaluation of employee performance?

28. Are performance reviews conducted at regular intervals for all personnel?

Facilities

29. Do the quarters appear to be well lighted; have adequate seating, work, and storage space; be well ventilated; and have a reasonable temperature?

30. Is the noise level in every area acceptable?

31. Are soundproof areas available for meetings, interviews, training, and the like?

EXHIBIT 6-5 (Continued)

Yes / No / DNA

32. On the whole, do the conditions of the quarters appear to be conducive to good EDP work?

33. Are the facilities protected against unauthorized access?

34. Are system documentation and other important materials protected against unauthorized access?

Project Planning and Control

35. Is there a written project control procedure?

36. Are there schedules that describe the tasks currently being performed and awaiting assignment?

37. Are there traffic documents showing planned products, expected completion dates, actual completion dates, and the like, for all tasks by each individual?

38. Do staff report time:
    by task?
    other?

39. Do task assignments, progress tracking, and performance measurment seem to be handled effectively on the whole?

40. Does the EDP manager meet regularly with his senior staff to review progress, problems, and plans?

41. Does the EDP manager (or members of his staff) review and approve the products of staff assignments (specifications, documentation, program tests, and the like?

42. Do procedures for quality control appear to be adequate?

Standards and Procedures

43. Are there written standards or procedures for the following (in each case, note also your rating of the standard itself and of its enforcement):
    feasibility studies
    programming
    file labeling
    use of computer libraries
    report and screen formats
    system documentation
    program documentation
    user instructions

EXHIBIT 6-5 (Continued)

Yes / No / DNA

data entry instructions

forms

operation instructions

program and system test

program/system change and change approval

job request by user

password control

System and Program Documentation

44. Is there a central file of system and program documentation?

45. Is the documentation:

well organized

complete

up-to-date

up to standard

secure against unauthorized access

46. Is it easy to find change requests and approvals for all changed programs?

47. Is the use of documentation by authorized personnel controlled through a signout procedure?

48. Does the operations staff have authorized access to the system and program documentation?

System Development and Maintenance Controls

49. Must EDP receive a written request with management approval before a new system is undertaken?

50. Does EDP require a written request for change before an existing system is altered?

51. Must users indicate written approval to proceed at the end of each of the following phases of system development (and maintenance, where applicable):

general design

detailed specification

system test

implementation

52. Are programmers denied access to:

operational programs and files

EXHIBIT 6-5 (Continued)

Yes / No / DNA

the computer room and tape (or disk or diskette) library

user passwords

input transactions

user terminals

user output

53. Are operations personnel denied access to:

system and program documentation

user passwords

user terminals

54. Are operations staff members precluded from executing any jobs other than those scheduled by or especially approved by the EDP manager?

55. Is an operator the only person authorized to operate the computer?

56. Is the operator the only EDP member authorized to access the user programs?

57. Must written approval be given to the operator before he can execute procedures that affect user programs?

Contingency Planning

58. Are backups of computer transaction files, master files, and programs taken at appropriate intervals?

59. Are other department resources like system software, program libraries, and password files backed up at appropriate intervals?

60. Are all backups scheduled and taken according to written operator procedures or automatically as part of documented system procedures?

61. Are there sound procedures for storage and rotation of backup media, and are there sufficient tapes, disks, and other media?

62. Is there a complete, up-to-date written emergency plan?

63. Has the emergency plan been tested?

64. Are materials necessary for recovery after loss of the computer site—documentation, storage media, instructions, special forms—ready, according to a written procedure?

65. Are materials necessary for recovery of computer operations after loss of the computer site maintained off-site in a secure area?

EXHIBIT 6-5 (Continued)

Yes / No / DNA

66. Are there written procedures for the maintenance of the emergency backup?

    Are they sound?

    Are they followed?

Other

67. Does the EDP manager routinely review computer history printouts, console printouts, operator logs, and other appropriate media to check that the computer is being properly used?

Perceptions of EDP

68. Are EDP costs reasonable?

69. Is EDP staff performance wholly satisfactory?

70. Are all urgent systems needs being addressed?

71. Are systems performing to specifications?

72. Is the EDP department able to keep up with corporate requirements?

73. Is turnover of EDP personnel satisfactory?

74. Is the EDP department up to date?

75. Does it compare favorably with competitors' departments?

76. Do users understand EDP problems?

EDP and the User

System

77. Does the user maintain adequate manual control over input and output?

78. Does the computer system adequately support the user through:

    batch controls

    activity reports

    thorough editing of data, including reasonableness checks

    complete and accurate reports according to specifications

    other

79. Are input forms and screens well designed?

EXHIBIT 6-5   (Continued)

Yes *No* *DNA*

80. Are printouts well designed, including adequate information for control, time and date of run, and end-of-report indications?

81. Are user instructions:

    readily available in the user facility

    complete (covering input procedures, controls, report use, and other points) and up-to-date

82. Was the system approved in writing by the user, based on his review of a system test before implementation?

83. Were all changes made subsequent to the implementation reviewed and approved in writing by the user?

84. Are user data input (or inquiry) devices adequately protected against unauthorized access?

85. Are passwords or other control means adequate and well maintained?

86. Can changes to master files be traced to the originating transactions and to the responsible individuals?

87. Are EDP staff excluded from access to programs, transactions, and passwords?

Perceptions of EDP

88. Is EDP staff performance wholly satisfactory?

89. Are all urgent systems needs being addressed?

90. Are systems performing to specifications?

91. Is the EDP department up to date?

92. Is there a good forum for the presentation of user needs and ideas?

Operations

Access Controls

93. Are only authorized personnel permitted entry to the computer room?

94. Are only operations staff authorized routine entry?

95. Is the facility kept locked?

96. Is there a visitors log?

EXHIBIT 6-5 (Continued)

Job Scheduling

97. Are all regularly scheduled batch jobs or operator maintenance functions in an operations schedule?

98. Are all nonscheduled jobs operated only with written approval?

Procedures

99. Is there a written operator procedure for each regularly run job?

100. Does each procedure contain specific instructions for file handling, backup, restart after error, and operator control procedures?

101. Are the procedures up to date?

Media Storage

102. Does the facility have adequate storage facilities for media (tape, disk, and the like)?

103. Is access to the storage facility well controlled?

104. Are the media well labeled and logically organized?

Hardware and Software Performance

105. Does operations keep a record of hardware and software problems?

106. Does operations maintain records of system utilization and capacities?

Physical Controls

107. Is the computer facility well organized and well maintained?

108. Is the facility free of safety hazards?

109. Is there adequate protection against:
    fire
    theft, vandalism

Perceptions of EDP

110. Is EDP staff performance wholly satisfactory?

111. Are all urgent systems needs being addressed?

112. Are systems performing to specifications?

EXHIBIT 6-5 (Continued)

113. Is the EDP department up to date?

114. Does it compare favorably with competitors' departments?

115. Do programmers and users understand the problems of the operations staff?

116. Do programmers and users often expect too much of the operations staff?

Programming and Analysis

Development and Maintenance Controls

117. Are system design standards used during the development of a system?

118. Are documentation standards used?

119. Are programming standards followed?

120. Does the EDP manager (or other senior staff member) review programmer products for adherence to standards?

121. Are specifications approved in writing before programming begins, by:

the user

the EDP manager

122. Are schedules set and/or approved by the EDP manager for systems development and maintenance tasks?

123. Does the programmer participate adequately in the setting of schedules?

124. Is programmer performance reviewed regularly against scheduled performance?

125. Are programmers authorized access to user live programs and/or computer files?

126. Do adequate controls exist to safeguard user programs and computer files against access by programmers?

127. Is there an attempt to segregate test and development activities from "live" operations, such as through the use of separate program libraries or separate physical storage devices.

Perception of EDP

128. Is adequate time given to the development of specifications prior to programming?

EXHIBIT 6-5 (Continued)

Yes / No / DNA

129. Is EDP properly staffed:
     in number of positions filled
     in level of skills

130. Is EDP staff performance wholly satisfactory?

131. Are all urgent systems needs being addressed?

132. Are systems performing to specifications?

133. Is the EDP department able to keep up with corporate requirements?

134. Is turnover of EDP personnel satisfactory?

135. Is the EDP department up to date?

136. Does it compare favorably with competitors' departments?

Data Entry

Access Controls and Input Handling

137. Are non-data entry personnel adequately restricted from the data entry area?

138. Are input forms, cards, tapes, and other records securely maintained before, during, and after processing?

139. Are input forms and output media logged in and out of the data entry facility?

Procedures

140. Are data entry personnel required to sign forms or otherwise indicate responsibility for their work?

141. Are there written descriptions of all data entry procedures?

142. Are all written procedures:
     up to date?
     complete?

143. Are all jobs either scheduled or accepted on a written-request basis?

144. Are records kept of operator performance?

145. When verification is required, is an operator other than the original entry person always selected?

Hardware Performance

146. Are records kept of machine problems?

EXHIBIT 6-5 (Continued)

147. Are records kept of machine utilization and capacities?

Perception

148. Do users usually provide input on time?

149. Are forms (or screens) well designed for data entry?

150. Is the data entry facility up to date?

151. Is the data entry facility able to keep up with corporate requirements?

152. Are staff well trained?

153. Is staff turnover reasonable?

154. Is the data entry facility used properly?

Data Control

General

155. Is there a data control group (or designated person)?

156. Does someone with sufficient independence of EDP operations, programming, data entry, and user operations perform the following:

receive user input materials, then log and distribute them to data entry or EDP operations

review input for completeness and authorization

receive output from data entry or EDP operations, then log and distribute it

review output for completeness and proper controls

157. Is there a systematic procedure to ensure the distribution to users of all output?

158. Are there written control-group procedures covering duties of the group?

159. Are these procedures followed?

Perceptions

160. Does operations provide timely and high-quality service to the user?

161. Does the data entry facility provide timely and high-quality service to the user?

162. Does the user adhere to cutoff schedules?

163. Does the user prepare input carefully, according to specifications?

164. Is there a good working relationship between the users and:

operations

data entry

165. Is there an overall interest in maintaining good controls on the part of:

the user

the operations staff

through 19), it would be preferable to have the president or another highly placed officer respond.

Position of EDP (Questions 1 and 2). The central idea here is to see whether EDP is most effectively placed within the organization. Question 2 ("is the EDP department independent?") addresses a particular area of weakness that arises frequently when the EDP manager reports to an operational unit manager who unduly influences the setting of EDP priorities.

Planning and Budgeting (Questions 3 through 5). EDP should be brought into the planning and budgeting process. The EDP department and its equipment and staff represent an expensive asset which demands constant attention to ensure a decent return on investment.

Does EDP have written corporate or department objectives to support its planning? If so, the objectives should be reviewed and compared for consistency with current and long-term plans.

Control (Questions 6 through 11). Is adequate attention paid by top management to EDP activities? Or is the department allowed to drift? There should be systematic high-level attention to the directions and performance of EDP to ensure that corporate objectives are addressed effectively. Users should participate in the review process and contribute to shaping EDP policy.

Perceptions of EDP (Questions 12 through 19). Unfavorable perception of EDP by top management may well be the reason for the operational audit. Look not only for substandard performance by EDP, but also for communications problems and inadequate top-level management of the EDP function to explain negative perception. Top-management satisfaction with EDP combined with user dissatisfaction (see the User Perception of EDP section) may suggest inadequate user participation.

EDP MANAGEMENT

These questions are for the EDP manager. The auditor must schedule adequate time not simply to complete the interview, which has many questions, but also to check the accuracy of the answers through examination of records, forms, documentation, written standards, facilities, and the like.

Organization and Staffing (Questions 20 through 28).   The emphasis of this segment is on the EDP staff——number, quality, training——and on the EDP manager's procedures for their evaluation. A "sleeper" question (here, Number 21) regarding separation of duties recurs in different terms throughout the questionnaire. Here it inquires whether separation of functions is evidenced by job descriptions. (If job descriptions were collected in the Data Collection phase before the interview, you will know the answer already.)

The question of separation of functions (or, segregation of duties) is one of the most important areas for the EDP operational auditor. It is one of the areas of control most frequently violated by EDP managers, often in the name of efficiency.

One of the most important concepts for the auditor to keep in mind is that the programmer is a computer user. He has no more or less right to the computer than any other user; all programmers should be excluded from operations. For example, the programmer has no more right to access the computer programs and records of the warehouse than does the company's personnel manager. Thus the programmer should be prevented from using special skills and knowledge of the computer to access operational programs and computer files. The EDP manager must ensure that programmers get proper support to enable them to work efficiently and effectively with only test versions of programs and files.

Facilities (Questions 29 through 34).   Look at the facility (not the computer room, that comes later) closely in a walk-through with the EDP manager. Is it a secure and comfortable place to work? If not, it may impair the efficiency of the staff.

Project Planning and Control (Questions 35 through 42). Does the EDP manager use sound procedures for managing the work of the staff? Are there records of assignments and progress or does he keep everything in his head? Does the manager show appropriate concern for quality and timeliness of products? Repeated negative answers probably indicate serious problems in effectiveness.

Standards and Procedures (Question 43). The use of standards promotes efficiency by reducing programmer/analyst system development time and programming time; they don't have to reinvent the wheel. Standards and procedures promote effectiveness if they are well conceived and their use is enforced by ensuring that all necessary procedures are followed and accomplished with acceptable quality.

Standards help new staff members get off to a good start by reducing the amount of time required for training and counseling and achieving full productivity. Standards, which set criteria for measuring product acceptability and indicate the proper format of documents, and procedures, which outline the steps required to accomplish a task, should not be confused with end products. The standard for report formats may be judged to be excellent, but the reports themselves may be poor because of failure to enforce the standard.

It takes an experienced auditor to judge whether a standard is acceptable, which is the first problem in Question 43. It takes less experience to determine whether the standard is being enforced, which is the second problem in Question 43.

System and Program Documentation. The earlier collection of Applications List and Brief Descriptions (Exhibits 6-3 and 6-4) will be especially helpful here. The questions relating to the existence of a central, secure, well-organized and well-operated facility for documentation storage will now be easy to answer by observation.

Well-maintained files can be key factors in efficient maintenance of programs, rapid training of new staff in existing systems, and smooth conversion of systems to new machines and software. If the files are not complete, and in particular if recent systems do not have good documentation, watch for excessive time and cost for systems maintenance and for user complaints about EDP department performance.

System Development and Maintenance Controls. The broad areas of concern here are with (1) a strict definition of the role of the user in the review and approval processes, (2) the restriction of the programmer to a test (rather than operating) environment, and (3) the limitation of the operator to schedule jobs, except as especially authorized.

Exhibit 6-6 illustrates a recommended approach to the development of a new system. (Following the numbers), the exhibit begins at 1 with the user filing a request for a new system with the steering committee, a group representing all users. The committee notifies the EDP manager of the request and obtains estimates of cost and impact on the EDP budget (3). Meanwhile, the committee evaluates (2) the request, weighs the cost and impact data, and (4) recommends action to top management. Management (5) considers the recommendation and (6) notifies the user, the committee, and the EDP manager of its decision. When approval to proceed is given, the user arranges to (7) provide any technical support EDP may require. The steering committee (8) updates its agenda of current projects, and the EDP manager begins the job-long process of (9) planning and controlling the activities of analysts and programmers. Programmers and analysts work on their assigned tasks producing (10) documentation and test results for (11) review by the EDP manager. When the EDP manager is satisfied that the product is good (12), he submits it to the user for review and approval (13). Only when all approvals are obtained in writing (14) does the EDP manager (15) issue the user instructions, operator instructions and data entry instructions, and (16) give written approval to the operator to transcribe the approved test version of the program for the library of operational programs.

Contingency Planning.   This segment asks about the adequacy of several kinds of backup procedures: (1) those for the user computer files, for system and application programs, and other systems-required data, and (2) those for disaster conditions where the entire computer site is lost. It is the EDP manager's responsibility to verify periodically that the procedures for backup are sound and being followed. The number and quality of the procedures should be assessed for cost and adequacy of protection. This is an area for the experienced EDP operational auditor.

The creation and maintenance of a plan for recovery of operations after loss of the computer site is an important job of the EDP manager. He should keep an up-to-date written list of the following:

Locations and contacts for backup computer and data entry facilities

Operator backup activities

Operator, data entry staff, and user tasks

The plan should be tested to see whether it works, and all backup materials (including documentation) should be stored off-site.

Other.   Question 67 raises the question of the proper use of the computer, including: efficiency, adherence to schedules, adherence to specified

EXHIBIT 6-6

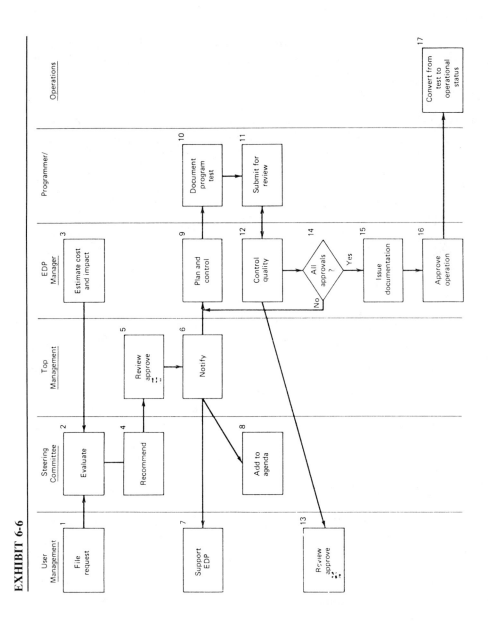

procedures, and restriction to authorized jobs and authorized personnel. It is unlikely that the EDP manager can supervise operations closely enough to be sure that the system is at all times being used properly. So the manager should use the media available to detect any undesirable use; modern systems software usually provides for the automatic maintenance by the computer of a log of all jobs executed. The EDP manager can either read an edited printout or review the whole log on a terminal.

Perceptions of EDP (Questions 68 through 76). If the EDP manager's view of the department is quite different from that of management and users, he probably has a communications problem.

EDP AND THE USER

This section should be administered once for each user application reviewed. It is unlikely that either systems characteristics or user perceptions will be the same in all user departments.

System. The role of the user in responding to these questions is principally to make materials available to the auditor and to demonstrate procedures such as control procedures, batching, terminal sign-on procedures, and data preparation and entry procedures. The auditor should also solicit the opinion of the user staff on system characteristics, but he must remember that a positive response may not always denote a positive situation, particularly when the user is unaware of problems.

Positive systems characteristics are evident in the questions. Negative responses point to several possible areas needing correction: user participation in systems development is inadequate, analyst and programmer skills are inadequate, standards are not being employed, the EDP manager is lax in quality control, the EDP manager is not following sound job control procedures, or a combination of the above.

Questions 85 and 87 are directed mainly to the terminal user. The password system should ensure that only authorized individuals can operate the terminal; that each individual is assigned a unique, private, personal password and a related, non-secret identity, which are necessary for sign-on; and that sufficient additional password protection of systems and data files be used to limit access to them to authorized individuals. Records of activity at the terminal should carry the public (non-secret) identity of the individual.

Passwords should be alterable by the user at a terminal by means of a special procedure, or by a security officer who is independent of operations, programming, and other users.

Programmers should not have access to user passwords. If the user has disclosed a password to a programmer (perhaps in discussing a problem at a terminal), it should be changed. Again, programmers should never, whatever their role in creating a system, be allowed routine access to operational programs.

Perceptions of EDP (Questions 88 through 92).   Other user perceptions than the ones covered in the questions may arise during the interview and should be noted. For example, a user who is resigned to generally unsatisfactory service from the EDP department may have accommodated himself to minor problems. If the user does not complain about these small problems, the auditor should take adequate time to be sure of correct responses.

OPERATIONS

These questions are intended mainly for computer operators. The auditor must examine the materials indicated in the questions before recording responses. Some sample materials (like the checklists and applications) may have already been collected. Others should be copied and added to the working papers as necessary during the interview.

Access Controls (Questions 93 through 96).   No one but operators and the EDP manager should have routine access to the computer room. The doors to the computer room should be locked at all times and only operators and the manager should have the means to open them. The operator is the custodian of the equipment, the programs, and other materials of the computer facility, all of which require the protection of good access controls.

The EDP manager should ensure that users and programmers are restricted from access to the computer. Any visitor should be authorized by the EDP manager and should sign a log maintained by the operator. The auditor can usually see very easily over the course of several day's auditing whether access controls are being observed.

Job Scheduling (Questions 97 and 98).   The EDP manager is responsible for determining which jobs the computer operator may execute. The manager should furnish the operator with a daily schedule of approved regular jobs and insist that the operator obtain approval for any job request that is not scheduled. The auditor should be able to compare history logs with the schedules and approval slips to verify that only approved jobs were executed.

It is possible for an operator to become so familiar with a routine that he does not need to refer to a schedule for guidance. Nevertheless, schedules should be produced to provide a record of the EDP manager's policy.

Procedures (Questions 99 through 101). Complete written instructions for the execution of every job should be available at the computer. The operator should be required to get permission to take any action not specifically covered by the instructions. It is essential that procedures be kept up to date in case a substitute operator must be used.

Media Storage (Questions 102 through 104). Ideally, storage media (tapes, disks, and the like) are kept in a separate library manned by personnel independent of programming and operations. Media should be provided to operations only on specific user request or in response to requests generated and printed (or displayed) automatically by the application system itself. This helps prevent an operator from switching files on purpose or by accident.

Many small- and medium-sized companies cannot justify the costs of space and personnel to provide a separate library and thus must risk letting the operator maintain the storage media. Whatever the method used, the questions in this section are applicable. If the operator is responsible for the storage media, then good organization, good labeling, and adequate space are essential in preventing their accidental mishandling.

Hardware and Software Performance (Questions 105 and 106). Operations should provide the EDP manager with information needed to assess hardware and software performance and suitability to corporate needs. If the EDP manager has not requested that performance records be kept, it may indicate a lack of proper attention to planning.

Physical Controls (Questions 107 through 109). The computer facility should have an orderly appearance, with separate places for incoming jobs, work in process, and jobs ready for distribution. Poor physical organization leads to time wasted in setup and increased numbers of errors requiring re-runs. It should be possible to walk easily through the working areas without tripping over exposed wiring or stepping over materials and equipment.

Hand-held or built-in fire extinguishers should be provided in the computer room. External doors and windows should be strong enough to withstand forcible entry.

Perceptions of EDP (Questions 110 through 116).   Listen to operators' comments for signs of a lack of organization in systems development. Systems problems invariably increase the operator's workload.

PROGRAMMING AND ANALYSIS

These questions should be asked of a number of programmers and analysts and after observing their working habits.

Development and Maintenance Controls (Questions 117 through 127).   Development and maintenance of systems is the principal responsibility of programmers and analysts. The question of standards and adherence to standards as evidenced by documentation was raised with the EDP manager, so there should be no surprises in this area from the programmers and analysts. Nevertheless, this staff is also asked whether standards are being followed during the course of development and maintenance, and problems in the standards may be discovered in the process.

Questions 122 through 124 follow up on similar questions asked of the EDP manager. The programmers and analysts will provide substantial insight into the effectiveness of the system for job control. The last several questions of the group address access and separation of functions controls from the programmers' perspective.

Perception of EDP (Questions 128 through 136).   Only the first of these questions is somewhat new. It attempts to discover whether, in the programmer's opinion, at least, there is proper attention to the development of specifications. A negative answer may indicate an EDP manager planning problem.

DATA ENTRY

These questions should be addressed to the head of the data entry facility.

Access Controls and Input Handling (Questions 137 through 139).   User transactions should be carefully handled while in possession of the data entry facility. Protection of user materials and the equipment require that access to the facility be carefully controlled.

Materials should be handled and stored with care to prevent loss or misplacement of transactions or output media. Logs should be maintained that track materials into and out of the facility.

Procedures (Questions 140 through 145).   Good procedures are important to the smooth running of a data entry shop. Operators should have ready access to data entry procedures that are complete and up to date. Otherwise time is lost when problems or questions arise, and new personnel take longer to become productive.

Hardware Performance (Questions 146 and 147).   The manager of the data entry facility should keep records relating to machine repairs, the frequency of service calls, and out-of-service time to be used when considering the merits of new service arrangements and new equipment. Records should be maintained of operator throughput, machine capacities, and other characteristics that will assist in making judgments about the cost effectiveness of proposed new equipment and techniques. The manager should be prepared at all times to estimate the impact on the staff and on production of accepting additional work.

Perceptions (Questions 148 through 154).   Perceptions of problems in scheduling, forms design, and overall use of the facility may be traceable to inadequate consultation by programmers and users with the data entry staff during systems design. Staffing problems, training problems, and failure to provide for necessary new equipment will lead to problems for the users in the form of higher error levels and slower service.

DATA CONTROL

General (Questions 155 through 159).   The data control function is one of the important elements in maintaining good segregation of duties controls and in providing an efficient means of handling EDP department routine contacts with user departments about operational matters. The data control function usually provides more efficient and effective control over receipt and distribution of materials. With an overall perspective of user and EDP coordination problems, the data control group can provide valuable assistance to the EDP manager. The auditor should review and get samples of the control documents and review the procedures to evaluate their suitability and the extent to which they are being followed.

Perception (Questions 160 through 165).   A data control group can provide a valuable insight into user and EDP department relationships, the adequacy of EDP service, and the adherence to schedules by the user.

EXHIBIT 6-7   Weakness Definition and Recommendations

Client Name:_____

Date: _____

Area: _____

Weakness

Nature: _____

_____

_____

Effect: _____

_____

_____

Cost Potential: _____

Risk: _____

Solution

Nature: _____

_____

_____

Effect: _____

_____

_____

Estimated Cost: _____

Key Personnel: _____

The form is completed as follows:

Client Name and Date: self explanatory.

Area: top management, EDP management, operations, etc.——from the questionnaire.

Weakness:

Nature: a description of omissions and errors.

Effect: Impact of the weakness on effectiveness and efficiency.

Cost Potential: a dollar cost estimate of the effect, if possible, or a relative estimate such as "high," "moderate," or "low." The cost should be related to a period of time.

Risk: where applicable, such as with a poor control procedure that may allow a defalcation, a characterization of the risk of the problem as high moderate, or low.

EXHIBIT 6-7 (Continued)

Solution:

Nature: a description of the proposed solution.

Effect: a description of the changes that will occur as a result of the solution.

Estimated Cost: if possible, a dollar figure, but otherwise a relative cost.

Key Personnel: the people likely to be involved in effecting the solution.

Where relative terms ("high," "moderate," "low") are used for costs, the auditor should use them in a consistent way, each translatable into a given percentage of the company's gross income, for example.

A one-page summary of all the Weaknesses and Recommendations may be prepared in a form like that of Exhibit 6-8. If organized in decreasing order of importance, using Cost Potential, for example, as a means, management can see quickly the potential benefits of implementing the recommendations.

Complete this summary form by copying Area and the Weakness and Solution Costs from the other forms. Summarize the Weakness Nature and the Solution Nature in two- or three-word phrases.

The EDP Operational Audit Summary Results form makes a good introductory sheet to the Weakness Definition and Recommendations forms. They may be combined and included in the final report to management, as well as used effectively in discussions of findings.

Presentation of Recommendations

The typical EDP operational audit will require the auditor to recommend changes to management that will increase the effectiveness and efficiency of the EDP department. It is not the purpose of this section to indicate what kinds of suggestions should be made; those must be based on the scope of the engagement, the EDP problems, and the expertise and perspectives of the auditor. But there are techniques for presentation of the recommendations that are almost universally applicable, that can promote understanding by the client of the recommendations, and that therefore lead to a more successful engagement. (See Exhibit 6-7 for an example.)

On reviewing the completed questionnaires and working papers, the auditor will be faced with the task of isolating problems, describing them in a manner that is understandable (and constructive in tone), and conceiving and describing solutions that are sensible and cost-effective.

The first step we would suggest is for the auditor to proceed section by section through the completed questionnaire and, as a problem area is encountered, summarize it in a form such as that illustrated in Exhibit 6-8. The set of forms produced in this way, after final reworking, including the

EXHIBIT 6-8 EDP Operational Audit Summary Results

Area	Weakness		Solution	
	Nature	Cost	Nature	Cost

consolidation of any related problems identified at different stages, can be typed and used for discussion of findings and recommendations with management.

SUGGESTED REFERENCES

AICPA. *Operational Auditing by CPA Firms,* Exposure Draft. Report of AICPA Special Committee on Operational and Management Auditing. New York, 18 June 1980.

AICPA. *Operational Reviews of the Electronic Data Processing Function.* Management Advisory Services Special Report. New York, 1978.

The Canadian Institute of Chartered Accountants. *Computer Control Guidelines.* Toronto, Canada, 1971.

The Canadian Institute of Chartered Accountants. *Computer Audit Guidelines.* Toronto, Canada, 1975.

seven

THE ENERGY AUDIT

Historically, energy conservation has not been a very important topic in the United States. Energy was abundant and cheap. That changed during the 1970s, when industrial energy users experienced a sixfold increase in energy costs during that decade, and the Arab oil embargo made shortages of energy a reality. Consequently, energy costs are a matter of major concern today. Consumers now realize that supplies of fossil energy are limited and that prices may continue to rise. In addition, reliance on foreign oil is having a detrimental effect on the country's balance of payments. Therefore, energy conservation is not only economical, but also patriotic.

The effectiveness of a company's energy management program depends on support from top management. Many companies have attempted hit-or-miss programs that lasted a few months. However, now energy conservation must be recognized not as just a penny saver, but as a program that is critical to the future of the organization. Energy costs are so high that permanent conservation programs can provide substantial returns.

Much has been written about energy conservation during the past decade, but most of the literature has been technical or geared toward the engineering market. The engineers' view of energy conservation is needed, of course, but also needed is more generalization of the applications of engineering research. When most companies think of cost control, they think of accountants. Therefore, the companies frequently call upon the management advisory services department of CPA firms and internal operational auditors to perform energy audits.

Present federal legislation encourages voluntary energy audits and there is some indication that the future may bring mandatory reporting of energy uses and conservation practices. Consequently, accountants may become even more active in the area of energy conservation. Thus CPA firms should get a head start on the energy issue now.

Although some engineering firms offer energy audits, CPA firms have been retained by many companies worried about the cost implications of the energy crunch. CPAs are in a good position to perform energy audits because accountants are skilled in performing audits and cost studies. Incentives in recent tax law bring energy audits into the accounting sphere. In essence, an energy conservation program is another type of management control system.

An energy audit makes a natural adjunct to the traditional financial audit and many practitioners may want to urge their clients to consider buying the extra service. The auditor knows the extent of the client's operations and is usually familiar with energy conservation practices followed by similar companies. Thus the CPA is qualified to perform an energy audit and should be able to assist clients by identifying wasteful uses of energy. CPAs bring a broad management outlook to the problems of energy usage. Additionally, CPAs usually have direct access to top management, whose support is needed to implement an energy conservation program.

The format of this chapter is slightly different from the other chapters in Part 2 in that its subject, energy, is not a separate functional area of the company. There is no "energy department" as such, but every department uses energy to some extent. An energy audit is somewhat similar to the preliminary stage of an operational audit in that the auditor must survey every department and determine which area appears to have the most potential for saving energy costs. Then, the auditor goes into these areas to show the client where there are opportunities to reduce costs and increase profits. Most of the auditor's recommendations can be implemented without reducing production or adding capital equipment. The accountant's energy audit is not really a technical energy audit, which is complex enough to require structural or process-oriented changes. Technical audits, althouth based partially on cost and other financial data, are dependent on engineering determinations. For projects that require technical analysis, a client would be best served by a cooperative engagement between a CPA firm and an engineering firm. Some large CPA firms that specialize in energy audits even have engineers on the management advisory services staff who are capable of performing the technical analysis.

Even when a technical energy audit is performed by an engineering firm, the CPA will need to help the engineers use the proper cost and rate-of-return figures in their recommendations. This author has reviewed a great deal of the engineering literature on the subject of energy-cost control; most of it either ignores the whole subject of the rate of return on energy investments or else recommends the payback method in deciding whether to invest. Rarely are the more sophisticated capital budgeting methods mentioned. Consequently, the CPA can perform a valuable service merely by urging that clients evaluate proposed investments in energy conservation equipment in the same manner as other capital investment projects.

Although there are numerous ways for a CPA to become involved in energy conservation and management, his role in the energy audit is discussed here. An energy audit generally begins with an inventory of all energy uses at a plant in order to identify the greatest opportunities for conservation and cost savings. The inventory should detail each area where energy is used, how much is used, and for what. Most engineers translate the energy usage into BTUs (British Thermal Units). However, an accountant would probably be better off sticking to quantity and cost of fuel used. For those who do wish to convert all types of energy into one common denominator, the following equivalents can be used:

Electricity: 1 kilowatt hour = 3413 BTU
Natural Gas: 1 cubic foot = 1000 BTU
Oil: 1 Gallon = 140,000 BTU
Steam: 1 Pound = 1,000 BTU

After the initial inventory, the auditor revisits the locations where he found the greatest potential economies in energy. In this second stage, the auditor makes detailed inquiries about the efficiency with which energy is used. The questionnaire (Exhibit 7-1) in this chapter can be used for this in-depth stage of the energy audit. Because this energy audit is assumed to be part of a thorough operational audit of a facility or as an adjunct to a regular financial audit, the questionnaire does not cover technical subjects that would ordinarily be handled by an engineer in a technical survey. This questionnaire could be used in a joint CPA/engineer audit, if the engineering firm had its own technical guidelines.

Since energy audits provide a valuable service, an auditor should be alert for clients who have high energy costs but no formal energy management program. Such clients provide almost a sure opportunity for the auditor to develop his practice.

Some CPAs avoid undertaking energy audits because they lack experience in this field. This is often true of small firms which have no CPAs on the staff with an engineering background (most large firms do have a few management advisory services staffers with an engineering background). Because of lack of faith in their abilities, some practitioners may be willing to perform only a financial analysis type of energy study instead of a major energy audit. On the other hand, some auditors may feel that they

EXHIBIT 7-1   Energy Questionnaire

Yes No DNA

Policies and Procedures

1. Do you have an energy committee?

2. Is energy usage submetered by department?

3. Do you know what percentage of your Cost of Goods Sold (for each product) or your cost per customer is composed of energy costs?

4. Is the operation of the most energy-consuming equipment scheduled to avoid use during periods of peak energy demand?

5. Have you asked for energy conservation advice from local utility companies?

6. Have you considered means of recycling waste products as fuel?

7. Does the Receiving department transfer refrigerated items immediately to storage coolers?

8. Do you keep all heating and cooking equipment clean?

9. Have you considered installation of a solar heating system?

Buildings (Indoor Environment)

10. Have you made a thorough cost/benefit analysis of installing additional insulation on the walls? On the roof?

11. Are pipes and ductwork insulated?

12. Have you had infrared thermograph pictures made of company facilities?

13. Are storm windows used?

14. Are windows airtight when closed?

15. Are there curtains or drapes at the windows?

16. Have you considered eliminating some windows to cut down on heat loss?

17. Is the hot water thermostat for restrooms set at 120 degrees or less?

18. Are hot water faucets periodically checked to be sure they shut tight?

19. Do you consider the energy-use effects when choosing the color to paint a building?

125

EXHIBIT 7-1 *(Continued)*

Yes   No   DNA

20. Do you feel the heating and air conditioning systems are efficient?

21. Are certain rooms ever uncomfortably hot or cold compared with other rooms?

22. Do you change filters in the heaters and air conditioners on a periodic basis?

23. Do doors close automatically?

24. Do you keep thermostats at 68 degrees or less in winter and 78 degrees or higher in summer?

25. Do you turn heating down and air conditioning off when the buildings are closed?

26. Are automatic washers always filled to capacity before running?

27. Have you considered using wasted heat in some areas to heat other areas?

28. Have you done caulking and weatherstripping to prevent unnecessary air leakage?

29. Do you place draft catchers in front of cracks during cold weather?

30. Do you use window shades, blinds, awnings, and draperies as energy-control devices?

31. Could you use space heaters as an alternative to heating entire rooms?

32. Would a lower ceiling save energy?

33. Has any type of alternative working schedule been considered for purposes of reducing energy use?

Lighting

34. Are lighting levels unnecessarily high?

35. Are incandescent lights always turned off when no one is in a room?

36. Are fluorescent lights turned off when someone is going to be out of the room for more than 15 or 20 minutes?

37. Have you considered using an automatic device to turn unnecessary lights off in little-used areas?

38. Do you reduce artificial light in the daytime by using natural lighting?

EXHIBIT 7-1 (Continued)

Yes / No / DNA

39. Have you considered replacing incandescent lighting with fluorescent lighting, mercury vapor lights, or high pressure sodium lights?

40. Do rooms with high ceilings have hanging lamps to bring light closer to the areas needing illumination?

41. Have you considered rewiring rooms that have several lights on one switch so that separate switches can be used?

42. Does ceiling and wall color adequately reflect lighting?

43. Are light fixtures periodically cleaned?

44. Are trees and bushes that might be obscuring outdoor lighting periodically trimmed?

Vehicles

45. Do you consider gas mileage when you purchase new vehicles?

46. Do you encourage employees to use public transportation when it is available?

47. Do you have a speed limit (perhaps 50 mph.) for your employees driving company cars?

48. Do you discourage employees from "warming up" cars before driving away?

49. Are your vehicles kept in a garage?

50. Do you discourage employees from using the air conditioner except during extremely hot weather?

51. Do you try to pool the use of cars even when just running errands?

52. Do you ever check cars to be sure trunks are not overloaded with unneeded items?

53. Do you encourage drivers to coast to a halt rather than using the brakes?

54. Are your cars serviced regularly?

55. Are wheel alignments periodically checked?

56. Are tires kept at the proper pressure?

57. Have you considered acquiring diesel-powered vehicles?

58. Have you considered acquiring electric vehicles for in-town driving?

EXHIBIT 7-1 (Continued)

59. Have you considered motorcycles and bicycles as alternatives to cars and electric carts?

60. Are all trips made by employees necessary?

61. Do you evaluate the cost of pickup when buying from a distant vendor as opposed to a close one?

Landscaping

62. Would the planting of trees cut down on energy needs in summer and/or winter?

63. Are there foundation plantings around buildings?

64. Have you considered the use of vines to protect walls and roofs from the sun?

65. Would an earth bank, or other regrading, help protect a building?

66. Would the building of a wall (fence) help conserve energy?

are experts because they have read this chapter; there is a seeming simplicity about energy conservation that makes everyone feel like an expert. Although the questions in Exhibit 7-1 may make an energy audit seem easy, they still require the auditor's reasoned analysis. The questionnaire contains tools to identify possible areas of energy waste, but, not every negative answer indicates waste. The auditor must evaluate each negative response to determine whether, in fact, it points to the least costly way of accomplishing the company's objectives. Also, the auditor will need to ferret out many of the company's objectives for using energy. Unlike the functional areas covered in other chapters, energy use is rarely spelled out in a manual. As an example of an unwritten objective of energy usage, an auditor might be concerned because lights in the factory might be left on when the building is vacant. The auditor may at first fear that this represents carelessness and waste. But the lights may be left on because the night watchman and local police officials feel that the lights are a deterrent to crime. Thus, the objective may be to reduce crime at the expense of electricity. Because the auditor has to doublecheck cases like this, even nontechnical energy audits are more difficult than might appear to the unsophisticated observer.

Many people tend to equate energy conservation with storm windows and insulation. These can be important aids, but there are many more complex energy conservation considerations. The questionnaire examines a wide variety of practices that can help a company save energy. Not all of the principles will be applicable in all climates, at least not when analyzed on a cost-benefit basis. For instance, a Hawaiian company probably would not need storm windows, nor would a company located high in the mountains be overly concerned with air conditioner usage. Therefore, the auditor must exercise judgment in tailoring the questionnaire to each client. It should be noted that the auditor will probably not find any one individual who can knowledgeably answer all of the questions. Because energy is used in all departments, the policies maintained may differ considerably from one section to the next. The sections of the questionnaire are:

Policies and procedures
Buildings (indoor environment)
Lighting
Vehicles
Landscaping

POLICIES AND PROCEDURES

The first question asks whether the organization has an energy management team (or committee). The group should be composed of a building's top official, such as plant manager, the chief accountant, the building engineer or maintenance supervisor, and a representative from each major department occupying the building. The purpose of this committee is to achieve as complete a cross section as possible of persons having experience with the conditions and characteristics of the building. The committee should periodically meet to make suggestions for reducing energy consumption. The committee should also be responsible for helping to win the cooperation of other employees in any energy-saving programs.

The second question is concerned with whether energy use is submetered by department. Some companies, for instance, use one meter to measure all electricity used in the plant. However, with such a system, it is difficult to pinpoint how or where energy is being used. Therefore, an organization should have a submeter in each department or each room so that energy use can be more closely monitored. With submeters, an in-depth analysis can be made of energy-use trends.

Question 3 asks whether management knows what portion of its products' cost is for energy. The important factor here is whether the respondents know the answer to the question. Both production employees and salespersons should be aware of how important energy costs are as a percentage of total production and distribution costs.

The fourth question inquires whether the use of the most energy-consuming equipment is scheduled during periods of off-peak energy demand. A disproportionately high portion of a company's bill is based on the amount of energy demanded during peak periods; the higher the use during peak periods, the higher the electric bill, regardless of the total quantity used during the billing period. Some utility companies even charge higher unit rates at peak times of the day; the savings from off-peak usage are even greater under these circumstances.

Some utility companies provide low-cost or free energy conservation advice to their customers. Question 5 asks whether the client has taken advantage of such a service.

The sixth question asks whether the company has made any analyses of the feasibility of recycling waste products as fuel. Many heating systems can incorporate waste wood and paper products as fuel. At a grain mill, corn cobs might be used as a fuel. In addition to saving on fuel costs, recycling can also cut down on the costs of disposing of the waste.

Question 7 applies to companies that deal in items that must be refrigerated. The Receiving department should be alerted to give high priority to refrigerated products. If an item is taken off a refrigerated truck and allowed to sit in the warm air for any length of time, it will get warm. Subsequently, the refrigerator in which the items are finally stored will have to work harder to get the products back down to the proper temperature. Thus, immediate transfer from refrigerated truck to refrigerated storage will save on energy costs.

The eighth question asks whether heating and cooking equipment is kept clean. Dirt and grease absorbs some of the heat emanating from heaters and cookers. Therefore, cleanliness can pare energy costs.

The subject of solar heating systems is examined in the final question of the Policies and Procedures section. Solar heating may be the energy source of the future, and some systems are already cost-efficient. Solar heating can result in substantial savings since its only costs are for the intitial equipment. This does not mean that all companies should switch to solar heat today, but there should at least be some managerial consideration of the idea. If a complete system is not economical at this time, there might still be savings available in solar-powered water heating systems. Solar-powered water heaters are currently the most widely used application of solar technology. The oldest use of solar power is in drying clothes. Thus the auditor might want to recommend that small motels and hospitals use solar power in their laundry departments. Companies should not be afraid to do things in new ways in order to save on energy costs, but old ways——like clotheslines——also have a lot to recommend them. Even windmills may be an economical approach. Although the Questionnaire does not ask about windmills, the auditor may wish to become familiar with the applications of wind technology.

BUILDINGS (INDOOR ENVIRONMENT)

The elimination of wasted energy in building use can be the major contribution made by the auditor in many types of companies. In cold climates, heating generally consumes the most energy and the auditor should place primary emphasis on saving heat. In warm climates, air conditioner usage tends to create the most waste, while in moderate climates, it may be lighting. Heating and air conditioning use up about one-third of all of the energy consumed in the United States. This subject is called the "building load" by architects and engineers. The building load is the amount of energy needed to maintain the indoor environment at desired levels, assuming that the building's systems are 100% efficient.

One of the primary principles of energy use in buildings is that many forms of energy use are interrelated. For example, a reduction in lighting may make the building cooler. Therefore, air conditioning costs will also be reduced but heating costs in winter will increase. Also, changes on one floor may affect other floors of the building. For example, this author once worked in a company where a huge oven was installed directly under the accounting department. In the winter, the accountants did not have to turn the heat on in order to be comfortable, but in the summer, no amount of air conditioning could keep them cool.

One of the best ways of reducing energy costs is by installing insulation. Thus, the first three questions in the Buildings section are concerned with insulation. Not only should the roof and walls be insulated, but also pipes, ductwork, and water heaters. One way to determine whether additional insulation is needed is to have an infrared themograph picture made of buildings. This service is offered by some utility companies and by engineers who conduct energy audits.

Questions 13 through 16 are concerned with windows. Windows can permit heating and air conditioning to escape from the building. Thus, storm windows should be used to cut down on heat loss (Question 13), and windows should be air tight to prevent drafts (Question 14). The auditor can check for air tightness by holding a lighted match or candle in front of window-sill cracks. If the flame flickers, there is a draft. One way to stop drafts is with a draft catcher (Question 29). A draft catcher is a sausage- or snake-shaped cloth bag that is filled with cotton or sand and placed in front of cracks. Caulking and weatherstripping (the subject of Question 28) is another means of eliminating wasteful air flows. Curtains or drapes at the windows will cut down on drafts and keep sunlight from heating a room during the summertime (Question 15). If a company is experiencing a great deal of heat loss through windows, it might even consider eliminating some of the windows (Question 16); windows could either be boarded over or restructured in a more formal remodeling effort. Benefits of eliminating windows, however, would have to be weighed against any concomitant increase in light bills.

Questions 17 and 18 are concerned with the heating of water. Savings can be generated by keeping the water heater thermostat turned as low as possible. Water used in restrooms does not have to be any hotter than 120 degrees. Using hot water wisely also helps cut the water bill.

Question 19 asks whether energy conservation is considered when buildings are painted. A dark color will absorb the sun's heat, while light colors will reflect the heat. Of course, it is not practical to paint every spring and fall, but companies in warm climates should have light colored buildings and buildings in cold climates should be painted dark colors.

Questions 20 and 21 ask whether heating and air conditioning systems are efficient. Although Question 20 asks the respondents for an opinion, it may overlap Question 21.

Several minor ways of saving energy are examined by questions 22 through 24. Periodic changing of air filters is one of the ways (Question 22). Question 23 asks whether doors close automatically. A low-cost spring apparatus can keep indoor air from escaping outside when someone forgets to close the door. Question 24 is based on the recommendation that has been circulated by utility companies and the federal government for several years. Thermostats set at 68 degrees in winter and 78 degrees in summer will save energy while maintaining supposedly comfortable working conditions. There are exceptions, however, to the advisability of these thermostat settings. For example, some computers must be kept at a temperature less than 78 degrees, while some typists may have trouble keeping their fingers nimble at a 68 degree setting.

Question 25 asks whether heating and air conditioning are shut off when no one is working. Some heat may have to be maintained in buildings to keep pipes from freezing, but a low temperature generally represents a saving over a high temperature.

Question 26 is applicable only to companies which use dishwashers or clothes washers. Running them only when full can provide considerable savings to restaurants, hotels and motels, hospitals, and other businesses which maintain washing facilities.

Question 27 asks whether there has been any consideration given to the idea of using wasted heat from machinery and equipment to heat other areas of the plant. Although this technique would usually require planning by the plant engineer, the costs of installing the necessary ductwork are often quite low. An example of this that has become common not only in businesses, but homes as well, is the deflection of clothes dryer exhaust back into a room. This can be accomplished for under 10 dollars.

Using draperies is examined again in Question 30, along with window shades, blinds, and awnings. These devices can be useful not only in cutting down on winter drafts, but also in constructively controlling the power of the sun. For example, drapes and shades that are kept closed on winter nights to keep out the cold, can be opened in the morning on the south-facing windows to let in the warmth of the sun and natural light. In the summer, blocking the sun from entering a room will reduce the amount of air conditioning needed.

Question 31 asks whether space heaters are used as an alternative to heating entire rooms. Space heaters are not as efficient as larger heating systems in cost per unit of heat. However, if only a handful of employees are working (perhaps on a night shift or a weekend), there is no reason to heat the entire plant or office. Instead, a few space heaters could serve the purpose at a lower cost.

High ceilings also waste energy during the winter months. Therefore, in an old building with a high ceiling (Question 32), the installation of a new hanging ceiling may produce a quick payback, at least in colder climates.

The final question in the Buildings section of the questionnaire asks whether there has been any consideration given to the establishment of an alternative working schedule that would conserve energy. For example, a four-day ten-hour-per-day schedule during the coldest winter months (in cold climates) or hottest summer months (in hot climates) would allow the company to shut down for three-day weekends. Not only would weekly heating and air conditioning costs be reduced, but employees would probably be thankful for the long weekends. So far, schools have led the way in adopting these four-day energy-saving schedules; this may be because schools are not-for-profit organizations that cannot easily pass the higher energy costs along to the customer.

LIGHTING

Lighting accounts for about 10% of this nation's energy usage, and there are many excellent opportunities for decreasing the cost of lighting—and by methods that require no additional investment. One of the simplest ways is to turn off lights when they are not needed. The first five questions (34 through 38) are concerned with this simple but important idea. The first question—"Are lights too bright?"—can be answered either subjectively (the auditor has to wear a green eyeshade in order to see) or by measurement with a simple pocket light meter. The measurement allows the lighting levels to be compared with the levels recommended by the Illuminating Engineering Society. Light meters can be purchased readily and require no special skills to operate.

Question 39 asks whether there has been consideration to the advisability of replacing incandescent bulbs with either fluorescent lights, mercury vapor lights, or high-pressure sodium lights. As an example of the resultant potential efficiencies, fluorescent bulbs are four times more efficient than a standard incandescent bulb because more energy is transformed into light and less into heat. Mercury lamps are used most often for outdoor lighting (for example, in parking lots), but can be used indoors as well; in fact, mercury bulbs can replace standard indoor incandescent bulbs. Mercury bulbs have a long life and provide twice the energy efficiency of incandescent bulbs. High-pressure sodium lights are the newest development in lighting and the most efficient form on the market. These lights are most suitable for outdoor use since they cast a strong yellow light which dulls or grays the colors of red and blue objects.

Despite the potential in energy usage offered by these newer forms of lighting, the auditor must be cautious in making recommendations. Just because a bulb is more energy efficient to operate does not necessarily mean that it is more cost efficient when the purchase price of the bulb is considered. For example, would a new bulb that used one-tenth the energy of an older bulb be a good investment if the new bulb cost $1,000? Any recommendation made by the auditor should take into account the same factors as a capital budgeting decision, even if the suggestion involves only buying different light bulbs.

Question 40 asks whether rooms with high ceilings have hanging lamps which bring the light closer to the work areas. Smaller wattage bulbs can then be used. Rewiring can also help reduce lighting costs in rooms where several lights are attached to one switch. This means that many lights are used when only one may be needed. Thus the more switches controlling the lights, the lower the energy costs will tend to be.

The reflective ability of wall and ceiling surfaces is examined in Question 42. Lighter colors generally reflect better and reduce the need for artificial light. Question 43 asks whether light fixtures are cleaned on a regular basis. Dirt on a bulb reduces the amount of light it casts. Therefore, dirty bulbs reduce lighting efficiency and raise costs.

The final question of the section, dealing with outdoor lighting, asks whether trees and bushes are trimmed to prevent them from casting too much shade. A company can reduce the number of outdoor lights if trees or bushes do not surround the lighted area.

VEHICLES

Most companies have at least one car or truck—major users of energy throughout America. Thus the Vehicles section of the operational audit questionnaire is of importance to most organizations. Most of the subjects covered in the questionnaire are familiar; during the past decade, oil companies, the federal government, and automobile manufacturers have placed a great deal of emphasis on gasoline conservation. Thus, the auditor will find nothing new in this section, but will be able to organize the material in a way that will permit easy analysis of all ways in which the client can save gasoline. Question 45 asks whether the company considers mileage when purchasing new cars. An affirmative answer would be an indication to the auditor that the company was at least to some degree energy conscious. Other simple concepts that deserve checking include encouraging the use of public transportation (Question 46) and driving at a moderate speed (Question 47).

Questions 48 and 49 are concerned with the warmth of engines. Car motors do not need to be warmed up very long before they are driven. Garaging a car will eliminate all warm-up time. Thus, cars should be kept in a garage wherever possible and drivers should be discouraged from wasting gasoline by warming up cars excessively.

Question 50 asks whether employees are discouraged from using the car air conditioner except during extremely hot weather. During many times of the year, an air conditioner is not needed, but may be used as a matter of habit. This author has often seen drivers switch the air conditioner on and roll the windows down. Since the use of the air conditioner consumes extra gasoline, air conditioner usage should be discouraged.

Question 51 inquires whether a company tries to get its employees to car pool when running company errands. For example, when the mail clerk goes to the post office, he might be able to give the accounting clerk a ride to the bank.

Since car weight is a factor in the amount of gasoline used, it makes sense to load the car as lightly as possible. Question 52 asks whether car trunks are ever checked for unneeded items. Sometimes trunks are used as storage areas, but it costs money to carry unnecessary junk around town everyday.

The driving practices of employees are examined in Question 53, which asks whether drivers are encouraged to coast partway to a halt rather than braking all the way. Coasting part of the distance is more economical than driving at a high speed, then applying the brakes.

Questions 54 through 56 are routine car service questions. If a car is tuned up and lubricated regularly, has its wheel alignment checked, and has its tires filled at the proper pressure, it will use less gas.

Vehicles powered by alternative sources of energy are considered by Questions 57 through 59. One possibility is using diesel-powered vehicles (Question 57). Diesel cars have a higher initial purchase price than gasoline-powered cars, but they get much better mileage and the fuel is slightly cheaper per gallon. Electric vehicles are another possibility; present technology permits them to be helpful in driving around town and around the plant. Bicycles and motorcycles are another possibility (Question 59). At first, the idea of investing in bicycles might seem whimsical, but for traveling around the plant, they might be the fastest vehicles as well as the cheapest.

Question 60 asks whether all car trips made by employees are necessary. This is related to Question 51, since some trips can be merged by pooling errands. Some trips can be eliminated by making a phone call instead or asking for delivery.

The final Vehicles question is whether the cost of pickup and delivery is considered when buying items from a distant vendor as opposed to a nearby one. For example, a company may buy from a wholesaler on the other side of town. However, it might be preferable at times to buy from a retail store down the street when only a few items are needed. The cost of gas for a trip to the other side of town may more than offset the wholesale-price savings.

LANDSCAPING

The final questionnaire section deals with landscaping. Trees and plantings can make our lives more pleasant. They can not only beautify the surroundings, but also modify the climate. Too often we rely on technology to save energy, when the proper use of nature can accomplish the same purpose. In fact, good landscaping can be one of the best ways for a company to reduce its energy costs.

Have you ever sat under a shady tree on a hot day? As you are cooler when sitting in the shade, so a building is cooler in the shade. Lessening the force of the wind is another way that trees can help a company save energy. Some studies have shown that a windbreak can save 30% to 35% of the cost of heating and air conditioning a building. And since heating and air conditioning account for 33% of all energy used in this country, it makes good sense to use windbreaks whenever possible.

The first question in the Landscaping section of the questionnaire asks whether the planting of trees could cut down on energy needs. This could be accomplished in two ways. First, trees could be planted that would provide shade to parts of the building. The shade would make the building cooler in the summer, and thus cut down the cost of air conditioning. These trees should be deciduous (i.e., not evergreen) because the shade would be undesirable during the winter months (an evergreen tree would provide year-round shade). U.S. Forest Service studies have found that a single tree can produce enough Btu's for cooling in one day as an average-room air conditioner running for 100 hours. Thus each tree shading a building can decrease air conditioning requirements remarkably.

In order to obstruct the wind, at least two or three rows of evergreen trees (e.g., pine, cedar, and hemlock) should be planted between the building and the direction of the prevailing winter winds (this is generally on the north and west sides of the building). This windbreak can reduce effective wind speed anywhere from 50% to 90%, depending on the height of the trees and their distance from the building. Unchecked, the faster wind blows, the faster a building loses heat even if it is well insulated. In particularly windy climates, a windbreak within 20 to 50 feet of a building can reduce heating costs by at least 40%.

Question 63 asks whether there are any foundation plantings around buildings. The dead air space created by putting shrubs next to a building makes a good insulator. To be effective, foundation plantings should be within three feet of a building. Again, they should face the prevailing winds.

Question 64 asks whether there has been any consideration given to the idea of growing vines on the roof and walls of a building. Grape vines are popular, but kudzu would be just as good in the South. The vines should be planted on the south and west walls and allowed to grow over the roof. The temperature behind the vines will be at least 10 degrees cooler than on an unprotected roof or wall. And if grapes are grown, the company can provide a perquisite to employees by letting them pick the grapes.

The idea of putting an earthbank up against a building is explored in Question 65. Earth is an excellent insulator. In fact, sod buildings are one of the most energy-efficient structures. If a building has a wall without windows, it might be possible to pile dirt against the wall. In fact, in some cases, the entire building can be built underground. Underground buildings are very energy efficient.

The final question asks whether a stone wall would help save energy costs. If a company does not have room to plant trees as a windbreak, it can get the same benefits by putting up a solid wall to intercept the prevailing winter winds. The higher the wall and the closer to the building the better.

Landscaping provides an unrecognized opportunity for saving energy costs. The effect of trees on temperature can be dramatic. The aesthetic aspects of good landscaping must also be considered, too. The cool, peaceful setting of a small group of trees provides benefits in mental well being, as well as climate control.

SUMMARY

All companies are affected by the pinch in energy supplies and the uptrending costs. A company's ability to reduce its energy costs depends on its understanding of energy's effects on costs. An operational audit of energy usage is designed to educate management in ways energy use can be curtailed. Energy savings can be achieved if all employees participate in conservation programs. This can be best achieved by starting with top management and then gaining support downward throughout the organization.

Because of the tremendous increase in energy costs in the past 10 years, it is an important subject for operational auditors. This chapter has emphasized an operational audit of energy usage, not a complete technical energy audit. Any auditor can analyze energy as a part of an operational audit, but some firms have gone a step further and purchased the technical equipment necessary to perform a complete energy audit. Such equipment includes energy usage monitors, simple pocket light meters, and infrared thermographic cameras. For firms that wish to gain additional expertise in the field, the three excellent Government publications listed below provide detailed guides to energy management. They are available from the Superintendent of Documents, U.S. Government Printing Office, Washington, D.C. 20402.

Architects and Engineers Guide to Energy Conservation in Existing Buildings (stock number 061-000-00394-1)
Guide to Energy Conservation for Grocery Stores (FEA/D-76/096)
Guide to Energy Conservation for Food Service (041-018-00127-1).

Even if energy costs continue to rise, a smart manager can save money by implementing conservation procedures. Much of the energy management job involves pure common sense and an awareness of the problem. An operational auditor can help the company become aware of its energy problems. The auditor's recommendations can result in considerable savings because most good energy conservation practices cost very little to implement.

eight

MAILROOM

The manner in which a company handles its mail can sometimes provide an indication of how the entire operation is managed. This is because, in a sense, the administrative process begins and ends in the mailroom. Unfortunately, the mailroom is often overlooked in any administrative shake-up. Most operational audits ignore the mailroom. Even some of the experts participating in bringing out this book disagree that the subject is important. But an anecdote will prove the point.

A few years ago, while conducting a mail survey of not-for-profit hospitals, this author received over 10% of his 1,000 responses in return envelopes that had been run through the hospitals' postage machines. The return envelopes were postage-paid business reply envelopes provided by the researcher. In other words, because of mailroom inefficiency, over 100 hospitals had paid 28 cents each to return a questionnaire for which the researcher had provided a postage-paid envelope. Most of these hospitals were operating at near breakeven or at a loss, but they were spending money unnecessarily in the mailroom.

In addition to using unneeded postage, the mailroom can be wasting money in other ways. Whenever the mailroom fails to process mail quickly and efficiently, it jeopardizes the company's competitive position. For example, if invoices or statements are mailed a day later than necessary, then the corresponding customer payments may also be a day later in arriving. By the same token, if incoming mail is not distributed to the proper departments as soon as it arrives, there will be a delay in processing and depositing customers' checks. These few inefficiencies in the mailroom can materially affect the company's cash flow and aggravate its interest load.

Despite the importance of the mailroom, it is traditionally the most neglected department in a company. The mailroom is often viewed as a messy, haphazard operation, and it is relegated to the dingiest room or lowest depths of the building. Too little thought is given to installing modern equipment or motivating employees. The workers are criticized for their inefficiencies, but rarely complimented when a job is well done. In short, this central department should get more managerial attention. With both postal rates and pay scales rising so fast, management can no longer ignore the problem of mailroom inefficiency. A cost-conscious organization can look for solutions in a variety of areas. Fortunately, most of the remedies are quite simple. Some of the ideas represent old-fashioned common business sense. Some of the suggestions can apply to companies that have well-managed mailrooms. There is often some need for periodic analysis owing to the frequent change and turnover within the enterprise, combined with the periodic breakthroughs in the methods and equipment available for processing mail.

Exhibit 8-1 illustrates the operational audit questionnaire for use in the mailroom. The questionnaire has four sections:

General
Equipment and materials
Personnel
Internal mailings

GENERAL

The first question checks that the organization does have a mailroom. Although a mailroom as such is not needed by all companies, most outfits would probably benefit from a separate department. Approximately half of the companies in West Germany and France have separate, fully equipped mailrooms. The percentages for the United States and Britain are lower.

As implied by Question 2, the mailroom should be in an easily accessible location. For maximum efficiency, the facility should be located near the flow of traffic, but also accessible to Postal Service deliverers. It is also a good idea to locate the mailroom on one of the lower levels of a building so that gravity-fed chutes can be used to move mail quickly to the processing area.

Question 3 asks whether the mailroom is used for business mail only. This is one of the most time-consuming problems confronting mailroom employees. Valuable time is lost when other employees ask to have personal envelopes stamped or packages wrapped. For this reason, company policy should forbid stamping and wrapping personal items. This is not to say that employees should not be able to leave personal mail in the mailroom for it to be picked up by Postal Service employees. Most

EXHIBIT 8-1   Mailroom Questionnaire

General

1. Is there a separate mailroom area?

2. Is the mailroom in an easily accessible location?

3. Is the mailroom used for business mail only?

4. Is a regular mailing schedule maintained and followed consistently?

5. Do you encourage early-in-the-day mailing?

6. Do you check all outgoing mail to be sure that it bears a ZIP code?

7. Are you careful about not running business reply (prepaid) envelopes through the postage meter?

8. Do you save unused envelopes that have been metered for a refund?

9. Do you presort mail before taking it to the Post Office?

10. Do you date-stamp incoming mail?

11. Have you considered using a bank lock-box service for incoming checks?

12. Are you aware of the Postal Service's Express Mail Service, which guarantees overnight delivery?

13. Do you qualify for a bulk-mail special rate?

14. Do you know the number of pieces required to qualify for bulk-rate savings?

15. Are packages containing breakables marked Fragile?

16. Do you piggyback first-class letters with packages?

17. When you have many letters to the same address (such as a branch plant), do you mail them in one large envelope?

18. Do you distribute first-class mail prior to distributing other mail?

19. Do you have a special Business Reply Advance Deposit account at the post office?

20. Are you eligible for your own separate ZIP code?

21. Do you ever send Air Mail letters to an address within the United States?

22. Do you know the minimum and maximum size requirements as prescribed by the Postal Service?

EXHIBIT 8-1 (Continued)

Yes / No / DNA

23. Do you make only limited use of Special Delivery service?

24. Do you know the difference betwen Registered Mail and Certified Mail?

25. Do you ever obtain a Certificate of Mailing when you need proof of mailing before a deadline?

26. Do you have a specific policy as to when insurance is obtained on packages mailed?

27. Have you considered the possibility of using Mailgrams?

28. Have you had a Postal Service representative visit your mailroom to suggest ways that errors or waste can be eliminated?

29. Have you had mailing equipment dealers (from Pitney Bowes, for example) visit you to demonstrate better ways to operate a mailroom?

30. Is there a Mail User's Council in your area?

31. Do you have a bulk-mail permit?

32. Have you investigated the possibility of using an independent mailing service instead of the Postal Service?

33. Do you know your average cost of mailing each piece of mail?

34. Is there a reference manual explaining all mail-handling operations?

35. Are you aware that postage for subsequent ounces of first-class mail costs less than the first ounce?

36. Do you keep a record of incoming and outgoing mail volume?

37. Do you save insurance receipts?

Equipment and Materials

38. Is the mailroom large enough to do an adequate job?

39. Do you have an automatic postage meter?

40. Do you have postage scales?

41. Do you have automated opening machines?

42. Do you have an automated inserting/sealing machine?

43. Do you have a letter-bomb detector?

44. Do you have an automated addressing system?

45. Do you have some type of trolley or wagon with which to carry mail around the plant?

46. Are sorting bins used for incoming mail?

47. Do you have enough equipment?

48. Is equipment up to date enough to be as cost efficient as new models?

49. Is mailroom furniture specifically for mailroom use?

50. Have you obtained Postal Service trays for mailing first-class letters?

51. Do you keep a variety of envelope sizes on hand in order to fit the envelope to the item being mailed?

52. Are your postage scales periodically checked for accuracy?

53. Does one person have final responsibility for the postage meter?

54. Are your mailing lists periodically updated?

55. Do you print Address Correction Requested on the outside of your envelopes?

56. Is there a company policy to route advice of address changes to the mailroom in order to update mailing lists?

57. Is cushioning material packed into boxes containing breakable items?

58. Are you weight-conscious with respect to the grade of paper and envelopes used for mailing reports?

59. Do you advance the date on your postage meter the first thing each morning?

60. Is there any control over use of the copying machine?

61. Do you have postal rate lists for all classes of mail available within the department?

62. Do you use postcards instead of letters when sending short messages?

63. Do you use only regulation-size postcards?

64. Is there a specific area in each office set aside for receiving and sending mail?

65. Do you use staples instead of (heavier) paper clips on outgoing mail?

66. Is the mailroom kept in neat order?

67. Is there adequate lighting in the mailroom?

Yes	No	DNA	EXHIBIT 8-1 (Continued)

Personnel

68. Are mailroom employees selected for their intelligence and maturity?

69. Is there high morale in the department?

70. Do you feel department employees maintain confidentiality with respect to job-related information?

71. Are there written job descriptions for every position in the department?

72. Do new employees receive any type of formal training?

73. Do employees have an overabundance of idle time?

Internal Mailings

74. Do you ever try to reduce "paper pollution" by cutting down on unnecessary internal mailings?

75. Do you have reusable envelopes for use with intracompany mail?

76. Are mailings to employees made in-house rather than through the Postal Service?

77. Are intracompany mail envelopes a different color from those for outgoing mail?

78. Is there any type of numbering system to facilitate delivery of intracompany mail?

79. Do you prepare a routing list for mail that should be seen by several individuals, instead of making copies?

companies do allow employees to make personal mailings from the company's premises. Such mail should bear a stamp before it reaches the mailroom. Some executives argue that it does not hurt a company to provide stamping and packing services to employees, who then reimburse the company. But this policy creates a new problem: who is responsible for internal control over the funds generated? The best policy is for a company to forbid stamping and wrapping of personal mail.

The fourth question inquires as to whether a regular mail route schedule is maintained. It is important for outgoing mail to be ready when the Postal Service comes to pick it up. By the same token, if a company employee has to deliver the mail to the Post Office, the delivery should be made early enough that the mail can be processed by postal workers before the Postal Service trucks depart for distant cities. Thus it is important for company mail clerks to have a regular schedule that all other employees can conform to. A day of delivery time can sometimes be saved by posting mail just a few minutes earlier. With respect to incoming mail, many companies like to have mail delivered to the departments the first thing each morning. This may necessitate the mailroom employees coming in an hour or so earlier than other employees. In any case, there should be a regular schedule of deliveries and collections.

Question 5 asks whether there is any encouragement of early-in-the-day mailing. Since post offices usually get much of the day's mail around 5:00 p.m., there is a delay in delivery of anything mailed near that hour. Therefore, a well-managed mailroom has company employees mail outgoing material early in the day, preferably before noon. Such a policy will get mail to its destination sooner.

Using a ZIP code on outgoing mail can speed up delivery by a couple of days. Thus, Question 6 asks whether mailroom employees check outgoing mail for a ZIP code. Mail clerks should encourage all departments to use ZIP codes. If a ZIP code is not known, it can be looked up in a ZIP code directory, which should be available in the mailroom. The job of checking for ZIP codes sounds like tedious work, but it is preferable to delaying a letter for several days at the post office.

Question 7 asks whether business reply envelopes are inadvertently fed through the postage meter. Paying double postage on prepaid envelopes is a common inefficiency.

The eighth question asks whether envelopes which have been erroneously metered are saved for refund. If they are taken to the Post Office, a refund can be obtained equal to 90% of the metered amount. Spoiled envelopes are worth saving.

Question 9 asks whether mail is ever presorted before being taken to the Post Office. Mail gets on its way more quickly if it is presorted by ZIP code. Pressure-sensitive stickers can be obtained from the Post Office for designating each group of mail. Presorting reduces the amount of handling that must be done by the Postal Service employees.

The tenth question is whether incoming mail is stamped with the date of receipt. When there can be no confusion about the date mail was received, company employees are more apt to reply quickly. These timely replies can, in turn, cut down on the number of "rush" jobs for the mailroom staff.

Question 11 deals with bank lock-box service. If a company uses a lock-box service for incoming customer checks, the quantity of incoming mail which has to be processed by the mailroom is reduced. Also, internal control over cash receipts is improved and cash inflows are sped up.

Question 12, which deals with the employees' awareness of Express Mail service, is a question that can be used to gauge the overall capability of mailroom staff. The Postal Service's Express Mail service guarantees overnight delivery. When an emergency package must be delivered the next business day, or there is a last-minute deadline, Express Mail service can often make the delivery at a lower cost than private air express or bus services. (Express Mail service is not available in all cities.)

Questions 13 and 14 ask whether the organization can take advantage of the special rates available for bulk mail. These rates are available on 200 identical pieces mailed at one time. This applies to first-, second-, and third-class mail.

Question 15, asking whether the word Fragile is stamped on packages containing breakables, suggests one of the ways mailroom inefficiency can reflect badly on other departments. When broken goods are delivered to a customer, the company loses not only the cost of the merchandise, but probably customer goodwill as well. The word Fragile stamped on a package does not always improve the treatment received by the package, but it can help.

The sixteenth question inquires whether first-class letters are sent piggyback along with non-first-class packages. A package containing a letter is supposed to be sent at the first-class mail rate, unless the package is marked First Class Mail Enclosed. Then, only the letter needs first-class postage. The remainder of the contents can be sent at lower rates.

Question 17 asks whether many letters to one address, such as a branch plant, are mailed in a single large envelope in order to save postage. The individual letters in separate, unstamped, envelopes may be directed to different individuals at that address.

Question 18 asks whether first-class mail is distributed prior to other classes of mail. Since first-class mail is theoretically the most important mail, it should be distributed first. Unfortunately, many mail-room clerks tend to distribute second-, third-, and fourth-class mail first because these classes usually represent bulky items. By distributing the bulky pieces first, the mail clerk appears to be getting a lot more accomplished than if he routed the first-class mail. Unfortunately, this inefficient practice sometimes delays the progress of important mail until the mailroom clerk has spare time.

Some companies would benefit from a special Business Reply Advance Deposit account—the subject asked about in Question 19. If a company provides business reply envelopes for its customers, the company must pay the first-class mail rate plus a surcharge when the customers utilize the envelopes. The company can pay the surcharge either when the envelope is delivered or in advance by maintaining a Business Reply Advance Deposit account at the Post Office. The deposit system reduces the surcharge, so it would be preferable for some companies to pay the advance deposit. Companies that use the reply envelopes frequently would benefit. The Postal Service charges an annual accounting fee to companies that have an account. Because of the annual fee, a company would have to receive about 1,000 business reply envelopes each year before it would save by maintaining the advance deposit account.

The twentieth question deals with a subject many people are not aware of: "are you eligible for your own ZIP code?" If an organization has a large volume of incoming mail (at least 1,000 letters a day), it can qualify for its own ZIP code. A separate ZIP code cuts down on the amount of handling mail must receive from the Postal Service.

Question 21 can be classified as a "trick" question. Unlike the other questions on the questionnaire, the desirable answer to question 21 is No. The reason for this is that there is no longer a domestic air mail service classification. A company should not pay for a nonexistent service. In fact, most first-class mail now travels by air, and at first-class rates—not air-mail rates.

Question 22 asks whether mailroom employees are familiar with new minimum and maximum-size requirements prescribed by the Postal Service. If an envelope or parcel is too large, an additional fee is charged. Too small an envelope or parcel will be returned to the sender. All new stationery orders should be checked to be certain requested envelopes are of the proper size.

Questions 23 through 27 ask about the utilization of some of the special services offered by the Postal Service. Since Special Delivery is an expensive service, it should be used only on a limited basis. Less well known are the categories of Registered Mail and Certified Mail. Registered Mail provides insurance and a receipt for first-class mail. Certified Mail is appropriate for an item of no intrinsic value, but for which a signed receipt from the recipient is needed. Probably the least known (and lowest-cost) service is the Certificate of Mailing. A Certificate of Mailing provides proof of mailing and costs only a few cents. The certificate should be obtained any time proof is needed of mailing an item by a certain deadline. Accountants, for example, should urge their tax clients to use the certificate service any time they are responding to the Internal Revenue Service concerning a tax audit.

Insurance service, the subject of Question 26 and Question 37, is available on third- and fourth-class mail in amounts up to $200 of declared value. The receipts for insurance should be kept on file for a substantial period of time—or until proof is received that the parcel has been received by the addressee.

Question 27 asks whether the organization has considered the possibility of using Mailgrams when next-day delivery is required. A Mailgram is a combination letter/telegram. It costs less than a telegram but much more than a letter. To send a Mailgram, a message is given in person to a Western Union office or called in to a Western Union operator. The message is then sent electronically to the Post Office that serves the addressee. The message is then delivered the next business day along with regular first-class mail.

Questions 28 and 29 ask whether Postal Service representatives or mailing equipment manufacturers (such as Pitney Bowes) have ever been called in for free advice. Both can provide assistance in improving mailroom operations, although the equipment salesman's methods will probably involve a recommendation for new devices. If the salesman can justify his recommendations with dollar-benefit proof, however, his advice should be given consideration.

Question 30 asks whether there is a Mail User's Council in the area. A council is an organization of mail users and Postal Service officials that meets periodically to discuss mutual problems. Through films, lectures, and training sessions, a council can help mailroom employees perform a better job. Membership in a council is available at no charge, but councils exist only in large cities.

The subject of Question 32 is whether the organization has considered using any delivery service other than or in addition to the Postal Service. The best known of the postal-type services is United Parcel Service. Others operate on a local basis.

Questions 33 and 36 are concerned with the cost of operating a mailroom. In order to operate efficiently, the mailroom manager should know how much it costs to process each piece of mail. Of course, a calculation of average cost requires first a knowledge of how many pieces of incoming and outgoing mail are processed each day. Thus, a log should be compiled of mailroom volume.

Question 34, asking about the existence of a departmental procedures manual, could appropriately be asked of any department. A detailed manual facilitates the orientation and training of new employees.

Question 35 asks whether mailroom employees are aware that postage for the second and subsequent ounces of first-class mail cost less than for the first ounce. The authors have witnessed dozens of mailroom employees placing twice as much postage on two-ounce letters than on one-ounce letters. The rates do not require this, however, as the first ounce is always higher than subsequent ounces. In a further variation on this theme, a mail clerk was seen placing too much postage on two-ounce letters. Informed of his error, he responded that he knew the correct rates, but he was putting the extra postage on in hope that the letters would get special handling by the Post Office. This does not happen; the extra dimes do not buy better service.

EQUIPMENT AND MATERIALS

As any postal equipment salesman will tell you, an efficient and effective mailroom requires a certain amount of equipment. Questions 38 through 50 ask about the availability of equipment and other facilities. Most of the questions are rather self-explanatory. The operational auditor should keep in mind, however, that not all of the equipment would be suitable for all organizations. For example, a company which uses a bank lock-box service might not need an automated opening machine (Question 41). On the other hand, companies with large volumes of incoming mail can select from a variety of machine sizes ranging up to one that will open 500 envelopes a minute. In fact, most types of postal equipment are available in sizes ranging from small table-top machines suitable for mom-and-pop businesses up to room-size machines suitable for large international corporations.

The one piece of equipment mentioned in the questionnaire that might puzzle some readers is the letter-bomb detector (Question 43). These machines are not common in the United States, but are widely used in Great Britain, where they sell for the equivalent of less than $1,000. Auditors should probably at least mention the detectors to clients in order to call their attention to the existence of such machines.

Following the questions concerning equipment are several which deal with materials and supplies used in the mailroom, and with procedures surrounding the use of equipment. Question 51 asks whether a variety of envelope sizes is kept on hand in order to match the envelope to the size of the material being mailed. Other things being equal, a larger envelope costs more to purchase and costs more to mail. Therefore, a variety of envelope sizes can result in twofold savings. Question 58 is similar to Question 51 in that it asks whether the company is weight-conscious with respect to the grade of envelopes and paper used in mailings.

Question 52 asks whether the postage scales are periodically checked for accuracy. With heavy use, even the best scale can become inaccurate, and an error multiplied can cost a company a great deal of postage money.

Internal control is the subject of Question 53, which asks whether one person has the final responsibility for the use of the postage meter. A company generally has a sizable investment in prepaid postage in its postage meter. Since this investment is subject to misappropriation by employees, it is important that only one person have a key to the machine.

Questions 54 through 56 deal with the subject of updating mailing lists. Many organizations waste money by mailing catalogs and other material to addresses that are no longer correct. Thus, periodic updating of lists is essential. One way to do this is to print Address Correction Requested on outgoing envelopes. Undeliverable letters will then be returned with a corrected address. There is a small charge for this service, but it is well worth the price if the same list is to be reused.

Question 57 is another one dealing with the packaging of fragile items. Some form of cushioning such as wadded-up newspapers, foam, or "popcorn" should be used to protect breakable items.

Question 59 asks whether the date on the postage meter is advanced each morning. Although the Postal Service sometimes forgives an incorrect date, the law requires metered mail to be deposited at the Post Office on the date shown on the metered postmark. A routine practice of changing the date the first thing every morning could avoid many problems.

Question 60 echoes those appearing in other chapters concerning control over copying machine use. Because the mailroom is often the location of a copier shared by several departments, some record of copier use is essential.

All mailrooms should have an up-to-date list of postal rates for all classes of mail. Unfortunately, Question 61 will occasionally be answered negatively despite the obvious need for correct postal rate information.

The alternative of postcards is examined in Questions 62 and 63. Since the rate for postcards is about one-third less than first-class letters, it pays to use postcards whenever short messages are being sent. Regulation-size postcards should be used because larger cards must be sent at regular first-class envelope rates.

There should be a specific area in every office set aside for receiving and depositing mail. This subject is examined in Question 64. The mail clerk's routine is simplified if he or she knows where mail is supposed to be in order to be picked up.

Questions 65 through 67 deal with minor points that can occasionally save an organization money or result in greater efficiency. For example, staples are lighter than paper clips; therefore, the use of staples in outgoing mail can help lower postage costs (Question 65). Neatness and adequate lighting are important in a mailroom because without them, it would be easy to misplace important pieces of mail.

PERSONNEL

Everyone has heard success stories about the poor but hard-working lad who started in the company mailroom and worked his way up to president. Because this is such an unusual situation, it may be assumed that the reason most mailboys don't make it to the top is because the boys (or girls) do not have the intellectual ability to make the climb. In fact, in some companies, the mail clerk is still viewed as a delivery boy who will never rise above that rank. Such thinking is not in the best interests of the organization. Mailroom employees should be stable individuals with a personal drive and a desire to advance. Mailroom employees need to learn productivity and quality control. With the mailroom as the nucleus of an organization's activities, mailroom employees should be helped to understand the important role they play in the success of the company. Although mailroom activities may at first appear to be routine and monotonous chores, there is no need for morale problems. If employees are inspired with the notion that the mailroom is an excellent place to learn how the whole organization operates, there should be no difficulty in providing motivation—particularly if mailroom employees who show promise are promoted to more responsible positions. The mailroom really is a good place to start a career. The employee has the opportunity to learn about the inner workings of the organization and to be visible to many officials who might play a role in his future success.

The questions in the personnel section of the questionnaire are self-explanatory. Perhaps Question 70 deserves special mention. Mailroom employees should respect the confidentiality of the information with which they come in contact. In some companies, the mailroom employees become "gossip brokers," because of their many contacts throughout the organization. Such extracurricular activities should be guarded against not only because of the danger of leaks of important information to outsiders, but also to keep the mail clerk from developing an unofficial power structure in the company. Access to information can make a low-level employee very important to power-grabbers within the organization.

INTERNAL MAILINGS

The final section of the questionnaire deals with in-house mailings. Although postage is not incurred on intraplant mailings, it does entail a significant cost in the form of employee time and supplies used. The first question in this section asks whether mailroom employees ever try to cut "paper pollution" by eliminating unnecessary internal mailings. Mailroom employees may notice that certain recurring reports are thrown in the wastebasket as soon as they are received. A mailroom clerk can save the company some paper costs by removing the recipient's name from the list receiving that report (after discussing the question with the managers sending and receiving the reports). This would not only save paper, but would also cut down on the work of the janitorial staff.

Question 75 asks whether reusable envelopes are used for intracompany mail. Typical envelopes of this type have a space for the name and department of the addressee. The envelopes are not sealed. To reuse an envelope simply requires scratching out the name of the previous addressee and writing in the new one.

A company can save a great deal of money by making mailings to employees through intra company mail rather than through the Postal Service. This idea is examined in Question 76. The envelopes used for intracompany mail should be a different color from the envelopes used for outgoing mail (Question 77). The color differential makes the task of the mail clerk easier and increases efficiency, because it reduces the chance that in-house mail will go to the Post Office.

Question 78 asks whether there is any type of numbering system to simplify the delivery of mail to departments within the company. A numbering system may not be needed in small companies, but greatly facilitates delivery in larger organizations.

The final question is concerned with whether a routing slip is used instead of making copies of mail directed to several individuals. This rule does not apply to important mail, which might not reach the bottom name on the list for several days. Thus, the routing slip should be used only when timeliness is not a critical factor.

SUMMARY

Because of the repetitive nature of much of mailroom work, there are many opportunities for increased efficiency and effectiveness. Many activities are similar from one organization to the next, so a generalized operational audit questionnaire can help increase overall productivity in the mailroom.

Cost-consciousness in the mailroom is partly a matter of education. If mailroom employees are taught to be alert to cases of inefficiency, the remedy they suggest will provide a return over an extended period of time. In fact, mailroom employees are in a position to help cut costs in all departments. Through adequate initial training, periodic retraining, a good procedures manual, and occasional visits by outside experts, the mailroom staff can make a major contribution in most organizations. With the mailroom at the center of most administrative activities, proper management can help the whole organization prosper.

nine

MARKETING

Marketing costs represent a relatively large expense in many organizations, but they have received much less analytic study than other functional areas. Of course, there are inherent problems in trying to measure efficiency and effectiveness of a department whose primary output is creativity. And, because standard measures of marketing efficiency and effectiveness are not available to most managers, they have tended to avoid the department altogether. Managers have preferred to concentrate on the functional areas of the organization where cost pressures are greater, the benefits are readily quantifiable, and the subject matter is familiar. Advertising costs, in particular, have received little serious discussion in accounting and management circles. Consequently, despite all the advances in information systems in recent years, marketing managers have not benefited.

Meanwhile, the scope of marketing has broadened in recent decades. The objective is not merely to sell the company's products to those who demand them, but also to create demand where none existed, and to discover demands that are not currently being met and develop a product that can be introduced to fill the unmet needs.

The importance of marketing cost analysis has increased because of a new concept called marketing management. In this concept, the marketing manager plays a key role in every aspect of the production and distribution cycle. First, the marketing department is responsible for finding out what the consumer wants. A product must then be invented and test marketed. Subsequent to a successful test marketing comes an introduction (usually expensive) to the entire market.

Since the role of marketing has increased, the corresponding costs have increased. It costs much more to survey customer needs, develop a new product, test market that product, and then introduce it to a national market than it did to sell a product which had already been manufactured. Unfortunately, the escalation in costs has gone undetected and unchecked at many companies. Therefore, the operational auditor has an excellent opportunity to provide a valuable new service to an organization.

Both managers and operational auditors need to be aware of some of the anomalies in running a marketing department. For one thing, marketing costs per unit of product tend to rise as sales increase. This is the opposite of the impact on production costs, which tend to decrease as volume increases. The reason unit marketing costs rise with increased volume is because the costs arise from attempts to break down the consumer's threshold of resistance. Some consumers have a low resistance threshold and will buy the product as soon as the marketing program begins. However, once these low-threshold consumers have been skimmed off, subsequent sales can come only after greater and greater media blitzes, all of which cost money.

Further complicating the measurement of marketing efficiency and effectiveness is the fact that many promotional costs are incurred for purposes of obtaining results in the future. In other words, there is a considerable time lag between cause and effect.

Do Advertising Expenditures Have Carry-Over Effects?   Intuitively, it is believable that most advertising campaigns of top quality have some carry-over effect on future sales. In fact, this characteristic of an advertising campaign is important in the evaluation of its effectiveness. Although certain components of a campaign may not yield a high return in the current period, they may produce future sales of the product. Advertising creates brand loyalty. There is a great deal of evidence to confirm this statement. During the years of World War II and the Korean War, many consumer goods manufacturers continued to advertise their consumer products despite the fact that they were producing only war materials for the duration. Why would these companies have advertised if they did not believe that the advertising would benefit future sales? The accountant properly wrote off the advertising costs as expenses in the year they were paid even though no revenues could be attributed that year to the costs, nor were they expected to be. The only objective was to keep the company's name and products in the public eye so that when consumer goods could be produced again, the consumer would purchase the advertised items.

The idea of advertising carry-over is not an unsubstantiated belief. Many empirical studies have proven the existence of such carry-over. The most comprehensive statistical examination of advertising carry-over was a study that dealt with the advertising activities of the Lydia Pinkham Company, an internationally known manufacturer and seller of medicinal vegetable compounds. Using a large amount of advertising, the Lydia

Pinkham Company was an appropriate subject for a study of advertising carry-over. Using the technique of multiple regression, Palda found that there was considerable lag between advertising expenditures[1] and their effect. Similar results were reported in a DuPont study of the effectiveness of Teflon cookware commercials.[2]

There are at least four reasons why sales often occur some time after the related advertising. First, advertising impressions may build up over time until the consumer is eventually persuaded to purchase the product advertised. In other words, there is a threshold of resistance that must be broken down. Each advertisement, from the first in a series to the last, plays a role in penetrating that barrier. Second, when advertising was instrumental in introducing a product to a consumer who later develops some brand loyalty to the product, repeat purchases can be attributed to the original advertising: no additional advertising was necessary to convince the buyer to make an additional purchase. Third, at the time a product is advertised, a customer may not be in the market for the product, but he may buy it later when the need arises. He may keep the catalog or mentally file the advertisement in the meanwhile. Fourth (a corollary of the third), a quite long lag may result if the product can be used only by certain age groups; for instance, children may not buy cigarettes or beer, but they become brand conscious and carry-over may result.

Other Complications.   There are other factors that complicate an analysis of marketing efficiency and effectiveness. For one thing, there is a lack of uniformity in marketing approaches. Every product requires the use of different techniques, and many companies like to vary their marketing mix from one year to the next (although there are numerous successful exceptions to this rule). The marketing process is simply not standardized. Each company's process is different, so their costs are different. These differences usually reflect unique competitive situations. Alternatives available in selecting a marketing mix make it almost impossible to make meaningful comparisons among companies' mixes, even though the companies may be marketing the same product. For example, one company may charge a high price and incur high marketing cost. A competitor may sell the same product at a lower price without incurring high marketing costs. If the companies earn the same amount of profit,

---

[1]Kristian S. Palda, *The Measurement of Cumulative Advertising Effect* (Englewood Cliffs, New Jersey: Prentice-Hall, 1964).
[2]James C. Becknell and Robert W. McIsaac, "Test Marketing Cookware Coated With Teflon," *Journal of Advertising Research*, III (September 1963), p. 2.

can it be said that the high-cost marketing program was less efficient than the low-cost program?

Although there are numerous problems in performing an operational audit of a marketing department, the job is not impossible. The output of a marketing department is more variable than the output of a production department, but there are some areas with a degree of uniformity. The questionnaire illustrated in Exhibit 9-1 covers some of the areas in which an operational auditor can assist a marketing manager. The questionnaire for Marketing differs somewhat from those in previous chapters in that it measures creativity more than areas of office management. Some of the sections of the questionnaire correspond to the segments of the typical marketing mix. The eight sections in total are:

General questions
Staff
Advertising
Advertising agency relationships
Distribution Activities
Pricing
Packaging
Accounting

GENERAL

The first two questions deal with marketing objectives and strategies. A marketing department needs to have measurable objectives. Too often, the objectives are to "maximize sales." Objectives expressed in such generalities, however, make it impossible to determine whether the objectives are achieved. Marketing goals should be stated in objective terms and accompanied by specific strategies as to how the objectives will be met. Marketing personnel should then be periodically evaluated in terms of their progress in achieving these goals.

The third question asks whether written job descriptions are available for every position in the department. Although this is important for every department, it is perhaps even more important for Marketing because of the variety of tasks performed.

Question 4 asks about the manner in which sales budgets are prepared. Sales forecasts should be based upon a careful analysis of economic conditions and the competitive environment in the company's market areas. This careful analysis, however, is not always done. Instead, last year's budget is raised by 5% or 10% and called a new budget. Useful budgets are based on realistic assumptions.

Yes	No	DNA	

EXHIBIT 9-1   Marketing Questionnaire

General

1. Are marketing objectives and product strategies available in writing?

2. Are product marketing strategies periodically updated?

3. Are job descriptions available for all positions in the department?

4. Are sales forecasts (budgets) prepared after diligent research?

5. Does the company have a means of obtaining market intelligence?

6. Are competitors' actions kept under surveillance?

7. Do you know your market share for every product of your company?

8. Do you know your marketing costs by product and by market segment?

9. Are your marketing objectives both long- and short-term?

Staff

10. Are all personnel properly qualified?

11. Are records and reports adequate for control of the work performed?

12. Are marketing personnel encouraged to participate in professional organizations and continuing education programs?

13. Does the company provide professional publications to employees?

14. Is supervision within the department adequate?

15. Are job duties clearly understood?

16. What is the annual turnover rate for departmental employees?

17. What is the annual turnover rate for salesmen?

Advertising

18. Are advertising activities coordinated with other phases of the marketing mix and with production?

19. Does the company have advertising objectives?

20. Does the company analyze the results of advertising activities by means of some type of advertising response model?

21. Are advertising budgets developed?

159

22. Are the budgets used as a means of project control?

23. Have you considered "pooled marketing" agreements with noncompeting firms?

Advertising Agency Relationships

24. Does the company use an advertising agency?

25. Are agency agreements covered by written contracts?

26. Are agency billings properly supported by company authorizations and proof of service?

27. Is company communication with the agency adequate?

28. Are media charges independently checked on a periodic basis to ensure propriety of the rates charged?

29. Has company given consideration to establishing its own in-house advertising agency?

Distribution Activities

30. Do you know your marketing costs by channel of distribution?

31. Is there any type of training program for new salesmen?

32. Are there refresher courses for veteran salesmen?

33. Does each salesman know enough about the product to do his job most effectively?

34. If there is any type of dealer support program, does it meet the needs of the dealers?

35. Are customers currently being adequately serviced?

36. Is the sales force utilized to help ascertain customer needs and complaints?

37. Are salesmen's expense accounts periodically audited?

38. Is there any evaluation of warranty claims or warranty programs?

39. Do you think company products are being marketed in the proper locations?

40. Have you investigated the possibility of entering the foreign (export) market?

41. Have you considered using independent sales representatives instead of employing salesmen?

EXHIBIT 9-1 (Continued)

Yes / No / DNA

42. Are any types of transportation studies performed to ensure delivery at the lowest cost?

43. Are deliveries always made on time?

44. Are salesmen notified of any anticipated delays in delivery schedules?

45. Are realistic sales quotas set for salesmen?

46. Does the company distribute information on successful sales approaches so that all salesmen can learn from them?

Pricing

47. Are pricing alternatives ever test marketed?

48. Do you know the price elasticity of the company's products?

49. Do you consider a product's position in its life cycle when establishing a price?

50. Are you familiar with the requirements of the Robinson-Patman Act?

Packaging

51. Does the design of product packages enhance sales?

52. Does the package attract buyers?

53. Do packages adequately protect their contents?

54. Does the company conduct any type of packaging research?

Accounting

55. Do you receive the type of information you need from the accounting department?

56. Does your accountant provide internal reports that defer the costs of marketing programs that are expected to show long-term results (as opposed to expensing the costs as they are incurred)?

57. Are marketing costs reported by function?

58. Are promotional costs such as "cents-off" coupons recorded as expenses instead of as a deduction from revenues?

59. Is short-run profit emphasized as the sole objective of marketing activities?

Questions 5 through 7 concern the marketing employees' knowledge of their market and the actions of competitors. A company should either have a program of surveillance over competitors' actions or subscribe to an independent service that provides such information. Large companies do both: they have their own market research team and they also buy information from outsiders. There are several large outfits that provide market share statistics which are advertised in most professional marketing journals.

The eighth question inquires whether a company calculates its marketing costs by product and by market segment. The computation of these costs is not an easy task because of the many interacting cost components within a company's product line. However, a knowledge of costs by product is necessary for an accurate evaluation of marketing efforts. Unfortunately, marketing cost analysis has not always been a popular topic among either accountants or marketing people. The complex environment in which marketing costs are incurred makes it tricky to allocate costs in a meaningful manner. However, difficulty does not mean impossibility, and the absence of traditional cost reporting tools does not preclude all reporting of marketing costs. Marketing costs must be reported and analyzed in much the same manner as production costs. The costs of marketing are now so great that effective control is mandatory.

Question 9—an extension of question 1—asks whether the company has both long- and short-term marketing objectives. Since marketing programs are generally thought to provide both long- and short-term benefits, it is only natural that separate goals be stated for each time frame. Although it may be difficult to state objectives for future years in terms of dollars of sales, projected market share or estimated unit sales may be appropriate formulations of long-term plans.

STAFF

The subject of marketing staff is explored in questions 10 through 17. Questions 10 (qualifications of staff), 11 ("are reports adequate for control?"), 14 (adequacy of supervision), and 15 ("are assignments understood?") could be applicable to all departments, but are perhaps more important to Marketing because of the intangible nature of much of the marketing department's output. Marketing personnel must be highly creative, a factor that sometimes results in lax supervision because managers focus more on creative results than on the work habits of subordinates. Question 11 should be emphasized because of the shortage of good accounting information. If staffers feel that they do not have adequate reports, this should be communicated to the controller.

Questions 12 and 13 ask whether continuing education and professional advancement are encouraged. Marketing employees should be urged to join such organizations as the American Marketing Association and to subscribe to magazines like *Advertising Age*. Since marketing is a creative occupation, employees should be given every opportunity to gain inspiration.

The department's annual turnover rate is examined in Questions 16 and 17. Because of the creative nature of the work, some degree of turnover is more acceptable in the Marketing department than in other functional areas. However, because of a company's investment in training employees, too much turnover becomes expensive.

ADVERTISING

Although advertising is not the only activity carried out in a marketing department, it is an important one. Advertising is often a bewildering tool. Expenditures for advertising in the United States amount to about 2% of the Gross National Product. Unfortunately, much of this money is spent without any examination of the results achieved. The measurement of advertising impact is difficult because advertising has both an immediate and a lagged response. The measurement problem is complicated also by the difficulty of isolating advertising from the rest of a marketing mix.

A company usually encounters five advertising decision problems: (1) determination of advertising objectives, (2) creation of suitable copy, (3) choice of appropriate media, (4) timing the message for optimum effectiveness, and (5) spending the proper amount on advertising. The operational auditor cannot help solve all of these problems, but the first and last are his realm.

One way for advertising to be more cost effective is to coordinate it with production plans and the other elements of the marketing mix (the subject of Question 18). The best marketing campaign in the world cannot succeed if there are no marketable products on the shelf. Therefore, an advertising campaign should be coordinated with the production departments to be sure that the right goods will be available to fill the newly created demand. Too often, companies have carved out a huge market for a product only to discover that none of the advertised goods was available, nor did the manufacturing division have any immediate plans to produce additional units. Other parts of the marketing mix also need to be coordinated with advertising programs; for example, increased sales visits should accompany a stepped-up advertising campaign, because the advertisements will make it easier for salesmen to get in the door. Advertising campaigns also should be built around price reductions or packaging changes.

Question 19 asks whether the company has any written advertising objectives. There should be specific objectives of what is expected of advertising campaigns. Objectives might include creating brand preference, triggering immediate sales, or disseminating information to potential buyers. In other words, is the advertising supposed to make the customer buy right away, or is it supposed to lay the groundwork for future sales when the potential customer is in the market for the company's product?

Advertising response models are the subject of Question 20. Since so much money is allocated to advertising, it is simply good management to ascertain the level of response to various advertising campaigns. The measurement of advertising effectiveness is not an easy task because of the lagged impact of many campaigns and the interrelationship of the elements in the marketing mix. But it is not impossible. Aided by computers, numerous quantitative models have been developed to help to analyze variables that were once considered unmeasurable.

One model developed by marketing academicians is the advertising decay model. There are at least three different types of advertising decay models that might prove useful. These are (1) advertising awareness or advertising attitude models, (2) multivariate regression models, and (3) experimental design models. Although all advertising decay models have limitations, any of the types can be serviceable if the user is aware of the assumptions implicit in each model.

Awareness Models

Advertising awareness (and the attitude-type) models are useful in predicting advertising exposure and the diminishing response rate of advertisements. Basically, an awareness type of advertising decay model defines the exposure level of advertising as being some fraction of the prior period's exposure level based on the rate by which consumers forget an advertisement they have seen (assuming that they see no additional advertising).

Marketing departments of major companies, as well as many advertising agencies, have their own sets of statistics on exposure carryover of advertising. A major assumption of this model, however, is that a consumer's awareness of the existence of an advertisement is synonomous with a future sale to that consumer. This is obviously a fallacious assumption, but a necessary one.

The benefits of advertising may be carried over for many years. A recent example of a long carry-over was Ipana toothpaste. Bristol-Myers Corporation produced Ipana between 1915 and 1968. During the 1930s and 1940s Ipana was the largest selling toothpaste in the country. Its sponsorship of such radio shows as Duffy's Tavern, Mr. District Attorney, and the Eddie Cantor Show made Ipana a household name. During the late 1950s and early 1960s Ipana began to struggle. Competitors introduced whiteners and brighteners and other ingredients to transform the toothpaste user into a sex symbol. Finally, Bristol-Myers stopped production of Ipana in 1968 in order to switch its promotional efforts to its own "extra-white" varieties of toothpaste.

In 1969 a Minneapolis, Minnesota, chemical manufacturer began producing its own toothpaste. The company called its new toothpaste "Ipana" and packaged the product in a tube similar to that of the old Ipana. The formula of the new toothpaste was in no way similar to that of the original Ipana, but the chemical company could legally adopt the name of Ipana, because it was no longer being used by Bristol-Myers. Consumer response to the introduction of the new toothpaste was instantaneous. With no advertising whatsoever, the new Ipana quickly carved for itself a major niche in the Minnesota toothpaste market. The reason for the quick acceptance was the legions of brand-loyal customers that had been created by the radio advertising three decades earlier. At last report, the Minnesota company had widened its distribution area to the entire Midwest, without significant promotional expenditures.

Advantages of Awareness Models. The primary advantage of awareness models over the other types of advertising models is their availability. Many firms already have such information available for purposes of determining the effectiveness of various advertising programs. The amount of decay is determinable either through interviews or simulations. The simulation method is often used by advertising agencies to try to compare the effectiveness of several proposed advertising campaigns. Although awareness models may not always correlate advertising to future sales, such models are generally useful for comparison purposes. Most companies could use the awareness models in one form or another if they could discern the connection between advertisement awareness and future sales.

Limitations of Awareness Models. The major limitation to the use of awareness models for accounting purposes is the problem of knowing whether or not the model is actually measuring the attribute in question. Say 20% of the potential customers exposed to an advertisement remember it after a period of time. That does not necessarily mean that 20% of the sales remain to be made. It can usually be assumed that no further sales will result from the forgotten portion of the advertising, but it is not known whether any sales will result from the remembered group.

There is also controversy about whether awareness of an advertisement is as important a factor as a favorable attitude toward the advertisement. It is difficult to conduct an interview to determine this without biasing the person being interviewed. There is also the problem of whether an interview should be conducted with aided recall or with unaided recall. In other words, should the interviewer show a person a copy of an advertisement and ask whether that particular advertisement was read, or should the interviewer simply ask what advertisements the interviewee has read lately. In conclusion, the reliability and validity of awareness models must be taken with a grain of salt.

Multiple Regression Techniques

Another alternative exists for a company that has been operating for several years. A company that has historical sales and advertising data available for a series of years may apply multiple regression techniques to the data to determine what percentage of revenues derive from the advertising of the current period and what portion from earlier advertising.

The use of regression analysis requires a *ceteris paribus* (other things being equal) assumption, however, thus limiting its applicability. A company that frequently switched its advertising outlays from one medium to another would not be safe in applying regression techniques, since the effect of the current media devices might not be similar to that of the media used in prior periods. Assuming that the advertising media employed by a firm have been comparatively stable over a period of time, the use of multiple regression can be a rather elementary task.

Advantages of Regression Analysis. Multiple regression analysis may provide a simple method of determining the carryover effect of advertising, particularly that portion which is attributable to learning by the consumer. If a company has a track record on which regression analysis can be based, then advertising benefits can be correlated with the revenues that are subsequently produced. Although the limitations of the method are numerous, many companies will find that these limitations can be either overcome or overlooked in practice. One advantage—yet a factor that might also be a limitation—is that regression analysis can be performed on most computers via canned programs. Although this availability is a distinct advantage, the ease of computer usage may cause the analyst to overlook the basic assumptions inherent in regression analysis.

Limitations to Regression Analysis.   There are several limitations to the use of regression techniques. First, a company must have been in business for at least a number of months in order to have data available on which to apply regression techniques. Secondly, regression analysis assumes that the relationships of the past will continue in the future, including changes in nonadvertising sales efforts as well as advertising. Owing to this *ceteris paribus* assumption, the use of multiple regression may not provide strict scientific accuracy. Third, a linear relationship must exist between sales and the independent variables. A fourth factor to keep in mind is that high positive correlations do not necessarily indicate cause-and-effect relationships. In our example at hand, advertising may be the cause of sales, or sales may be the cause of advertising, or both factors may be correlated with a third variable, or possibly the relationship is due strictly to chance occurrences. Finally, it is not proper to try to predict a dependent variable in any area outside the relevant range: the relevant range is usually perceived as the area within which observations were made.

Despite the multitude of limitations, regression analysis can be the most efficient means of measuring effectiveness if there is an awareness of the underlying assumptions and the capability to control the relationships of the input data.

Experimental Design Models

Still another method that might be used is the experimental model. An experiment is conducted to determine what portion of a firm's advertising expenditures results in sales in future periods, no matter what the reason for the carryover might be. An accountant need not be concerned with whether the carryover effects are attributable, for example, to brand loyalty or to a continually weakening brand resistance. The important finding is whether carryover effects do exist.

Advantages of the Experimental Design Method.   The use of an experiment to determine the rate at which sales will decline if advertising is stopped should prove to be a quite accurate determinant of the value of past advertising expenditures, but rarely have such experiments been conducted.

Limitations of the Experimental Design Method. The model puts too much reliance on the one most recent period. It implies that the results of the most recent period are similar to all other periods. Cost and time are other limitations of using an experimental model. An experimental model must be undertaken well in advance of the time when the information is desired. No doubt, cost-benefit analysis would show that only in rare circumstances would the use of an experiment be profitable. Therefore, it is the opinion of this author that the use of experimental models to determine the decay effect of advertising results would not be tenable. Such studies would ordinarily not pay for themselves as far as accounting is concerned. Perhaps in instances of corporate consolidation or reorganization the expense could be justified.

Question 21 asks whether advertising budgets are developed. There should be an estimate of sales for each level of advertising expenditure. This is simplified if the response rate to advertising is known. Once a flexible advertising and sales budget has been prepared, the optimum level is selected—the optimum level being that point where marginal cost is equal to marginal revenue. Once a budget has been established, it should be used as a control tool (Question 22).

In Question 23, the respondents are asked whether there has been any consideration of adopting "pooled marketing" agreements with noncompeting companies. In a pooled marketing venture, two organizations advertise each other's products. For example, American Express ads urge credit card holders to rent Avis cars. Avis ads, in return, recommend their car rental fees be paid by American Express credit cards. These are complementary advertisements which simultaneously help both companies. Thus, both companies get twice the exposure for a given price. National Car Rental had a similar arrangement with Hilton Hotels. Pooled marketing arrangements can be helpful on the local level as well as the national level. For instance, some small motels place brochures from a local restaurant in their rooms; the restaurant reciprocates with motel brochures.

ADVERTISING AGENCY RELATIONSHIPS

Supposedly, many advertising agency services do not cost the advertiser anything. The agency is paid a fee (typically 15%) by the media in which an advertisement appears. Since a company incurs few additional costs in giving the work it used to do to an ad agency, there is good reason for hiring an agency. Therefore, a negative response to question 24 ("is an agency used"?) may not indicate a problem, but the company should be asked why an agency is not used. After all, if costs are no greater, it would seem advantageous to have someone else do the paper work. (This is not always true. Some companies feel that they do not have enough proximity to the market when they use an advertising intermediary. Part of the reason for this feeling may be the lack of adequate communication, the subject of Question 27.) Another advantage of using an ad agency, particularly for a small company, is that the agency can often provide creative ideas, artists, photographers, and other key people at a lower cost than an organization could hire its own in-house people. (Agencies do charge for creative services; it is generally only the dealings with the media that are free to the advertiser.)

Questions 25 and 26 deal with the business side of a relationship with an ad agency. There should be a written contract that spells out exactly what services are to be provided by the agency and which services are to be charged for. Also, agency billing should be correlated to company authorization and proof of service. To the accounts payable department, the proof of service (perhaps a tear sheet) should be viewed as a substitute for a receiving report.

Periodically, media charges should be independently checked to ensure the propriety of the rates charged (the subject is examined by Question 28). Charges are set by the media (such as TV stations and magazines). Thus the company should ask their media for their current rates. The rates should correspond to the amount charged by the agency.

Question 29 takes the other tack in asking whether the company has considered the idea of establishing an in-house advertising agency. Since an agency receives 15% of the cost of running each ad (from the media), it means that an advertiser who owned an agency as a subsidiary would save that 15% (less the additional administrative expenses incurred). This author was once asked by a client to perform an audit of media charges (like that mentioned in Question 28). The media charges turned out to be correct, but what was interesting was the fact that the company was in effect paying its agency about $30,000 a year (15% of the $200,000 annual media outlays), despite the fact that the company had its own in-house advertising department. I did not see much need for the agency. The advertising director explained that this was the first year an outside agency had been used, yet media charges were no higher than in the past. Actually, the company was receiving free use of the agency since magazines (the media in question) charge the same rates whether an agency is used or not. Thus only the magazines were making less money after the agency was retained. Given that background knowledge, my next recommendation was to form an advertising agency as a company subsidiary. The subsidiary was soon established in the form of a part-time secretary who was paid $3,000 a year. The company not only began receiving the $30,000 that had previously gone to the magazines and the agency, but also the enterprising secretary soon recruited a few local agency clients who generated enough additional revenue to pay almost her full salary. Thus, any company with a knowledgeable advertising staff should give consideration to forming an advertising agency subsidiary.

DISTRIBUTION ACTIVITIES

Distribution is one of the major considerations in a marketing mix. There are many channels of distribution that an organization might use, including mail order, door-to-door sales, grocery stores, discount stores, company-owned stores, wholesale and retail. Whatever channels are used, a company should know the cost by channel, as examined in Question 30. Unfortunately, many companies use numerous channels, but know their distribution costs only in total, not by individual channel. With detailed cost records, it may be found that some channels are not paying their way.

Questions 31 through 33 are concerned with the knowledgability of the company's salesmen. There should be some type of training program for new salesmen to familiarize them with product attributes and proven selling techniques. Refresher courses can benefit veteran salesmen.

Question 34 asks whether dealer support programs meet the needs of the dealers. Do the programs really support the efforts of sellers, or do they give only lip service to the concept? Question 35 deals with a similar topic, asking whether customers are currently receiving adequate service. In most businesses, service by the seller is a strong competitive tool. A higher price can often be justified by better service.

Customer needs and complaints are the subject of Question 36. The sales staff is closer to the customer than anyone else in the company is. Thus it makes sense to use the sales staff as an information link back to the company. Probably the best system is to have the sales staff periodically communicate all complaints and requests from customers.

Questions 37 and 38 are basically internal control questions. Salesmen's expense accounts should be periodically audited to be sure that claims are truly business-related. Also it is a good idea to evaluate warranty claims for authenticity. In addition, warranty programs should be periodically evaluated to be certain that they meet the needs of customers and are cost-effective for the company.

Question 39 asks for an opinion on whether the company's products are being marketed in the proper locations. This question rarely yields a constructive alternative suggestion, but occasionally the auditor may uncover a good idea which has been overlooked because of a communication breakdown or personal politics.

The advisability of entering the foreign (export) market is examined in Question 40. Exports have never been a prime consideration for most U.S. companies, because profits rarely depended on them. With one of the world's largest group of consumers, plus efficient transportation and distribution facilities, the United States has been a natural, familiar market for American companies. Companies have often been able to prosper without having to learn new ways of doing business in other parts of the world. In other countries, virtually every business performs some export activities, but many managers of U.S. businesses view export sales as being of marginal importance. In the past, it was possible to expand a company without reaching into the international market. Now, successful companies are those that take advantage of every sales opportunity, and the biggest opportunity of all is often in foreign markets. Because the cost of Mideast petroleum is tipping the trade balance in the United States, exporting can be not only a profitable activity but a patriotic one as well. In fact, to encourage export sales, the U.S. Congress has passed a law that provides preferential tax treatment for exporters. Businesses of all types can take advantage of these tax provisions by forming a subsidiary corporation that is operated as a Domestic International Sales Corporation (DISC). Basically, a DISC is allowed to defer payment of taxes on much of its export income.

Question 41 asks whether the company has considered using independent sales representatives instead of or in addition to company-paid salesmen. The use of sales reps would make selling costs, including travel, strictly variable since costs (commissions) would be based on sales made. Many companies use both their own sales staff and some independent representatives. Local sales reps are used in areas where the market is not large enough to warrant the use of a company employee. Question 41 is not intended to imply that it is preferable to use reps instead of company employees. The question is designed to find out rather whether the company has made an evaluation of the merits of the two approaches.

Delivery problems are the subject of questions 42 through 44. First, there should be periodic studies performed of delivery rate structures to ensure deliveries are being made at the lowest possible cost for that quality of service. This becomes especially important when the company has multiple factories shipping the same products, or multiple facilities. Linear programming models have been developed to assist a company in making cost-effective delivery decisions. On a related topic, if it is known that a delivery is going to be late, the salesman involved should be alerted.

Perhaps he can head off any problems that might arise as a result of the delay.

Question 45 asks whether realistic sales quotas are set for salesmen. "Realistic" involves an opinion, but there should be some policy regarding quotas. Like any standard, a sales quota should be neither too easy to achieve, nor impossibly difficult. Quotas usually motivate best when they are challenging but reachable.

The final question in the Distribution section asks whether the company sends information to all its salesmen on successful approaches developed by members of its sales force. The company will benefit, and the salesman who originated the new approach will take pride in the recognition awarded his idea. It might even be helpful to reward the salesmen whose ideas are used as an added incentive to share their best sales techniques.

PRICING

Pricing is an integral part of the marketing mix, and pricing alternatives should be test marketed (Question 47) in the same way that new products, packages, and advertising campaigns are. Without knowing its products' price elasticity (Question 48), a company may fail to charge the price that will maximize profits. As a rather extreme example, a small troubled company found that it could actually increase its volume by raising prices. This author had advised the small client to double all his prices immediately. The client had no cost accounting system and so had no idea what it cost to produce its products. Consequently, the company was selling several items below cost. The company was near bankruptcy. After the suggestion to double all prices was implemented, sales volume in units quintupled. As a result, the owners became millionaires within months. Apparently what happened was that the company's products were perceived as luxury goods after the prices were raised. At a lower price, the same items were considered cheap trash. Thus companies should test their pricing alternatives in order to determine the price elasticity of demand.

Question 49 inquires whether a product's position in its life cycle is considered when establishing a price. Most marketing professionals are familiar with the concept of the product life cycle. It is simply a schematic history of a product's sales over the life of the product. The historical data typically produce a one-humped curve when sales are plotted as a function of time. The product's life begins, with very low sales, during the market development or introduction period. Sales then accelerate quickly during the growth stage. The growth stage is followed by the maturity stage when sales reach their peak and level off. The last stage is the decline stage, when sales fall and the product is eventually withdrawn from production. As a product progresses through these stages of its life, its price elasticity will probably change. During the introductory stage, prices can be kept high since there are no competitors and few products to sell. During the growth stage prices can be reduced, but kept high enough to enhance profits. As the product reaches its mature stage, many competitors have entered the market and prices must be reduced to the lowest possible level. Finally, during the decline stage, prices must be raised because unit costs go up as production decreases; meanwhile, there are fewer competitors left in the market, so there is less difficulty in raising prices. In summary, knowing a product's place in its life cycle is an excellent aid in pricing.

The final question in the Pricing section asks whether the respondent is familiar with the requirements of the Robinson-Patman Anti-Price Discrimination Act. This act prohibits quoting different prices to competing customers unless there are actual differences in delivery costs or manufacturing costs. Both the buyer and the seller would be liable for treble damages if a competitor could prove price discrimination. Therefore, marketers should be aware of the requirements of the Robinson-Patman Act.

PACKAGING

There are only four questions in the Packaging section of the questionnaire, none of which elicits many "no" answers, in this author's experience. The packaging questions are designed mainly to determine whether the company does any packaging research, and whether its packages are intended to attract customers as well as protect the contents. If an auditor does encounter any negative responses to a question in the Packaging section, the source is usually a conflict between Questions 52 and 53. Some companies view packaging mainly as a means of attracting customers. Other companies stress the protective function of packaging. In reality, a package should both attract buyers and protect the product.

ACCOUNTING

Marketing managers have rarely had useful accounting information in their field. This is due partially to a lack of interest by both marketing managers and accountants, and partially to a lack of communication between the two groups. The questions in this section are designed to elicit information that can be communicated to the Accounting department. If the accountant knows what type of information is needed by the marketing manager, the chance of that material being made available is improved.

The auditor should not be too surprised to receive numerous negative responses to the questions in the Accounting section. This author has never received a positive response to Question 56, for example ("Are long-term marketing costs deferred?"). However, numerous marketing professionals have expressed an interest in receiving reports showing deferment of marketing costs. This desire can be communicated to the controller's office.

The final question asks whether short-run profit is emphasized as the sole objective of marketing activities. The ideal answer to this question is "no" but not a flat "no." Most marketers are rated by top management on the basis of their short-run results, because companies usually have to make sales in each period in order to survive. In the best of all possible worlds, the Marketing department would achieve short-run objectives and simultaneously set the stage for the long-run progress of the company.

SUMMARY

Many marketing departments are managed by people who are artists, rather than analysts. These people are creative. They can spend money, but rarely know the return on their investment. With marketing costs becoming an increasingly large part of a company's total expenditures, there is a growing need to assess the efficiency and effectiveness of marketing operations. The operational auditor can provide a major service by bringing order out of the chaos that prevails in many marketing departments.

Yet, efficiency and effectiveness are not easy to measure in this department. Marketing is one of the last functions in the typical business to come under management scrutiny. Many of the variables in the marketing process do not lend themselves to scientific management as readily as production activities do. Although marketing management is complicated, it is not impossible. If analysts with the proper skills are given access to a marketing department, they can effect a material improvement. Recognition that efficiency and effectiveness can be measured is a step in the right direction. The operational auditor may find the Marketing department to be more of a challenge than any other department, but the potential rewards make the undertaking well worthwhile.

ten

PAYROLL

The payroll department is one department on which all employees are experts. If the department is inefficient or inaccurate, someone (or everyone) is going to know about it eventually. Since the duties of the payroll department are of a repetitive nature, a small failing can recur often enough to be quite costly over time. The Payroll department plays an important role in the company's success because Payroll is interrelated with every other department. The efficient operation of every department is dependent on a smooth-running payroll function. Payroll also has legal implications, inasmuch as the Payroll department is responsible for adhering to many federal laws (such as tax laws and the Wage and Hour law).

Exhibit 10-1 depicts an operational audit questionnaire, which was constructed from suggestions obtained in a survey of 150 payroll department heads. The operational audit questionnaire for Payroll consists of five sections:

Controls
Procedures
Physical facilities
Personnel
General

The section on internal controls has a great deal of overlap with the internal controls tested in connection with the company's annual financial audit, illustrating the close relationship between the operational audit and the annual financial audit. (Indeed, the operational audit makes a perfect adjunct to the annual financial audit.) Note that most of the questions are designed so that a "yes" answer indicates a good department and a "no" answer indicates a possible deficiency. The "Does Not Apply" (DNA) column is used when a question is not applicable to the company being

EXHIBIT 10-1 Payroll Questionnaire

Controls

1. Are employee time cards used? Is an automatic time clock used?

2. Does anyone oversee the clocking-in process? Is the job of overseer rotated regularly?

3. Is an employee's starting salary authorized in writing by a qualified official?

4. Are salary changes authorized in writing?

5. Are dismissals and resignations reported to payroll immediately in writing?

6. Are time card (or time sheet) clerical calculations ever audited?

7. Are all payroll department employees bonded?

8. Are all employees paid by check?

9. Are payroll checks prenumbered?

10. Are payroll checks signed by someone other than the preparer?

11. Are payroll checks kept locked up when not being used? How many people have keys to the vault?

12. Is a check protector used?

13. Does someone other than those with access to the payroll checks reconcile the bank account monthly?

14. Does the reconciliation of the bank account include a check for double endorsements on payroll checks?

15. Is there a set procedure for handling unclaimed paychecks?

16. Is there a special procedure for issuing corrected checks when errors occur? What is the procedure?

17. Are payroll employees required to take a vacation at least annually?

18. Are payroll checks distributed by someone other than the payroll employees?

19. Is the preparation of payroll relatively free of errors?

Procedures

20. Is payroll always completed on time?

21. Does the department receive all time cards and other payroll information prior to the time they are needed?

EXHIBIT 10-1 (Continued)

Yes / No / DNA

22. Are time cards kept long enough to meet legal requirements of the Wage and Hour Law and other regulations?

23. Is a separate payroll bank account used?

24. Has the possibility of reducing the frequency of pay been considered?

25. Has the possibility of using a computer service center or a "one-write" system been examined?

26. Are payroll figures reported by department?

27. Is a trend analysis ever made of gross payroll figures?

28. Are quarterly tax reports always filed on time? Are W-2 forms always issued prior to January 31?

29. Are withholding tax deposits always made on time?

30. Are quarterly reports always typed within a reasonable length of time after they have been prepared?

31. Are problems that affect work discussed with the heads of the departments that are at fault?

32. Does the payroll department operate without overtime work?

33. Is necessary overtime within the department authorized by a responsible official?

Physical Facilities

34. Are the physical facilities of the department adequate?

35. Is an adequate number of office machines available when they are needed?

36. Can additional office machines be borrowed from other departments if needed during extra-busy periods?

37. Is all equipment fully utilized?

38. Would reducing the number of machines diminish efficiency?

39. Is there a specific procedure to follow when the purchase of new machines is necessary?

40. Does the department regularly dispose of supplies that it will not need in the foreseeable future or perhaps never use?

41. Are the employees of the department well qualified to perform the duties that are required of them?

42. Do you feel that all employees within the department keep the information that they come in contact with confidential?

EXHIBIT 10-1 (Continued)

43. Do you feel the working atmosphere in the department is relaxed and open?

44. Is continuing education encouraged?

45. Has the workload been evenly distributed so that all employees in the department work steadily and efficiently?

46. Is the department adequately staffed?

47. Has the use of temporary employees been considered for helping meet end-of-quarter deadlines?

48. Is it fairly easy to hire new employees when they are needed?

49. Do payroll department employees "float" to other departments during slack periods? Would such floating be feasible?

50. Do employees of other departments "float" to the payroll department during busy periods?

51. Are department employees familiar with the requirements of the federal Wage and Hour Law?

52. Is the employee turnover rate known?

53. Is the employee absenteeism rate known?

54. Are duties of Payroll personnel rotated regularly?

General

55. Is there a written procedures manual detailing procedures and objectives for every job performed in the department?

56. Is there an open line of communication between the department head and the individuals to whom the department head reports?

57. Are payroll reports organized in such a way as to be useful management tools?

58. Are there adequate written job descriptions and defined areas of responsibility?

59. Is some type of personnel budget used in the department?

60. Is payroll advised of the payroll budget for each department so that there is an up-to-date knowledge of the allotted amounts?

61. Are the employee payroll record forms designed to accommodate all necessary information?

62. Is all of the information contained in the payroll records needed?

Yes	No	DNA	EXHIBIT 10-1 (Continued)
			63. Is the company eligible for merit reductions in state Unemployment Insurance taxes?
			64. Are the effects on merit reductions weighed in considering layoffs?
			65. Is the company eligible for merit reductions in Workmen's Compensation rates?
			66. Is the effect on the merit rating ever considered when minor work-related injuries occur?
			67. How often are errors made in the preparation of payroll?
			68. Are W-4 Forms on file for each company employee?
			69. Are signed receipts required when payroll is paid in cash?
			70. What problems, if any, do you feel exist in the payroll department?

audited; this last column can be used also when an interviewee does not know the answer to a question.

CONTROLS

The questions in the Controls section of the questionnaire are fairly self-explanatory. Questions 1 and 2 deal with time clocks. The use of time clocks permits greater efficiency, fewer errors, and less opportunity for employee fraud. Someone should oversee the clocking-in process to be sure that employees are not clocking-in for friends or nonexistent employees. Questions 3, 4, and 5 are concerned with the Payroll department's communication with the Personnel department (or whoever does the hiring and firing). Without good communication between the Personnel department and Payroll, an employee might be paid for a period after his termination. Question 6 asks whether time card clerical calculations are ever reviewed or audited. The need for this can be illustrated by an instance of a small error, resulting in several weeks' overpayments. A clerk's electronic calculator was not working properly: the calculator consistently added up production figures incorrectly. It was not until the clerk missed work owing to illness that a clerk on another machine discovered the errors, which had resulted in the company overpaying it's employees by several thousand dollars. The company decided to absorb the loss rather than try to recoup individually small amounts from over 100 employees.

Question 7 asks whether payroll employees are bonded—a policy that should be followed for all employees who deal with financial matters. Questions 8 through 12 are concerned with payroll checks and the control exercised over the checks. In most companies, all employees are paid by check, so a "no" to question 8 is a problem that the auditor will rarely encounter. The checks should be prenumbered by the printer in order to maintain control over unwritten checks. The importance of storing unused checks in a vault cannot be overemphasized (question 11). Newspapers often carry articles that stolen payroll checks are circulating in a community. Payroll checks are readily accepted by many merchants, thus making stealing payroll checks popular with the underworld.

Questions 13 and 14 inquire whether an in-depth bank reconciliation is performed each month. A good reconciler should examine the endorsements on paychecks to be sure that they are not endorsed twice—the second time by a payroll employee or a departmental foreman. In one recent incident, a payroll department supervisor embezzled about $100 per week for over two years by writing a check to a nonexistent employee. Every fraudulent check had the supervisor's endorsement; a simple check for double endorsements could have quickly stopped the fraud. With the endorsements not monitored, the company suffered a loss in excess of $10,000, because the supervisor was not bonded.

Unclaimed checks and corrected checks require special handling. Questions 15 and 16 ask about the special procedures surrounding these unusual situations. The auditor should document the procedures for unclaimed checks and erroneous checks, to be certain that there is no opportunity for misappropriation.

The area of internal control is further explored in Questions 17 through 19. Vacations and rotation of duties are required by law for some financial institutions. Such requirements are good internal control tools for any organization (Question 17). Even if an organization has to hire temporary help to fill in during vacation periods, the extra costs may be worthwhile.

PROCEDURES

The Procedures section of the payroll questionnaire is quite important due to the repetitive nature of most of the procedures performed. The payroll procedures and the Controls sections of the audit are especially important to the operational auditor, because payroll is often a fruitful area for fraud schemes. Question 20 concerning whether the payroll is completed on time is the most important as far as employees are concerned. A "no" answer here will certainly indicate a problem of dire proportion, but it does not pinpoint the cause of the problem. Question 21 might suggest one reason why the payroll is not prepared on time: a delay in the receipt of time cards can cause the entire payroll system to balk. If the individual who writes the checks has to stop writing and look for time cards, the work will be late.

Questions 22, 28, and 29 inquire into compliance with federal laws. If required reports and payments are not made on time, the company is subject to penalties. Records must be stored. The Wage and Hour Law, for example, requires employers to keep inactive time cards for several years. Without these records, a company may find itself assessed for back pay if an employee puts in a claim for overtime pay or says he was paid less than the minimum wage. In these and other instances, the company must be able to document the actual hours worked and rate received by each employee.

The timely payment of federal income tax withholding deposits (Question 29) is another key area. Late deposits can result in interest charges and heavy punitive fines. Question 30 explores the possibility that the delay in filing quarterly reports might be due to log jams in the secretarial pool. Question 23 asks whether a separate payroll account is used. The use of a separate bank account for payroll is not only a good internal control device, but also speeds the reconciliation of the bank accounts.

Other possibilities for minimizing payroll-preparation costs are examined in Questions 24 and 25. Obviously, these processing costs would be lower if pay were distributed less often. From a morale point of view, this is often difficult, because once a payroll schedule is established, the initial changeover often places a burden on the employees. However, just because a company has always paid its employees weekly is not enough reason to continue the practice. Computerization can also help. If a company does not have its own computer, there are service centers located throughout the nation that can process payroll checks at a very low cost.

Questions 26 and 27 explore the use of Payroll departmental reports. Gross payroll by department provides useful data for managers in making them aware of the cost of department activity. This is another example of information needed by management, but often not communicated to the proper individual.

The final questions in the section relate to use of overtime to complete the payroll on time. With the time constraints that typify the preparation of payroll, it is common to factor regular overtime (at premium rates) into the operating procedures. Overtime runs 50% more than straight time and should be avoided. As an alternative, adding a second shift or utilizing temporary employees should be considered.

PHYSICAL FACILITIES

The Physical Facilities category of the questionnaire asks whether adequate equipment is available and whether all available equipment is being utilized. These questions are largely self-explanatory, although it might be appropriate to underline the significance of Questions 35 and 36. These questions ask whether an adequate number of office machines is available when needed. The department should have machines when there is work to be performed. If the quantity of work available on slow days does not warrant the purchase of a full complement of machines, it may be possible to regularly borrow machines from other, nearby departments for use on busy days.

Question 40 examines the possibility that storage space is being wasted on supplies that will never be used. It is often difficult to convince people that expensive supplies should be scrapped, but the auditor should convey the concept of a sunk cost as it relates to these obsolete items. If supplies will probably not be used, then they should be disposed of.

PERSONNEL

Several of the questions in the Personnel category deal with the qualifications of workers and whether they are encouraged to continue their education. The confidentiality of company information is examined by Question 42. This is especially important for payroll employees, since they have access to salary figures for everyone in the organization. Gossiping by payroll employees should be forbidden.

Questions 49 and 50 are rather controversial in managerial circles. Since the workload in a payroll department often varies from day to day, some department heads feel that payroll employees could "float" to other departments on slow days, while employees from other departments could be borrowed on busy days.

There is a great deal of difference of opinion on this topic. Although the idea of floating employees makes sense, some department heads we surveyed feared that constant floating could cause morale problems that might result in long-run personnel costs greater than the anticipated savings. Still, it is a workable idea in theory.

Questions 52 and 53 inquire about the turnover and absenteeism rates. If the figures are available, the auditor should compare them to those of other firms. There is merit in a company that has statistics on its turnover and absenteeism rates readily available. So many organizations have no idea what their rates are, that an auditor can assume that a company that does know the figures either does not have a problem or is on the road to solving it.

The final question in the Personnel section of the questionnaire asks whether the duties of payroll workers are periodically rotated. Rotation of duties is an internal control technique that helps deter embezzlement.

GENERAL

The General category embraces several miscellaneous concepts. Questions 55 and 58 relate to procedures manuals and job descriptions. It is important that these be in written form to reduce the chance of misinterpretation. The formal job descriptions also make it easier to recruit qualified new employees since the nature of each job is clearly spelled out ahead of time.

Questions 57 and 60 relate to the reports prepared by the department. No department should lose sight of the fact that reports are prepared for the user. The preparer must have an awareness of what the user desires. Otherwise, the preparer has been inefficient, and he could diminish the user's efficiency as well.

The form of employee payroll records is examined by Questions 61 and 62. The format should accommodate all information that is needed—but no more. The auditor should also scan the payroll records for consistency with the array of current legal requirements.

Questions 63 through 66 are probably more appropriate for the Personnel department, but Payroll employees should have some familiarity with Unemployment Insurance tax merit ratings and Workmen's Compensation rating categories, according to many payroll department heads. Lower Unemployment rates are available to companies that maintain stable employment practices.

One of the most important questions is Number 67. Errors have to be corrected, but corrections cost money. When an error is made in the preparation of a paycheck, there is the additional cost of writing a second check plus the employee's loss of confidence in the payroll department.

The payroll department comes in contact with all employees. Consequently, the image of the Payroll department often becomes the image of the company as a whole. For public relations purposes, it is vital that the payroll department operate in an efficient manner. To do otherwise can be costly in indirect ways, as well as direct ones.

Although most companies pay their employees by check, there are still a few places where payment is made in cash. Question 69 inquires whether these companies obtain receipts from employees for the cash paid.

Since no prepared questionnaire can ever cover every possible problem situation, the auditor should ask all employees in the Payroll department the final question: "What problems do you feel exist in the department?" This gives the employees the opportunity to express their own personal grievances and to make suggestions for improving operations.

SUMMARY

Operational auditing can be the tool to help make the payroll department more efficient. By observation and by asking the proper questions, an outsider can often bolster a department's efficiency. In too many companies, the Payroll department head is so overburdened with work that he cannot step back to see the entire picture of the department's operation—the department head's first priority is to keep his desk clear of papers. An operational auditor does not have the daily responsibility, so can devote effort to improving the total system of a department.

eleven

PERSONNEL

Most organizations are composed of people who provide their services. Without these people, an entity cannot be successful. The skill, enthusiasm, and satisfaction of employees are vital. Since most companies comprise a variety of jobs, they need a special personnel department to hire new workers and coordinate employee relations.

A personnel department is more than just a necessary element of overhead costs. Modern personnel management endeavors to maximize the effectiveness of the work force through application of sound personnel policies and practices. A personnel department channels the human element to achieve company objectives and foster the overall success of the enterprise. Personnel work is a continuous responsibility. A constant alertness and awareness to human relations are important every day.

Although personnel work has always been useful, personnel departments are now almost a necessity, because the amount of regulatory oversight in Washington, as well as at state and local levels dictates so many personnel practices. The Civil Rights Act of 1964, ERISA (Employee Retirement Income Security Act), equal pay legislation, and OSHA (Occupational Safety and Health Act) have dramatically expanded the nature of the personnel manager's job. Unfortunately, not all personnel departments can meet all these challenges. Some personnel officers waste their efforts on superficial programs and excessive emphasis on records and paperwork. A good department's focus should be on policies and programs that meet company needs.

This is not to say that the daily, routine operation of the personnel department is not important; the work must be performed. But the clerical functions should be performed by the staff and not by the director of the personnel department. Where necessary, the manager should be an agent of change in the organization. In order to be an agent of change, the personnel manager must be familiar with developments occurring outside the company. An awareness of external changes, coupled with a knowledge of internal objectives, can promote greater achievement by the company.

For most companies, the employees are the valuable economic resource that makes the enterprise successful. The personnel department is responsible for obtaining this resource and keeping it valuable. A good personnel department employee realizes that it takes more than dollars to keep the labor force happy. Equally important are the morale, minds, and attitudes of workers. The individual rights of workers should be recognized, along with the employees' needs for self-fulfillment. More than any other department in the company, personnel is in a position to apply the findings of social science research. In fact, one duty of the personnel department should be to disseminate information to managers that might improve management style.

Basically, the activities of the personnel department can be summarized as follows:

Identification and fulfillment of manpower needs

Training and development

Wage and salary administration

Performance evaluation

Transfers and promotions

Terminations

Employee records

Fringe benefit programs

Employee morale

Health and safety programs

Labor relations

Communication with employees

Compliance with governmental regulations

The above jobs are quite varied, and some are difficult to measure. For these reasons, an objective operational auditor can provide a valuable service by evaluating the efficiency and effectiveness of the personnel department. In fact, an operational audit of almost any other department within an enterprise will indirectly provide insight into the personnel area, which usually interrelates with all other departments. Human resources are required for every department of every company. The personnel department is the manager of those resources.

The personnel department questionnaire for the in-depth audit is illustrated in Exhibit 11-1. The questions are grouped as follows:

General
Clerical operations
Department staff
Physical Facilities
Communication

GENERAL

The General questions are designed to determine the nature of the personnel function in a particular organization. The answers to the first three questions, plus 6 and 7, will give the auditor insight into the personnel function's standing in relation to other departments. The first question, "is there a centralized personnel function . . . ?" is the most basic question and will have been answered before the auditor gets to this in-depth stage of the audit. However, the second part of the question— ". . . through which all applicants must pass"—is the more important to the auditor at this stage of the operational audit. It seeks to elicit the response that the personnel department is separate from all other departments. Unfortunately, the personnel department is sometimes "affiliated" with the payroll department simply because both departments keep some employee records. This affiliation is inadvisable, because each of the two departments should have separate goals and objectives. Questions 6 and 7 ("does management rely on the department?" and "is personnel involved in all decisions affecting employees?"), if answered negatively, would indicate a weak personnel department. Some operating managers prefer to bypass the personnel department. Particularly in closely held companies top management makes all decisions affecting employees without consulting the personnel department. If this is allowed to happen, the effectiveness of the personnel function is reduced.

Questions 4 and 5 ask whether the personnel department employees have a clear idea of what they are supposed to be accomplishing. Regardless of how hard the people are working, they may not be operating at their maximum effectiveness if they do not know the goals. No matter how fast you are going, if you are going in the wrong direction, you will not reach your destination. Without definable objectives, a personnel department can busily chase its tail, without accomplishing much. The department should have three objectives. First, it should perform its

EXHIBIT 11-1   Personnel Questionnaire

Yes / No / DNA

General

1. Is there a centralized personnel function through which all job applicants must pass?

2. Is the Personnel department separate from Payroll?

3. Is the personnel department a "staff" function as opposed to a "line" function?

4. Does the Personnel department have definite goals and objectives?

5. Do the goals and objectives of the Personnel department foster the fulfillment of the goals and objectives of the organization?

6. Do you feel that management officials rely on the advice of the personnel department in areas of personnel management?

7. Is the personnel department involved in all management decisions affecting employees?

8. Does a procedures manual exist with written procedures and objectives for every job performed within the department?

9. Is there an up-to-date written statement of personnel policies and procedures available to all employees?

10. Are personnel policies as set forth in the employee handbook honestly and uniformly applied?

11. Are personnel policies written clearly so as to minimize the risk of misinterpretation?

12. Are personnel policies ever reviewed?

13. Are job descriptions available for every position in the company?

14. Is there a formal employee evaluation program?

15. Do you know your rates of employee turnover and absenteeism?

16. Are all personnel actions being processed in a timely and accurate manner?

17. Is the final responsibility to hire and fire held by one person?

18. Are all job applicants treated with consideration and courtesy?

19. Is there an established wage and salary program to ensure equitable rates of pay?

20. Do you feel the pay system is truly a merit system?

21. Do you ever compare your fringe benefit program with those of businesses in surrounding communities?

22. Do you have a set procedure for screening and accepting applicants?

23. Does the department utilize a standard evaluation measure for screening applicants?

24. Is the position control system based on, or correlated with the annual budget?

25. Do you feel the Personnel department has a role which is well accepted by management?

26. Is there a staff planning program?

27. Are future manpower needs forecast accurately enough to minimize the need for emergency recruiting?

28. Are benefit programs up to date?

29. Are turnover statistics available for every position in the organization?

30. What is the average duration of a vacancy?

31. Is there an established grievance procedure?

32. Is continuing education encouraged?

33. Is there some type of employee development program?

34. Does there appear to be a reserve of trained talent for key executive replacement?

35. Is an effort made to fill openings from within the organization before recruiting outsiders?

36. Is the performance of department heads appraised regularly?

37. Do you try to shorten the length of time that a position is left open?

38. Are pre-employment physical examinations given?

39. Is any personnel research being performed?

Clerical Operations

40. Are complete records kept for each employee?

41. Do the departmental records meet the recordkeeping requirements of governmental agencies?

EXHIBIT 11-1 (Continued)

42. Are recordkeeping and personnel forms designed to contain all necessary information?

43. Is all information contained in records and personnel forms necessary?

44. Are form sizes convenient for filing?

45. Is spacing on forms designed for easy typing?

46. Is all filing of records kept up to date?

47. Is the filing system easy to understand?

48. Is there a system for immediately determining what positions are vacant?

49. Do your position records permit finding each employee at all times?

50. Is there a system for updating information in personnel folders?

51. Is there an adequate system for recording promotions and transfers?

52. Is there a system for immediate notification of the Personnel department when an employee is terminated?

53. Are references of potential employees thoroughly checked?

Department Staff

54. Is there a job description for the director of personnel?

55. Are all department employees knowledgeable about personnel policies and employee benefits?

56. Do you feel all employees in the department are well qualified for their jobs?

57. Are department employees knowledgeable about Social Security rules and regulations?

58. Are all hirings made in compliance with EEO (Equal Employment Opportunity) guidelines?

59. Do you feel departmental employees are familiar with labor laws?

60. Is department staffing tailored to the workload?

61. Has work been evenly distributed, so that all employees in the department work steadily and efficiently?

EXHIBIT 11-1 (Continued)

62. Is there an established line of authority within the department so that work continues as usual when illness or termination occurs?

63. What is the employee turnover rate in the department?

64. What is the employee turnover rate for the entire organization?

Physical Facilities

65. Are the physical facilities of the department adequate?

66. Does the layout of the office suit the normal flow of work?

67. Do interviewers have their own private offices?

68. Is the department easy to reach by the public?

69. Is the department easy to reach by employees?

70. Do you have sufficient equipment in the department?

71. Is your budget for supplies and equipment large enough?

72. Do you feel your total departmental budget is adequate?

73. Do you have an excessive amount of equipment in your department?

74. Is there any control on copying machine use?

75. Is a record kept of the reason for each long distance phone call?

Communication

76. Do you feel company employees understand the personnel policies?

77. Are surveys ever made of employee feelings and impressions?

78. Do employees consider the personnel department a "total information center"?

79. Is there close coordination with the Payroll department?

80. Does the department have an open line of communication with all department heads and managers?

81. Does the personnel department maintain an open-door policy to all employees?

82. Do employees feel free to come to the personnel department with their problems?

83. Is there a formal orientation program for new employees?

EXHIBIT 11-1 (Continued)

84. Is there an internal newspaper or magazine for employees?

85. Is there a bulletin board available for communication of information to all employees?

86. Does the organization have a suggestion box? Are employees rewarded for accepted suggestions?

87. Is the future supervisor of a potential employee brought into the hiring process?

88. Is the nondiscrimination policy clearly stated and posted?

89. Are all reports you receive timely and informative?

90. Are all reports you prepare timely and informative?

91. Do other departments know where Personnel's responsibilities end and theirs begin?

92. Does the organization train supervisors to conduct proper employee-evaluation appraisal interviews?

93. Has the organization attempted to ascertain and document the various capabilities of its employees?

94. When a department manager asks for additional staff, is his request evaluated on its merits as well as on its impact on his departmental budget?

95. When a member of the personnel department screens a potential employee, is the applicant given a clear and complete picture of what the job entails? Do the Personnel department and the operating managers know which aspects of the position each will cover?

96. Do the applications provide enough information about past work experience and educational background to permit a valid assessment of the applicant's suitability for the post?

97. Does the Personnel department use tests to evaluate applicants? If so, do the test results of accepted applicants correlate with on-the-job performance?

98. Does the organization do any recruiting at the college level; if so, are its efforts organized, necessary, and cost-justified?

99. Do you have a formal safety program?

100. Does the department conduct exit interviews with employees who resign? If so, does it store and utilize the information gathered from those interviews?

Yes	No	DNA	EXHIBIT 11-1 (continued)
			101. When policy is changed, is the change relayed first to managers and then to their staff?
			102. Does the firm spend too much on overtime?
			103. Is an incentive plan in use? If so, is it equitable? Does it really succeed in motivating employees to perform better?
			104. Does the company subscribe to any personnel magazines for the edification of Personnel department employees?
			105. Does the Personnel department have the full support of top management?
			106. Do you sponsor social or recreational activities for employees (such as a company softball team)?
			107. Do you make line managers aware of new trends in behavioral science research that might have an impact on thier personal management style?

routine chores on a regular basis. This is usually not a problem; in fact, many departments spend a disproportionate amount of time on daily routine. Second, the department should be allocating some of its efforts to problem-solving activities. This type of objective refers to the manner in which the personnel department works on specific projects for the benefit of other departments. Third, the department should devote some of its energy to innovative ideas. This objective is difficult to quantify, but can result in the greatest contribution to the company. Innovative objectives include introducing new ideas, improving employee relations, and implementing new programs.

Question 8 is also concerned with the subject of department duties in asking about the availability of a procedures manual. A procedures manual helps to ensure that all employees handle a given kind of problem in much the same way.

Questions 9 through 12 deal with personnel policies. It is essential not only that policies exist (Question 9), but also that employees be aware of the policies. If generally recognized policies exist, then new problems can be solved correctly and different persons can solve a given problem in the same (correct) way. In effect, personnel policies are answers to questions that have not yet been asked. The idea of a uniform approach underlies all policies and procedures manuals, but nowhere is it more sensitive than with respect to treatment of employees. Question 10 asks for information on whether policies apply equally to all employees. Not only is it unethical to discriminate for or against specific employees, but it can also result in a damaging lawsuit against the company.

Question 13 inquires about the availability of a job description for every position in the company. This is extremely important. If the personnel department does not have access to a job description for an open position, it cannot effectively recruit qualified individuals. The job description should be sufficiently detailed to permit the personnel staff to determine the type of person best suited to the job. Job descriptions are also used to judge the effectiveness of incumbent personnel.

A formal employee evaluation program can promote good morale. Thus Question 14 should be answered affirmatively, and the program should call for regular meetings (on a semiannual or annual basis) between each employee and his or her immediate supervisor. The personnel department probably should monitor these schedules to be certain that the meetings take place—unfortunately, many managers tend to put off evaluation sessions with their employees.

Absenteeism, employee turnover, and the length of time a position remains unfilled are the topics examined in Questions 15, 29, 30, and 37. All four questions relate to the problem of an unfilled position. (Although these four questions are closely related, they are intentionally not grouped in one place on the questionnaire. By asking similar questions separately, it may be found that respondents change their opinions between questions.) If the personnel department has the statistics, then the problem is partially solved. If a vacancy remains unfilled for a considerable length of time, there may be reason to question whether the position really needs to be filled.

Questions 16, 17, and 18 involve internal operations of the personnel department. Question 16 asks about the promptness of the work performed by the department. Since a personnel department is a cost center, not a profit center, there is a tendency to stint the department when it needs new staff members. Therefore, the department may be falling behind in some of the elective aspects of its work. The subject of who has the final authority to hire is examined in Question 17. This role should be designated in the organization chart. Question 18 is a matter of common courtesy. An applicant who is well qualified for a particular job is usually well treated. However, an unqualified person is sometimes treated less courteously, because he is of no use to the company. Such discourtesy may come back to haunt the company. For example, the applicant may not consider the company in the future when it has an opening for which the applicant is qualified. Also, the applicant might be a potential customer for the company's product. Finally, an applicant who has been treated rudely is more likely to file some type of discrimination suit. Therefore, it pays to be nice to everybody.

The organization should have some type of formal pay system in order to stem problems of inequity (Question 19). The pay system should be based on merit (Question 20). Question 21 asks whether the personnel staff does any research to compare fringe benefits with those of other employers in the area. Such research should be conducted on a regular basis, but too often this activity is postponed when other duties are putting stress on personnel department workers. Question 28 is related to Question 21 in that it asks whether fringe benefit programs are up to date.

The screening of job applicants is the subject of Questions 22 and 23. There should be a set procedure for the screening of applicants. For example, the applicants should go to the personnel office first—not to the operating department that has the opening. Question 23 is designed to enable the auditor to learn whether any formal screening device is used. This subject is examined in more detail in Question 97.

Question 24 asks whether the position control system is correlated to the annual budget. The position control system should take into consideration budgetary constraints. There should also be a staff planning program (Question 26) that permits the department to know in advance when new hires are going to be needed. The subject of Question 27 is whether manpower forecasts are accurate enough to minimize emergency recruiting. Planning is even more important when new employees have to be company-trained before they can become productive.

Question 31 seeks to find out whether there is an established grievance procedure. Non-union companies might not have these procedures, but having them can help management head off problems before they develop into a unionization drive.

Further training and education of company employees is examined in Questions 32, 33, and 34. If a company does not encourage its employees to improve themselves, it cannot be expected that many employees will participate in educational activities on their own initiative. As a result, small companies in particular will tend to have a shortage of executive replacement talent (Question 34). It may take the auditor several years to convince his client of the importance of this problem, but eventually most will understand.

Question 38 deals with pre-employment physical examinations. With the present high cost of health insurance and Workmen's Compensation premiums, no organization can ignore the value of hiring healthy workers. For most companies, insurance premiums are based on the amount of claims filed; thus healthier employees mean lower insurance premiums. A physical examination may reveal conditions that would result also in greater employee absenteeism. There is no sense in hiring a person who will not be able to work every day.

The remainder of the questions in the General section involve relations with company employees, in particular, treating all workers equally and paying them an adequate salary. If an organization cannot answer "yes" to these questions, it may someday find itself with a problem on its hands: many unionization drives are based as much on claims of unfair treatment as on economic issues.

CLERICAL OPERATIONS

The section of the questionnaire on clerical operations relates to many of the activities performed in the personnel department. The necessary recordkeeping results in a great deal of paper flow. Questions 40, 41, and Questions 48 through 52 pertain to the quality and quantity of records kept. The personnel department should be a source of information on almost every topic concerning an employee. If the department has to answer "no" to one of these questions, then it is not in a position to fulfill all its duties. Question 40 ("is there a system for updating information in personnel folders?") is usually the biggest problem area, because it is often much harder to obtain information about current employees than about new employees. Questions 51 and 52 ask more specifically whether promotions, transfers, and terminations are promptly recorded.

Questions 42 through 45 involve the forms used. It is inconvenient to use several forms when one well-designed form would suffice. The questions which ask whether forms are properly designed for easy filing and typing (Questions 44 and 45) seem rather insignificant on the surface. However, much time can be saved if forms are properly planned. If forms are not the proper size for filing, they may have to be folded before filing, or expensive oversized filing cabinets may be required.

Questions 46 and 47 on the topics of whether filing is up to date and whether the filing system is easy to understand may help reveal whether a personnel department is properly staffed with well-trained employees. When daily chores are more pressing, filing is often postponed.

Question 53 asks whether an applicant's references are checked before the applicant is hired. The personnel department can stave off problems for other departments by following through on reference checks before approving an application. This step is easy to skip when a position has to be filled in a hurry. For example, one client recently suspected that a "CPA" he had hired a month earlier might not be totally qualified. A suspicious supervisor called the employee's alma mater to doublecheck that the man had graduated with a degree in accounting. The university reported that the individual had indeed been a student in liberal arts, but had never graduated and he had never taken a course in accounting. The "CPA" claim also proved to be a fabrication. Because references were not checked in this case, a delicate matter that could have been handled in a routine manner mushroomed into a very major problem.

Another client who failed to check references did give a preemployment screening test to an "engineer." The applicant passed the test and was immediately hired. After about two months, the engineering supervisor asked the personnel department for the new man's references. The supervisor doubted that the man had an engineering degree, because he was incompetent in the practical aspects of engineering. A call to the man's previous employer brought this response: "We fired him two months ago after finding out from his university that he had never attended engineering school." The chagrined personnel manager called the university for more details. It seemed that the self-proclaimed engineer had attended college for a couple of years as a math major. The math faculty remembered him as a "real whiz" at working problems. It was this ability to work math problems that enabled the applicant to pass the screening test. Even though checking references may often seem a waste of time, the one exception can be a big cost saver.

DEPARTMENT STAFF

The section on department staff relates to staff size and competency of personnel employees. Question 54 dealing with job descriptions could be asked in every department. Personnel department employees must be knowledgeable not only about company personnel policies and fringe benefits, but also about laws such as FICA (Social Security), EEO, OSHA, and minimum-wage requirements. Questions 55 through 59 deal specifically with the capabilities of department employees. Topics of importance include Social Security (Question 57), EEO guidelines (Question 58), and various labor laws (Question 59).

Questions 60 and 61 deal with the department workload. Many employees will reply that they are overworked, but the auditor should be alert for indications that certain members of the department are underworked. Uneven distribution of the workload is not only inefficient, but can also create morale problems.

Question 62 inquires whether the department has an organization chart. There should be some system to reshuffle staff in the event one slot is vacant, owing to long-term disability, for example.

The final two questions in this section (63 and 64) are ones that cannot be answered with a "yes" or a "no." Employee turnover can be costly to a company. Many employers do not know how much turnover is costing them because they do not know what their turnover rate is. If personnel employees know their company's turnover rate, the auditor can assume that any turnover problem is headed toward possible solution. If a company has to invest heavily in training new employees who leave shortly, it might be well advised to implement a human resources accounting system. These detailed records of how much was invested in every employee would permit an analysis of the true cost of employee turnover.

PHYSICAL FACILITIES

Questions relating to physical facilities are similar to the corresponding sections in other departments' questionnaires. Both Questions 65 and 67 deal with the adequacy of facilities. Most personnel experts agree that staff interviewers should have private offices for screening potential employees. If private offices are not possible, then small interview rooms should be available. Since applicants are asked to discuss personal matters, the privacy of a closed room helps to put the interviewee at ease. Questions 68 and 69 are especially appropriate for a personnel department since the department will be most valuable to employees if it is easily accessible to them.

Questions 74 and 75 deal with the chronic problems of control over copying machine use and personal long-distance telephone calls. It must be realized that reduction in use is not necessarily the objective of a control program. As a recent advertisement sponsored by AT&T pointed out, more use of long distance calls can save a company money (if the call substitutes for a personal trip). It is the personal use of a copying machine or long distance calls that the controls should be designed to deter.

COMMUNICATION

The final section of the personnel department questionnaire relates to communication. This is the most important section, because communication with all departments and with individual employees is an integral part of the department's function. The personnel function is usually a staff function, and as such, it exists only to help others. Without two-way communication, the personnel department cannot do its job. Therefore, Question 80, asking whether there is an open line of communication with all department heads, is one of the most important items in the entire questionnaire.

Question 88, concerning the posting of the company's nondiscrimination policy, is important for legal reasons. Questions 89 through 91 are also concerned with the Personnel department's communication with other departments, as is Question 101. The latter question asks whether a manager is notified of policy changes in advance of the lower-level staff. Managers who are not kept informed by the department are not likely to be supporters of the personnel department.

The remaining questions in the Communication section apply to communication with individual employees. In many companies, the only contact an employee has with top management is through the personnel department. The personnel department should be the one place where an employee can go with a grievance, suggestion, or question. Thus, the personnel department should maintain an open-door policy to all employees (Question 81). A house organ (Question 84), suggestion box (Question 85), and a frequently used bulletin board (Question 85) facilitate communication.

Subjective answers are required to Questions 76 and 78, which ask whether employees understand personnel policies and think of the department as a total-information center. In a sense, these can be more accurately answered by employees outside the Personnel department. Thus the auditor may want to ask the mail clerk or an office gossip what the employees really think about the department. Similarly, Question 82 dealing with employees' attitudes about confiding their problems may or may not be adequately answered by Personnel employees. The personnel staff may incorrectly believe that they are being exposed to all of the employees' problems.

Question 83 asks about the existence of a formal orientation program for new employees. Such a program is usually advisable in that it exposes all new hires to the same information about the company. If organization procedures and objectives are covered in the orientation program, the new employee cannot later rationalize less-than-adequate work by claiming ignorance.

The subject of supervisor training is examined in Question 92. Because many supervisors feel uncomfortable about holding appraisal interviews, the personnel department can provide a real service by teaching managers the proper way to evaluate subordinates.

Question 93 ("are employee capabilities documented?") is one that few departments can honestly answer in the affirmative. Yet it is a good idea; an organization that has collected and cataloged the various capabilities of its employees has a valuable data base. An organization will find it much easier to promote from within if the personnel department has documented and categorized the skills of all employees.

The budget should not be the only factor considered when a department wants to add another employee position (Question 94). Budget constraints are important, but there should be some bypass mechanism permitting a manager to hire a needed new employee even if his budget limitations have already been reached.

Questions 95 through 97 deal with procedures followed in interviewing job applicants. Potential employees should be given a clear understanding of what the job opening entails (Question 95), and the applicant should give the company a clear understanding, through his completed application form, of his background and qualifications. In particular, Question 97 (tests) is important. The law requires that if tests are used to evaluate applications, the examination must test the skills needed for the job.

Many companies spend a great deal of time and money recruiting new employees at colleges and universities. Question 98 asks whether such recruiting trips are really necessary, and if so, are they properly organized and cost-justified. (College recruiting trips can be occasions for personnel staffers to return to their alma mater for the homecoming football game.)

Question 98 asks about the existence of a formal safety program. Although the importance of employee safety and health has been recognized for decades, recent operational safety and health laws have heightened the concern. Mental health is also receiving consideration, along with physical health; both mental and physical health can affect productivity, so these areas must be an integral part of an employee relations program.

A formal safety program should also include a reporting system. The company's accident statistics should be periodically compared with those of other organizations. Statistics commonly maintained include (1) number of workdays lost and (2) injury-frequency rate. A good safety management program also includes a follow-up on each accident to determine possible cause. Some companies have a safety committee which investigates accidents to determine whether changes in operating procedures are necessary. An effective safety program includes employee training and information about the importance of safety. The program should emphasize not only factory hazards, but also noise levels, mental health, and office safety. If there is any doubt about the dollar-cost benefit of office safety, in one company the Workmen's Compensation insurance premiums were higher for accountants as a group than for the foundry workers. This reflected the fact that in a short period of time, two accountants had severely broken their hands while hitting a stapler. Since

Workmen's Compensation premiums vary with claims, the company was hit with higher premiums. Safety is important in all departments. Considering workmen's compensation premiums and lost time, an effective safety program can help control costs at most entities.

The 100th question asks whether an exit interview is conducted when an employee leaves the company. The information gathered at exit interviews should be stored and periodically analyzed for trends. A company loses an important asset when a valued employee leaves the organization. It is the responsibility of the personnel department to learn the reason for departure and ensure that it does not become part of a trend.

Questions 102 and 103 deal with compensation, such as overtime pay. Overtime pay is often an unnecessary cost in a well-managed company. If overtime is a regular part of the operating system, then additional permanent employees (perhaps part-time workers) should be hired to cut down on premium pay. Incentive compensation plans (Question 103) can also give rise to questions. Has the company considered the possibility of utilizing some type of incentive? If so, does the system lead to better performance by employees? These are the types of qestions that should be periodically examined by personnel staffers.

Question 104, asking whether the company subscribes to any personnel magazines, centers on the topic of the continuing education of company employees. Some employees will take the initiative to keep informed, even at their own expense. However, if all the professional employees are to keep up to date, then the company will have to foot at least part of the bill. The journals that would be of most value to personnel employees, include the following:

Personnel
American Management Association
135 West 50th Street
New York, NY 10020

The Personnel Administrator
19 Church Road
Berea, OH 44107

Personnel Journal
1131 Olympic Journal
Santa Monica, CA 90404

Personnel Psychology
3121 Cheek Road
Durham NC 27704

In addition to recommending the magazines to clients, the auditor may want to subscribe to one or more of them for his own office in order to keep up to date on innovations in personnel management

Whether the personnel department enjoys the full support of top management is asked in Question 105. If the answer to this question is "no," the auditor probably already knows the answer. A department cannot be totally effective without top management support. Thus if numerous other questions throughout the questionnaire have been answered negatively, this is probably an indication that full support is lacking.

Question 106, dealing with the sponsorship of employee athletic teams and other recreational activities, is directed toward the question of morale. Sometimes an investment in a bowling or softball team can provide handsome rewards. In addition to the morale benefits, the team can function also as an advertising tool.

The final question deals with communication with other departments. The personnel department is in a position to learn the latest trends in management techniques. New ideas should be routed to the line managers who can make best use of the techniques.

SUMMARY

The personnel department has a sensitive function in an organization. Clearly, this is an area where the operational auditor can provide an important service to management. The personnel department has a big responsibility—to see that the entire organization is properly staffed. And staffing is not all there is to the personnel manager's job. The personnel department is responsible also for maintaining and raising employee morale, implementing health and safety programs, providing management training programs, and helping the company cope with generally rising expectations. To these responsibilities are added questions of unionization, minority rights, women in the workplace, and an overabundance of federal regulations.

The operational auditor who is sensitive to the role of the personnel department realizes that it is basically a staff function which provides an extensive array of services to all other departments within an enterprise. Because of this diversity of tasks, it is difficult for a personnel department to be effectively and efficiently managed. Yet inasmuch as the personnel department comes in contact with all other departments, a problem in the personnel department can affect every other department. Thus if the operational auditor can help the personnel department become more efficient, then the entire organization will benefit.

In conclusion, an operational auditor should give a great deal of consideration to the problems of the personnel department. The auditor can often provide significant benefits in a department whose objectives are so manifold and impact so broad.

twelve

PRODUCTION PROCESS

The production or manufacturing process exists in those companies where raw materials are transformed by employees into a finished product. Examples include the largest steel mill and auto manufacturer down to the local bakery and print shop. The task of managing the production function is known as production management, and there have been many professional studies of production management. In recent years, the service sector has gained in importance; therefore, many students of the subject have expanded the scope of the production management field to include the service industry. Consequently the phrase "operations management" is sometimes used synonymously with "production management." The phrase "production/operations management" is occasionally used.

Production management is quite important in most organizations, but not in all. If an operational auditor were performing an engagement for a retail store client, for example, he could probably skip this chapter altogether. But in most other types of companies, the production function is often the major area of the business in terms of costs incurred (and in corresponding opportunities for cost savings). Unfortunately, the production function is not an easy area to audit. All companies are different. In some, raw materials may be the most significant input. In others, labor or technical equipment may be perceived as being more critical to the production process. Whatever the critical input may be, there is always a complicated interrelationship among all the factors of production. The operational auditor's contribution is to ensure the coordination of activities within the production departments and to check the coordination with other functional areas of the business (such as purchasing, personnel, marketing, and accounting).

Basically, the production process begins with an idea: a recognition of the need for a particular manufactured product. At this point, production management decides how the needed items are to be produced. This decision may involve such questions as whether to use a labor-intensive

204

method or a capital-intensive method. Once it has been determined how an item is to be produced, the next step is to acquire the needed inputs (materials, labor, and equipment). The next type of production management decision involves the area of routine operations. This includes the determination of output levels, production scheduling, and allocation of labor and equipment. As an example of this kind of decision, suppose a company that produces items in job lots has a backlog of orders. Which order should be filled first? Maintaining quality control, another area of routine production management, will be dealt with in a subsequent chapter. Handling of raw materials within the department, management of employees, and maintenance of equipment would also fall into the category of routine operations.

The final stage of the production process is periodic modification of the system to take into consideration changes in product demand, revised organization goals, new technology, or alternative inputs (such as change in raw material quality).

In summary, the production management process consists of the following stages:

Recognition of the need to have an item produced
Determination of how the item is to be produced
Acquisition of the needed inputs
Implementation of routine operations:
  Output levels
  Production scheduling
  Resource allocation
  Quality control
  Materials handling
  Administration of employees
  Equipment
  Cost control
  Liaison with supporting departments
Updating the system

This list might appear to place too little emphasis on cost control for orienting the operational auditor. However, this is not the case. Ultimately, the entire production process must be evaluated on the basis of cost control. This evaluation includes a careful analysis of costs and variances as grounds for corrective action. Familiarity with transfer pricing and standard costing is almost as essential for a production manager as for a cost accountant.

Maintaining the reliability of a production system ("maintenance of equipment") is another vital routine task. Sometimes as long as the output of a system is of an acceptable quality, it is easy for the manager to forget about the need for maintenance of buildings and equipment. In reality, maintenance is needed even when everything is operating smoothly. In order to prevent costly breakdowns, preventive maintenance can provide a great opportunity to save money. At the same time, preventive maintenance can sometimes require the use of what would otherwise be production time. Thus, the cost of planned preventive-maintenance downtime must be weighed against the cost of potential accidental downtime following mechanical breakdown. These are examples of the everyday decisions facing the production manager.

Scrap control can represent another area where the operational auditor can help the production manager. Production of scrap wastes materials and production labor inputs. Bulky and cumbersome to handle, scrap also increases disposal costs. On the other hand, a certain level of scrap output is sometimes acceptable in the most cost-effective production function. In other words, management may be willing to accept some waste in order to produce more efficiently, on the theory that the waste is a necessary cost of high-speed production, the waste being more than offset by the savings generated by greater production. Finding new ways of recycling or disposing of waste items is part of the management of scrap production. Unfortunately, line managers often cannot spare the time to investigate new uses for scrap products.

In investigating the production department, the operational auditor will no doubt find plenty of opportunity to assist management. Many of the opportunities for increased efficiency and effectiveness of expensive production facilities are too technical to be considered by the typical operational auditor. However, there are still many ways in which a nontechnical auditor can be helpful. The operational audit questionnaire for production (Exhibit 12-1) has five sections:

General
Materials
Labor
Equipment and facilities
Cost control and reports

(Quality control rates a separate chapter, Chapter 14, and Safety is covered in the chapter dealing with the personnel department, Chapter 11.)

EXHIBIT 12-1   Production Process Questionnaire

General

1. Is there a procedures manual?

2. Does the procedures manual specify the manner in which production requirements are to be received?

3. Do you feel the purchasing, receiving and personnel departments work efficiently?

4. Do you maintain good relations with the purchasing, receiving, and personnel departments?

5. Do you maintain good relations with the quality control department?

6. Do you find the suggestions of the Quality Control department to be helpful?

7. Do you consider alternatives to present manufacturing methods?

8. Do you do any planning for the long term (i.e., a year or more ahead)?

9. Do you use PERT or the critical path method to plan and control big projects?

10. Are you consulted about the probable cost of producing potential new products?

11. Are you given the opportunity to evaluate alternative production methods before new facilities and equipment are ordered?

12. Do you have a system to determine the sequence of production scheduling?

13. Are quantitative methods such as linear programming or queueing models ever used to evaluate production decisions?

14. Do you use an economic production quantity model to determine the size of production runs?

Materials

15. Are materials always available when needed?

16. Is there a specific system for requisitioning materials?

17. Do you perform any studies concerning the possible use of alternative materials (in both new products and those currently being produced)?

18. Are materials properly cared for while awaiting processing?

EXHIBIT 12-1 (Continued)

	Yes	No	DNA

19. Is there a procedure for handling scrap (waste)?

20. Is there excess waste or spoilage of materials?

21. Are spoiled materials disposed of or recycled in the most efficient manner?

22. Have you made a thorough analysis of waste control?

23. Has the amount of scrap given rise to some study of possible alternative production methods?

24. Is there adequate security over materials and scrap?

25. Are alternative methods of scrap disposal periodically evaluated?

Labor

26. Is the department adequately staffed?

27. Are employees well trained?

28. Is there excessive idle time?

29. Is there excessive overtime?

30. Is supervision adequate?

31. Is there good morale among employees?

32. Are labor relations satisfactory?

33. Do you have a specific method of allocating employees among various jobs?

34. Do you know how much the company has invested in human resources in your department via training programs?

35. Have you considered using temporary workers to speed work during rush periods?

36. Do you have an adequate incentive pay system for production labor?

Equipment and Facilities

37. Is there a preventive maintenance program?

38. Are maintenance services available when needed?

39. Do you have adequate equipment in the department?

40. Is it reasonably easy to acquire new equipment when needed?

41. Have you considered sharing rarely used tools and equipment with other departments or with other companies?

EXHIBIT 12-1 (Continued)

42. Are your production facilities laid out in the most appropriate manner?

43. Do you feel your facilities are safe enough for employees?

44. Is fire protection adequate?

Cost Control and Reports

45. Does higher management feel your cost-control performance is adequate?

46. Do you receive variance reports promptly enough for them to be helpful?

47. Do cost reports focus only on controllable costs?

48. Are reports detailed enough to be useful?

49. Do you maintain adequate records of the amount of scrap and byproducts?

50. Do you understand everything in the reports you receive?

GENERAL

The first two questions in the Production questionnaire establish whether the department has a procedures manual. The manual should be sufficiently detailed to specify procedures for obtaining production orders, scheduling orders, requisitioning materials, and hiring new employees. Having a written manual permits fixing responsibility when something goes wrong. The manual also serves as an orientation tool for new employees.

Questions 3 and 4 ask whether the respondent feels that the purchasing, receiving, and personnel departments work efficiently, and whether good relations are maintained with these departments. Because production management begins with a process of coordinating production inputs, it is important for good relations to be maintained with the departments that help provide the inputs. A negative response to Question 3 may indicate either (1) inefficiency in a support department or (2) poor communication between production and one or more of the other departments.

Questions 5 and 6 cover good relations with the quality control department. Quality control, which often has a negative image to production workers, should be viewed as a support department. The quality control inspectors are helping the production department put out an acceptable product. Their suggestions should be incorporated into daily production operations.

A negative response will often follow Question 7. Periodic studies should be made to determine whether current production methods should be changed. Constant updating of the production process is one of the responsibilities of the production manager, but it is easy for him to get into a rut once a production mix has been established. Reminding the production manager of the need to re-evaluate production methods is a major contribution the operational auditor can make to management.

Long-term planning is the subject of Question 8. If a company is capital intensive, new products may require costly new equipment, which should be budgeted far enough in advance to permit the arrangement of financing. Most companies budget their capital outlays at least a year in advance; therefore, the production department should be doing some related long-range planning. The production of proposed new products should also be carefully analyzed over a long period of time to plan the most efficient production mix. Again, this sort of analysis should take place well ahead of actual production. A lack of long-range planning may mean that a given production mix is not the most efficient one possible.

Question 9 asks whether PERT (Program Evaluation Review Technique) or the critical path method is used to plan and control big projects. This question is not usually applicable to all companies, but many companies could adapt the techniques in one of two ways. First, a company that produced large structures such as buildings and bridges could use the techniques in the routine manufacture of individual products. Second, a company might use the techniques to plan and control a new product introduction. The entire development process, for example, could be incorporated into a PERT system. The production manager could thus be sure that he had considered all possible steps in the development process.

Questions 10 and 11 concern the planning that takes place prior to the production of a new item. The production manager should be consulted about the estimated cost of a new product before a marketing researcher arbitrarily assigns, say, a 98-cent selling price to the item. The production manager should also be given sufficient time to evaluate various production alternatives before new equipment is ordered. In a hurry-up order, the most cost-effective production method may be overlooked until after unneeded equipment is purchased.

A system for production scheduling is the subject of question 12. The department should have some procedure for determining which job it will produce when. In some cases, a first-come, first-served policy is effective. At other times, it is better to run certain jobs at specific times, especially when the production run will require a long and costly set-up job first. A specific set of priorities for production scheduling not only helps the production department operate efficiently, but also permits the sales staff to notify customers of probable delivery dates.

Questions 13 and 14 ask whether any type of quantitative technique is used in evaluating production decisions. Linear programming would be particularly appropriate for a department that produces more than one product. It would be useful also in analyzing costs of products that require a mixture of several raw materials. For example, a dog food mixture of meat, meat by-products, cereal, and water could be formulated by means of linear programming to provide the desired level of nutrition at the lowest possible cost. Queing (waiting line) theory is often used in service establishments. For instance, a bank could use queing theory to determine how many tellers should be on duty at all times. The final question in this section asks whether an economic production quantity model is used. Most textbooks cover this topic under the heading "economic order quantity," but the same principles and formulas apply to production quantities in a manufacturing concern. The objective of an economic production quantity model is to minimize the total start-up costs plus inventory carrying costs. An EPQ model should be used by a company with significant start-up costs.

MATERIALS

The section on materials (which includes waste and scrap) opens with two questions about the availability of raw materials. There should be a set system of requisitioning materials, and materials should always be available when needed. Without one small component part, it could be necessary to shut down an entire production operation. Idle employees and idle equipment are expensive, and any delay or error in materials receiving could cost a company thousands of dollars.

Question 17 asks whether any studies are performed concerning the possible use of other materials in company products. Such studies should be performed both for planned new products and for established products. It is too easy to fall into a routine of using whatever was used last year, or whatever was used by the new-product development department. Periodic studies of alternative materials are indicative of a management team that is trying to update the production system.

Questions 18 and 19 ask whether materials and scrap are properly cared for. Most companies handle raw materials carefully, but many undervalue waste and scrap. The image of scrap causes some people to ignore it, despite the fact that it may have value. The same image problem affects internal control over materials and scrap (Questions 24). Most companies have adequate security over raw materials, but few have any security over waste and scrap. Obviously scrap or waste is worth much less than good materials or finished products, but the total value may still be many thousands of dollars. Consequently, due care should be exercised.

The remaining questions in this section concern the generation and the disposal of scrap. Question 20 asking whether there is excess waste or spoilage is in most cases an opinion question, but an occasional respondent may propose a solution that has not reached the proper ears. The auditor should determine whether periodic analyses are made of scrap creation and scrap disposal. Often these tasks are ignored because of the low value assigned to scrap.

LABOR

Most of the questions in the Labor section are quite clear. For example, Questions 26 and 27 ask whether the department is adequately staffed with well-trained employees. Question 30 similarly asks whether there is adequate supervision in the department. Negative responses to any of these questions will probably not be uncommon. The typical manager has long complained about an inadequate number of trained workers and supervisors. If the operational auditor agrees that there is a problem, top management is more likely to pay attention.

Questions 28 and 29 ask whether there is excessive idle time or overtime in the department. Both of these questions should be answered negatively. Unfortunately, many companies will have to respond affirmatively to both questions. Owing to machine breakdowns or materials shortages, a company incurs idle time. Then, in order to get production out on time, overtime costs have to be incurred.

Employee morale and labor relations are the subjects of Questions 31 and 32. Problems in these areas arise more often in production than in any other department of an organization. Therefore, a manager must work hard to generate high morale and maintain good labor relations.

Question 33 asks whether there is any specific method of allocating employees among various jobs. In less sophisticated shops, whoever is available is assigned to the most pressing job. However, such blind assignments do not take into consideration the differences among employees' skill levels and pay rates. In general, there should be some plan to match expertise and pay level to job assignment.

Question 34 can be described as a rhetorical question. Few, if any, respondents will know how much money the company has invested in their department's human resources. However, an appreciation on the part of managers as to the rough amount of the investment will be an inducement to maintain stable employment.

Question 35 asks whether the company has ever considered using temporary workers during rush periods. Many unskilled jobs can be performed by people who would welcome the opportunity for temporary employment. One of the author's clients manufactured toys. The rush season was during the summer, when toys were manufactured for Christmas giving. Utilizing the many hundreds of college students who were willing to work during the summer at a minimum wage, the company was able to keep year-round employment at about 100 people. It could readily gear up to over 450 employees for the rush period. Conversely, companies with a slow summer season can hire mothers of school-age children for nine months a year.

The final question in the Labor section asks whether any type of incentive pay system is used. Many types are described in cost accounting and production management textbooks: some methods reward individuals, some reward groups. Although these systems are not suitable for all production operations, there should at least be consideration given to the desirability of implementing some form of incentive pay. By the same token, companies that do have an incentive system should conduct periodic reviews to determine whether the added pay is truly boosting productivity.

EQUIPMENT AND FACILITIES

The first two questions in the Equipment section are concerned with preventive maintenance and access to maintenance services. Preventive maintenance is less often a problem area for a company that is operating at under-capacity rates, because maintenance chores make good "filler" work when there are no production jobs in process. However, for a department that is operating at or near capacity, the temptation to defer preventive maintenance is great: why shut down a machine for maintenance when the machine is running smoothly and the production is needed? The manager should consider whether the cost of a routine shutdown outweighs the cost of a possible unplanned breakdown. Generally, the latter is far more costly.

Question 39 asks whether there is adequate equipment available in the department, and Question 40 is concerned with procedures for acquiring needed new equipment. Some empire-builders always like to have more equipment, so the auditor should always delve into the rationale for proposed expansion. When purchases are made, there should be a prescribed procedure for justifying the acquisition.

The possibility of sharing rarely used equipment with other departments or with other companies is examined in Question 41. Although intracompany sharing by manufacturers is common, sharing with other companies is very rare. Some not-for-profit service organizations do occasionally share equipment. For example, hospitals may join with other hospitals in their community to purchase high-priced technical equipment that will not ordinarily have to be used by any one institution full time. There is no reason why manufacturers cannot do the same thing.

Question 42 asks whether production facilities are laid out in the most appropriate manner. This is an engineering or systems question, but a negative response might be indicative of a less-than-optimum operating situation, which could in turn lead to a systems engagement for the CPA firm at a later time.

Questions 43 and 44 are concerned with the safety of employees and with fire protection. Safety factors are considered in detail in Chapter 11, which should be referred to in case of a negative response to Questions 43 and 44. Safety and fire protection are very important in the production area. They are not detailed in this chapter simply in order to avoid overlap.

COST CONTROL AND REPORTS

The final section of the production questionnaire deals with cost control and reports. Cost control may have given rise to the operational audit. If higher management feels that the department's cost performance is inadequate, the auditor should ferret out the reason. Question 45 is not enough. A negative response should signal the auditor to be extra alert for cost-control problems.

One possible reason for poor cost performance can be that variance reports are received too late to be useful (Question 46). If a variance report is to be used as a control tool, it must be made available soon enough to permit timely changes to be made. Some well-run companies produce daily variance reports. Others distribute them monthly or even less often. Obviously, a two-month-old report is not a very good control device.

Some managers complain that their cost performance appears poor because the cost reports include noncontrollable, as well as controllable, costs. Most costs are "controllable" at some level of management, but the department head should be accountable for only those costs he is responsible for. Production managers also complain that they dislike receiving reports that are too general to be useful for control purposes. Detailed reports (the subject of Question 48) should be provided. This problem usually reflects poor communication between the production manager and Accounting, which normally has the data the production manager needs but does not realize he wants it.

Question 49 asks whether adequate records are maintained of scrap and by-products. This is another check on the adequacy of control over these inventory items.

The final question asks the respondents whether they understand everything in the reports they receive. The auditor may not always get an honest answer here, but a negative response could indicate one of two problems. One possibility is that the respondent needs to be oriented to the usefulness of the report. Alternatively, the parts of the report that are not understood may not be relevant, so the auditor can suggest that the report, or just the section that is not germane, be either eliminated, or not forwarded to departments where it is not applicable.

SUMMARY

Production management is a challenging occupation. The job requires the proper coordination of materials, people, and equipment. And since all of these inputs are constantly changing, the production manager also has to be willing to change. Thus, production management involves constant study. There always seems to be a better way to make a product and there are always new products to be produced.

The job of the production manager begins with the choice of the most efficient method of production, then obtaining production inputs, managing day-to-day operations, controlling costs, and constantly updating the system. All of this is complicated by the fact that production management has become more scientific. The effective manager needs to be familiar with EOQ models, linear programming, queueing theory, PERT, and the critical path method. Because many of these activities do not occur every day, the operational auditor can provide a real service by reminding managers of the many tools available.

One final comment: production management is not confined to manufacturing companies. Service industries also produce a product, albeit intangible. Therfore, much of this chapter is as applicable to a service company as to a manufacturer.

thirteen

PURCHASING

The purchasing department is another department with which all administrators and department heads are familiar. This is because an error or inefficiency in the purchasing department always affects at least one other department. The purchasing department normally begins a company's operating cycle. A basic objective of the purchasing department is to obtain the proper materials and supplies at the right price and at the right time. The procurement of supplies is a major business function, involving the coordination of the needs of many diverse departments with the offerings of many sellers. Because the duties of the purchasing department are of a continuing nature, a small inefficiency can be quite costly over a period of time

Exhibit 13-1 provides an operational audit questionnaire for use in determining whether a purchasing department is operating efficiently. The questionnaire was constructed on the basis of suggestions from 150 purchasing agents. The operational audit questionnaire for purchasing (Exhibit 13-1) consists of six sections:

General
Communication
Policies and procedures
Department staff
Vendors
Forms and reports

Most questions have been designed so that a "yes" answer indicates a good situation and a "no" answer suggests a possible inefficiency or area of ineffectiveness.

EXHIBIT 13-1   Purchasing Questionnaire

General

1. Does the company have a centralized purchasing system?

2. Is the purchasing function separate from receiving?

3. Are purchase orders used for all buying?

4. Does Purchasing always search for the best price and supply of the goods requested?

5. Have dollar-purchase approval limits been established?

6. Do you feel that other departments view the Purchasing department as a source of information on solving all types of materials problems?

7. Are purchase requests always executed on a timely basis?

8. Is the purchasing department oriented toward "service"?

9. How often does an out-of-stock situation occur?

10. Is overstocking a problem?

11. Do you try to acquire generic products, as opposed to brand-name products?

12. How much time is required to process a request for purchase?

13. What is the cost (or number of man-hours) per purchase order?

14. Is there an adequate file of catalogs and current price lists?

15. Is there an inventory control system?

16. Do you have records of the amount of time spent talking to salesmen?

17. Are purchases (both in dollars and number of orders) known for each department in the firm?

18. Is there a product evaluation committee? Is the purchasing agent a member of the committee?

19. Is copying machine use controlled?

20. Are you aware of the amount invested in inventory at all times so that money is not tied up for excessive periods of time?

21. Are price variances used as a measure of purchasing agent performance?

22. Are there rules against conflict of interest such as ownership by the purchasing agent of stock in suppliers?

EXHIBIT 13-1 (Continued)

Yes / No / DNA

23. Are the physical facilities of the department adequate?

24. Is an adequate amount of office equipment available in the department?

Communication

25. Does the Purchasing department have good relations with other departments?

26. Does the Purchasing department communicate well with Accounts Payable and with Receiving?

27. Do Accounts Payable clerks always have the information that they need from Purchasing?

28. Do you know the amount of budget available for each department in the firm?

Policies and Procedures

29. Is there a policy and procedures manual for the department?

30. Have you established uniform purchasing standards for the company so that all departments are treated equally?

31. Is there a special procedure for purchase of capital equipment?

32. Are purchase requisitions required before a purchase order can be filled out?

33. Is there a system for authorizing invoices that do not agree with orders as to price, terms, or freight?

34. Is there a company standardization committee to control product proliferation?

35. Do you utilize any type of economic order quantity (EOQ) procedure?

36. Do you try to buy products that meet the needs of several departments rather than stocking several brands of nearly identical items?

37. Do you try to maintain lean inventories while minimizing out-of-stock situations?

38. Do you ever make a value analysis of products to be sure that the products meet the intended need?

39. Do you take advantage of quantity discounts when available?

40. Would it be possible to pool your orders with those of other local companies in order to obtain quantity discounts?

EXHIBIT 13-1 (Continued)

41. Do you attempt to avoid rush orders?

42. Do you obtain competitive bids from vendors?

43. Are all provisions of bids considered, such as freight terms, discounts, and service?

44. Are exceptions to lowest bid allowed? How are such exceptions controlled?

45. Are quotations obtained from several vendors before an order is placed?

46. Do you feel that quantities purchased are always consistent with actual requirements?

47. Do you make purchases from several sources to ensure a steady source of supply?

48. Is there a follow-up procedure for orders not received promptly?

49. Do you regularly follow up when vendors back-order an item?

50. Do purchase orders normally include prices?

51. Is a record kept of instances when actual purchase price differs from expected purchase price?

52. Do you establish a usage rate on each item in order to help trim inventories?

53. Have you determined the level of safety stock for each item?

54. Are your files periodically purged of old records? Do you set aside one day a year as "space conservation day" to clean out files?

Department Staff

55. Is the department staff large enough?

56. Do you feel that all department employees are highly ethical?

57. Do employees in the department have a favorable attitude toward their job and company?

58. Is morale high in the department?

59. Do employees have an adequate knowledge of products they handle?

60. Do employees make an effort to keep informed about new items?

Yes / *No* / *DNA*

EXHIBIT 13-1 (Continued)

61. Does the firm subscribe to specialized journals for purchasing personnel?

62. Does the firm provide for continuing education of employees?

63. What is the employee turnover rate in the department?

64. What is the employee absence rate?

Vendors

65. Do you deal only with reputable vendors?

66. Do you have vendor performance files to indicate which are dependable in various situations?

67. Do you make certain that vendors guarantee their products before you place an order?

68. Is a statement of policy made available to vendors?

69. Are salesmen discouraged from contacting other department heads?

70. Is there any policy with respect to acceptance of gifts from vendors?

71. Is there an effort to develop new vendor sources?

72. Is the vendor list updated with reasonable frequency?

Forms and Reports

73. Are purchase order blanks prenumbered?

74. Is there a combined purchase order and receiving report?

75. Is there sufficient space on all forms (particularly purchase orders and purchase requisitions) for the information needed?

76. Are printed forms available for recording quotations and bids from vendors?

77. Is the spacing on forms correct for easy typing?

78. Are monthly purchase reports prepared? Does anyone read them?

79. Does the purchasing department maintain an equipment ledger for capital equipment?

80. Are blank purchasing forms properly safeguarded?

81. Are records maintained efficiently and effectively?

82. Are there printed purchase requisition forms?

GENERAL

The General section begins with questions relating to the overall organization of the purchasing department. The first two questions ("is there a centralized purchasing system?" and "is purchasing separate from receiving") should be answered positively, but Question 3 ("are purchase orders always used?") may not always result in a "yes." In some companies, such emergencies as rush orders or special orders can bypass the regular purchasing procedure and no purchase order is required. As a general rule, bypassing the regular channels can result in unnecessary purchases, high (noncompetitive) prices, and a breakdown in internal control. This is not to say that all purchases must always originate in the purchasing department. For instance, some companies give other departments the authority to make certain types of purchases: these departments have been delegated this purchasing authority on a permanent basis, and they follow procedures similar to those of the purchasing department (except that they use a different type of purchase order). A common example of a department authorized to make its own purchases is that of a marketing department authorized to buy advertising space. In cases like this, the theory is that the purchasing department has no special contribution to make to the transaction, so nothing would be gained by routing it through the purchasing agent.

The real problem occurs—too often—when a requisitioning department first conducts its own investigation regarding price and availability, then asks the purchasing agent to simply process the transaction. The purchasing agent often agrees, because he thinks his work has already been performed. However, such transactions are undesirable because they usurp the authority of the purchasing department even though on paper they appear to be normal. Question 4 is an attempt to uncover this situation.

Question 5 examines the amount of authority delegated to the purchasing department. The purchasing department should not be given a blank check, but rather should be limited in the amount it can spend on a given order. The approval of the president or vice-president, for example, might be required before an order over a certain dollar amount can be filled.

Questions 6, 7, and particularly 8, emphasize the fact that a purchasing department must be user-oriented. At this point it should be explained that similar questions are often listed in different places on the questionnaire. The reason for this is so that the respondent will not get the "drift" of what the auditor is seeking. In this way, the auditor may surprise the respondent into conflicting answers and thus obtain greater insight into a given situation. For example, Questions 10 and 20 are worded differently, but both deal with the problem of overstocking. The purchasing agent must understand that excess inventory costs the company money in the form of storage costs and interest. Question 11 pursues the objective of minimizing inventories in checking that one generic product is used for several departments instead of several brand-name items for each user. Question 15 inquires whether there is some type of inventory control system that the purchasing agent can use as a guide in buying. Examples of such systems vary from a sophisticated computerized perpetual inventory system to a simple two-bin system. Sophisticated or simple, any workable system is better than none at all.

Cost records are the topic of questions 12, 13, 16 and 17. The department should keep such important statistics as (1) preparation time and cost per purchase order and (2) amount of time spent talking to salesmen. In addition, the department should know whom it is requisitioning for. Thus it should keep track of purchases (in both dollars and number of orders) for all departments in the organization (Question 17). The awareness of such data is a major consideration in helping to control costs. When known, the time required to process a purchase order and the cost involved should be compared with industry averages and prior years' costs.

Question 18 asks whether there is a product evaluation committee. Composed of individuals from user departments, the committee evaluates products. This provides quality guidelines for the purchasing agent.

Questions 14, 23, and 24 examine the adequacy of the physical facilities of the department. Questions 23 and 24 are very general, but Question 14 zeroes in on the availability of vendor catalogs and price lists. The lack of a library of such materials may be evidence that the purchasing agent is not performing enough exploratory work prior to placing orders.

In Question 19, the respondents are asked whether there is any control over the use of the copying machine. In many organizations, employees get into the habit of using the copier for their own personal use. The cost of providing these free copies can get out of control if there is no attempt to control them. While performing an audit, this author once asked a department head whether there was any control over copier use. The department head responded that although there was no control, there was no problem. While we were talking, an employee copied 10 pages from a comic book. While we were laughing about "no problem," another employee copied his personal tax return. Needless to say, the department head implemented a control system the very next day.

Question 21 examines the problem of employee evaluation. One measure of purchasing agent performance is the extent of price variance. If the purchasing agent knows that price variances will be tallied, he has more incentive to obtain the lowest costs possible. Although the absolute amount of the price variance is an important evaluation tool, it should also be measured in relation to the total orders handled by the department. The year-to-year trend in this percentage should be analyzed.

POLICIES AND PROCEDURES

The section on policies and procedures begins by asking whether a formal manual exists. A manual fosters consistency of action within the department. Questions 30 through 34 pursue the topic of department policies. Department standards should ensure that all requisitioning departments are treated equally (Question 30). For example, written purchase requisition forms should be required before an order is submitted (Question 32). Question 31 ("is there a special procedure for purchase of capital equipment?") should be emphasized, because the purchase of capital equipment, involving a long-range decision, differs from the routine purchase of supplies.

Question 35, dealing with EOQ models, attempts to determine whether purchases are made on a haphazard or systematic basis. Question 36 may not be applicable to all companies, but many companies accumulate a proliferation of nearly identical items. Question 37 has been developed to determine whether out-of-stock costs are considered in purchase decisions. Question 52 (on usage rates) and 53 (on safety stock) are similar to Question 37 in that they relate to minimizing inventory carrying cost.

The subject of quantity discounts is examined in Questions 39 and 40. Even a small company can obtain discounts for buying in quantity. Many companies take advantage of quantity discounts by pooling their orders with other local businesses. If a company has several branches or locations, it may be able to obtain quantity discounts even though the vendor has to ship the goods to several points. A company might also consider pooling orders with nearby competitors who are also too small to qualify for quantity discounts.

Questions 41 through 45 pertain to efforts made by the purchasing department to get the lowest available cost. Avoiding the need for rush orders (Question 41) is one way to help keep costs at a minimum. The auditor should verify that bids and quotations (Questions 42 and 43) are obtained regularly. The procedure is easy to omit after suppliers have been established for each item, but annual requests for price quotations is a good policy.

A value judgment is required of the Purchasing staff in Question 46 in that they have to estimate whether quantities purchased are always consistent with requirements. Purchasing agents are often asked to order specific quantities of certain items. Occasionally, these requests represent excess quantities and the excess ends up as obsolete inventory. Conversely, some requisitioning departments consistently make their orders too small. Later, rush orders, at high freight rates, are necessary to maintain production schedules.

Question 47 asks whether several sources of supply are maintained for regular inventory items. There is a great deal of difference of opinion on this question. Some purchasing agents feel that the shutdown of one supplier can present problems for a company. Other purchasing agents consider this question relatively unimportant, apparently because low prices are more important than a variety of suppliers.

Questions 48 and 49 inquire about follow-up in cases of late supplies. Follow-up is necessary since extra costs are often incurred as a result of late deliveries.

Questions 50 and 51 pertain to purchase prices. If purchase prices are not specified in orders, there is a risk of overcharge. Prices should always appear on the purchase order. Questions 52 and 53 are similar to question 37 in that they relate to the goal of reduction of inventory carrying costs.

The final question in the section could apply to any department. All files should be periodically purged of old records. The records should be removed to a storage room or (ideally) put on microfilm, rather than be allowed to continue cluttering the filing space in the department. With the high cost of floor space and filing equipment, devoting one day a year to this housekeeping chore may prove quite economical.

DEPARTMENT STAFF

Most of the section of the questionnaire on department staff is self-explanatory. The question (56) regarding the ethics of purchasing department employees is quite important because there is so much opportunity for unethical behavior. Thus, purchasing employees must maintain not only a real independence from vendors, but also an appearance of independence. The problem of employee morale (Questions 57 and 58) is closely related to employee ethics. If staff morale is high, there is less reason for an employee to try to "ripoff" the company. Many instances of white collar crime result from an employee's sense of under-appreciation or unfair treatment. This kind of crime is committed as much for revenge as for money. In every sense, then, loyalty and high morale pay off in productivity in all departments.

Questions 59 and 60 (knowledge of products) are particularly important. Purchasing employees must make a conscious effort to keep abreast of products (both old and new) in order to do a good job for the company. One way to keep abreast of current developments is to subscribe to professional journals in both the purchasing field and the industry in which the company operates (Question 61).

VENDORS

Because purchasing employees have a great deal of contact with vendors, it is imperative that they have good relations. Questions 65, 66, and 67 deal with the reputation of vendors, the reliability of products, and their dependability. If vendors cannot be depended on, the company may find itself in a dangerous out-of-stock situation.

Question 68 inquires whether a purchasing policy statement is made available to vendors. This procedure can often reduce the amount of time that has to be spent talking to vendors. Question 69 also looks to the objective of reducing the amount of time company personnel spend with salesmen in asking whether an attempt is made to keep vendors from bothersome access to other department heads.

Question 70 concerns gifts from vendors. There should be a definite policy on this important subject. There is a very fine line between a "gift" and a "kickback." Copies of company policy relating to the acceptance of gifts should be made available to vendors, as well as employees.

New vendors should be sought (Question 71) in an attempt to cultivate new sources of products. The knowledgeable employee makes a constant effort to find new and better sources of supply. Question 72 dealing with updating the vendor list is a matter of internal good housekeeping. In an efficient department, the approved vendor list is updated frequently.

FORMS AND REPORTS

The section of the questionnaire concerning forms and reports emphasizes size and spacing of format (Questions 75 and 77). Questions 73 and 74 are concerned with internal control and convenience. If forms are prenumbered (Question 73), they can easily be accounted for if a question arises. One form (perhaps in different colors) can serve as both purchase order and receiving report. Question 76 asks if there are printed bid and quotation forms as an indication of whether the forms are being used regularly to help obtain competitive prices.

In Question 78 the importance of the reports generated is quizzed. Are all copies of reports really used, or would it be possible to cut down on the number of copies. Perhaps just one copy of some reports is sufficient. It could be placed in the files without being sent to anyone (particularly if few people read the report). This author once encountered a company which made 12 copies of every purchase order. It was found that four were sufficient.

The equipment ledger is the subject of Question 79. The ledger gives the purchasing department a list of all company equipment. Use of such a ledger may permit reduced equipment purchases by having user departments either share rarely used equipment, or arrange internal transfers of unneeded equipment.

Question 80 deals with internal control. Purchase order forms should be safeguarded in order to deter operating personnel from making unauthorized purchases. The subject of purchasing department housekeeping is asked about in Question 81: An efficient and effective department is usually typified by a well-organized recordkeeping system. The final question asks whether the company uses printed requisition forms (as opposed to scraps of paper and backs of envelopes). All requisitions should be in writing, and the best way to ensure this is to provide printed forms to all authorized employees.

SUMMARY

The purchasing department exists only for the benefit of the other departments. If the purchasing department increases its efficiency, it may help cut costs in all departments. Because almost every purchasing department faces the same problems, this general questionnaire can be helpful to any company.

Operational auditing can be a tool in making the purchasing department efficient. By means of observation and keen questions, an independent auditor can often suggest means of boosting efficiency and effectiveness. The purchasing agent can get so bogged down with routine work that he or she cannot see beyond the detail. The operational auditor does not have to worry about fulfilling routine tasks, and can concentrate on the overall smoothness of operation.

fourteen

QUALITY CONTROL

Quality control has become a major consideration in modern business because of industry's demand for higher production speeds combined with high-precision products. To ensure the desired level of quality, companies use both inspectors and statistical quality control techniques. Sometimes all products are inspected. Other times, only a sample is checked. A company tries to ship only high-quality products to its customers, but in some cases it is not economical to produce only high-quality products, because the most economical production method in terms of overall unit cost may factor in some spoilage. This is where the quality control department fits in as the inspection process weeds out the bad products.

Quality control (inspection) personnel are often viewed as policemen, do-gooders, purists, or narrow technical specialists. Too often, quality control personnel deserve these labels. However, significant changes have taken place in the field in recent years. No longer just inspectors, the people in the quality control department are becoming a monitoring, fact-finding, and reporting team. This development requires different skills from those needed in the past.

Many factors have played a role in the evolution of the quality control department. Among these are new consumer legislation, watchdogs like Ralph Nader, and tighter employee safety rules under OSHA. Declining productivity and the resulting bite on profits have also played a role. Product liability suits have put great pressure on quality control departments to boost product reliability.

In a sense, quality control is part of the production function and belongs in Chapter 12. Quality control is an integral part of the production process, but it is also related to the engineering function and to the marketing of the product. Quality control can be distinct from production, inasmuch as it concerns service enterprises as well as manufacturers. Too many people limit their conception of quality control to the inspection of finished products to determine their acceptability. There are many other aspects of a complete quality control program. Quality control begins with the design of a new product.

Once the design is deemed acceptable, the quality control department will be involved next in the inspection of the raw materials that will go into the product. The primary objective of inspecting raw materials is to protect the quality of the finished product, but the inspection can serve also as a basis for accepting the materials. Once the raw materials are accepted, the inspectors will play a role next in the production process, by inspecting the product at the intermediate stages in its development. Finally, the finished product will undergo scrutiny by quality control personnel prior to its shipment to the customer.

The costs of running a quality control department are quite high (incidentally, making the department an excellent candidate for an operational audit); however, the cost of not having a department is even higher. When quality deteriorates, the cost of materials and labor are wasted. The biggest cost of all—loss of customer goodwill—accrues if an unacceptable product is sold and delivered. An additional cost may result from any damages for losses sustained by the customer because of the unacceptable product. Thus quality control, although expensive, is a necessity for most companies. In essence, quality control activities contribute to the total profitability of the organization. The trick is to operate a quality control program at the lowest possible cost without sacrificing the benefits.

Quality control is more than just inspection. It is also prevention. The ultimate success of a quality control department will be determined by the speed, effectiveness, and permanence of the department's attack on the causes of poor quality. This gives the department the responsibility for identifying the causes of poor quality, determining who is responsible, and then implementing a solution. Once the causes of poor quality have been identified and corrected, the job of inspection is much easier: to monitor the system, not necessarily to separate good products from bad.

The first step in a quality control program is to define a level of acceptable quality. This decision is complicated by a variety of factors. For one, the sales staff will want an attractive product that can be sold at a competitive price. On the other hand, the engineering department will want to design a utilitarian product that will be durable, regardless of the selling price for such a product. The production foreman will want the product that can be most easily processed. The problem becomes one of choosing a desired level of acceptable quality from among all of the possible combinations available. Thus quality control does not necessarily focus on absolute quality, but on management's definition of quality given all of the cost and marketing constraints.

Once a desired level of quality has been defined, the quality control department determines the best combination of prevention and inspection activities to attain it. Preventive actions include training programs and locked-in machine settings. Inspection activities are performed not only to screen out unacceptable products, but also to monitor the effectiveness of the preventive measures. It is usually preferable to perform the inspection activities on a statistical sampling basis: every item does not have to be inspected, but generalizations can be made concerning the effectiveness of the preventive measures employed in the production process.

The operational auditor cannot solve every problem in a quality control department. In fact, in many technical organizations, the auditor's contribution is limited by his lack of expertise. However, the operational auditor can assist a department in many of the administrative details of the quality control program.

The quality control questionnaire (Exhibit 14-1) is divided into six sections:

General
Safety
Handling rejects
Subcontracts and receiving
Records and reports
Facilities and equipment

GENERAL

The General section of the questionnaire begins by asking whether the quality control department is kept informed of all quality specifications. There should be some formal procedure to notify the department of specifications on new products and changes in specifications on old products. Without a formal system of notification, a breakdown in communication could develop between engineering and quality control, and there would be no way to determine who was at fault.

The second question is designed to judge how broad the role of the quality control department is. The department should be doing more than just inspecting: it should also be eliminating the underlying causes of poor quality—obviously a more constructive activity than policing the quality of completed work.

In most companies, the quality control department uses sampling

Yes	No	DNA	

EXHIBIT 14-1 Quality Control Questionnaire

General

1. Is the Quality Control Department kept advised of all quality specifications?

2. Is there a prevention program to block the underlying causes of poor quality?

3. Is the statistical sampling method approved by a qualified statistician?

4. Is substandard work followed up in a systematic way?

5. Do you try to determine where the mistake originated in the plant?

6. Do you check on correction recommendations for follow through?

7. Is there adequate staff in the department?

8. Are relations with production workers kept on a cordial and cooperative footing?

9. Do production workers agree with the decisions of quality control employees?

10. Do you try to minimize quality control costs?

11. Are products packed in such a way as to avoid damage and deterioration during shipment?

12. Is there a first-piece inspection after set-up is completed?

13. Is it possible for production workers to make assembly inspections as they work?

Safety

14. Do your quality standards consider product safety and product liability?

15. Are safety goals included in your plans?

16. Do you know the product liability legal requirements in the states and countries where your products are sold?

17. Do your products bear warnings of potential hazards?

18. Have any product liability claims been made against the company in the past two years?

19. Do you offer optional safety equipment to accompany your products?

EXHIBIT 14-1 (Continued)

Yes / No / DNA

20. Does the company have product liability insurance?

21. Could you reduce your insurance costs by dropping a trouble-some product from your line?

22. In designing products, are you always mindful of the safety of the user?

23. Do you have a product safety council of product users?

24. Do you keep records on product safety and related complaints?

25. Do you keep a record of why customers return items?

Handling Rejects

26. Are rejections properly segregated and tagged?

27. Are rejected materials returned to vendors for credit?

28. Are rejects ever audited to verify that they are unacceptable?

29. Do you evaluate rejects to determine whether they can econom-ically be (a) reworked or (b) torn down and their parts reinserted in the production process?

30. Are rejected products sold at lower-than-normal prices as "seconds" or scrap?

31. When nonconforming products are shipped to the customer at his request, are the defects noted on the shipping documents?

Subcontracts and Receiving

32. Do you inspect all incoming materials on receipt?

33. Do you get samples of new materials before selecting a supplier?

34. Do you maintain some type of supplier performance rating?

35. Do you consult with suppliers about the need for higher-quality products?

36. Do you follow up after a vendor sends rejected materials to make sure the problem has been corrected?

37. Do receiving inspectors have written instructions that tell them how to do an adequate inspection of all materials received?

38. Are materials issued to Production only after passing Receiving inspection?

Yes	No	DNA	

EXHIBIT 14-1 (Continued)

Records and Reports

39. Are charts showing quality performance kept up to date?

40. Are adequate records kept of work performed?

41. Do inspection records show the number of items inspected, the number rejected, and the name of the inspector?

42. Do you record all first-piece and in-process inspections?

43. Are inspection records kept in the quality control department?

44. For job order products, are inspection records kept by job number?

Facilities and Equipment

45. Are facilities adequate?

46. Is equipment adequate to perform your job effectively?

47. Are inspection areas kept neat and orderly?

48. Are your gauges and test equipment periodically tested for accuracy?

49. Is there a written schedule for calibration of gauges and test equipment?

50. Are decals put on gauges and test instruments showing the date of last calibration and the due date of the next calibration?

51. Are out-of-service tools and gauges tagged to prevent their inadvertent use?

techniques, especially when the product has to be destroyed in order to be properly tested. The concern of Question 3 is whether sampling methods are statistically sound. The objective of statistical sampling is to permit a statement to be made—with a known degree of precision—about a whole population based on a limited examination. Judgment sampling may or may not be adequate. A company's sampling plan should be reviewed by a statistician qualified to assess how representative the samples are of all units produced.

Questions 4, 5, and 6 are similar to question 2 in that they inquire about regular follow-up on substandard work to determine where the mistake was made and by whom. These activities are part of any preventive program: negative answers here may precede a negative response to

Question 7 (adequacy of staff). Prevention objectives may be unmet because of a shortage of personnel. Questions 4 through 7 should be emphasized by the operational auditor: follow-up on substandard work can make a great contribution to company profits.

The relationship between quality control personnel and production workers is the subject of Questions 8 and 9. Production workers often feel threatened by the inspectors—perhaps sometimes rightly so. The best cure is to open the line of communication between the two groups. When production workers understand the reason for a rejection, they can produce better products in the future. The task of improving relations falls on the shoulders of the quality control employees.

Cost control is the subject of Question 10. Although effectiveness may be more important than efficiency in the quality control department, there is the same need to control costs as in any department. Unfortunately, cost control is sometimes subordinated to effectiveness.

Question 11 asks whether products are packaged in such a way as to avoid damage and deterioration during shipment. This extends the traditional role of the quality control department by expanding responsibility from high-quality finished product to delivery of the quality product. If a respondent denies that this question applies to his department, his answer is as deficient as a negative response.

Question 12 asks whether there is a first-piece inspection after a new set-up is complete. This is quite important inasmuch as there is no sense in producing an inferior product where the substandard feature is due to improper set-up of the machine or jig.

Production workers sometimes know on the spot when they have made an inferior product. They should be given the chance to reject their own work (Question 13). Letting production workers perform their own inspections reduces the demands on quality control departments. Worker inspection is especially important when inspection by the quality control department is on a sample basis.

SAFETY

The safety of a company's products and the potential for product liability suits are factors that continue to grow in importance. The quality control department must devote a great deal of effort to product safety. A good product safety program should try to minimize the number and severity of personal injuries caused by the company's products. Questions 14 and 15 inquire whether user safety is considered by the quality control department. A product safety program should seek to minimize not only direct costs (such as out-of-court settlements, damage payments, product recalls, and liability insurance), but also indirect penalties like unfavorable publicity.

Question 16 asks whether the employees are familiar with the product liability laws of each jurisdiction in which company business is conducted. Employees can probably never know all these facts, but they should be aware that most states and nations have a variety of product safety laws. Often the manufacturer will not know about the laws until he violates them. A small toy manufacturer, for instance, made a rag doll. The company received a letter from an official of a distant state warning that the dolls did not bear a label certifying that they were fireproof. Nor did the company have the requisite $75 permit to sell rag dolls in that state. The company's solution was to stop selling in that state since the dolls were not fireproof and the permit was too expensive for the volume of sales made in that state each year. Thus it is imperative that persons associated with quality control also be alert to various laws governing sales and uses of the company's products.

If a product is not totally safe under all circumstances, the hazards should be noted on a label (Question 17). Potential hazards should never be underplayed. A proper warning may some day be sufficient to win a legal action: it is much easier to prove negligence on the part of a user who was exposed to numerous warnings about the dangers of the product. If the product is used by individuals whose first language is not English, it is probably wise to include warnings in several other languages.

Question 18 (asking whether there have been any product liability claims in the prior two years) serves to alert the auditor to potential problems. Even if a company successfully defends a product liability case, the legal costs can be staggering. And the company may experience costly unfavorable publicity when a case is filed, even if the plaintiff subsequently withdraws the claim or loses the case. The auditor should not forget the old "where there's smoke, there's fire" doctrine: if the company is being sued, there is probably something wrong with the product even if the company is winning the cases.

The subject of whether a company offers to sell its customers optional safety equipment is explored in Question 19. This is a tricky question: an affirmative response may be bad. Some court decisions have indicated that if a buyer elects not to purchase optional safety equipment and someone is injured by the product, the seller can be held liable if it was reasonably foreseeable that the buyer would not buy the safety device. Therefore, it may be advisable to package the safety device with the product at a higher price.

Questions 20 and 21 ascertain the extent of product liability insurance coverage. Most companies can get such insurance. The problem is price, not availability. In order to keep insurance premiums to a minimum, it might occasionally be wise to drop a hazardous product or product line (particularly if the product is a low-profit item or an unprofitable item maintained just to round out a full product line).

Questions 22 through 25 examine the role of the customer in a company's quality control program. In addition to designing products with the safety of the user in mind, it is also usually a good idea to have a safety council made up of product users. The council can not only help spot potential trouble, but can also be used as sales and community relations tools. A company that felt that only idiots could have accidents with its products included several "idiots" in its safety council as a deterrent measure. If a company does not have a safety council, it may be able to garner many of the same benefits by carefully analyzing every complaint letter from customers. Even "crank" letters should be analyzed because the cranks may file lawsuits.

Product safety should be an integral part of every quality control program. The first objective of the quality control program is to deliver a high-quality product to the customer. The customer will not give the company a high mark for quality, however, if he is injured by the product.

HANDLING REJECTS

The first question in the Rejects section is whether rejected items are segregated from good items and tagged or marked so they will not be inadvertently used. Nothing is more irksome than to discover unacceptable products, and then have them mistaken for good items. If materials or parts are rejected by Receiving inspection, they should be quickly returned to the vendor (Question 27) to avoid any possibility of their use.

Question 28 asks whether anyone ever audits the work of the quality control department—or who checks the checkers? Such checks are an integral part of the entire program of control over rejected products (other aspects are analyzed in Questions 29 and 30). There should be an evaluation to determine whether rejected products can be reworked, or torn down and their parts reused in the production process. If unacceptable products can not be reworked or reused, can they be sold as "seconds" or scrap? Rejects are costly to a company; good management dictates an effort to pare this cost.

The final question in this section asks whether shipping documents are appropriately marked when nonconforming goods are shipped to the customer at his request. Proper labeling can avoid a misunderstanding at the customer's receiving department—which might otherwise reject the goods as unsatisfactory.

SUBCONTRACTS AND RECEIVING

The subjects of inspection in the receiving department and of subcontractors' work are examined in Questions 32 through 38. The first question asks whether all incoming materials are inspected. The auditor may want to observe the inspection process itself to supplement his interview responses from employees. This is advisable even if the company has a policy of inspecting all materials received, because the policy may be bypassed when several deliveries are coming in at once. The Receiving inspectors should have written instructions telling them how to adequately inspect all materials received (Question 37): without written instructions, an inspector may not know exactly what to look for. Question 38 also applies to receiving inspection in that it checks to be sure that no materials are used until they have passed inspection. Although most companies have policies requiring materials to be inspected before issuance, the policy is sometimes violated when production workers need the materials in a hurry. Unfortunately, the benefit of maintaining output may be outweighed by a loss on rejected finished products.

RECORDS AND REPORTS

Adequate records should be maintained to document the work of the quality control department. The first question in the section asks whether charts are kept up to date. This is quite important because many times remedial action is triggered at a certain level of rejections. Without up-to-date information, there will be a lag between the onset of a problem and its remedy.

Questions 40, 43, and 44 ask whether work records are adequate, maintained in the department, and filed by job number. Good records may some day help avoid a loss in a product liability suit.

The contents of inspection records is discussed in Question 41. Records should show the number of items inspected, the number rejected, and the name of the person making the inspection. This person is ultimately responsible for the inspection.

There probably should be separate records of all first-piece and in-process inspections. The reason for this is because errors at the beginning of a run can be quite expensive, since additional costs will be incurred for the benefit of the unacceptable products.

fifteen

RECEIVING AND MATERIALS HANDLING

Many business managers believe that they can make a profit simply by buying merchandise at a low price and reselling it at a higher price. However, this is rarely the case. The raw materials, merchandise, and parts must be received, processed, put into stock, rehandled, repacked, and shipped before they reach the final user. These intermediate steps often entail costly error and even loss. Only with trained people can the procedures be handled in an orderly manner. Although the handling of materials would seem to be a routine chore that does not require analysis, in fact, it approaches a science with tested principles that must be followed on a consistent basis.

First of all, when new facilities are being built, the proper flow of materials should be one of the primary factors in determining the size, shape, and configuration of the structure. For manufacturing companies, the best method of receiving and transferring materials should indicate how production machines are arranged: the proper placement of processing machines can significantly reduce handling costs. And once a materials handling system has been established, it should be reviewed periodically to determine whether efficiency can be increased.

Personnel in the receiving and materials handling department are responsible for moving the parts, raw materials, and finished products at the lowest possible cost. The staff must move these items at the proper time to ensure that they reach their destination when needed. Indeed, materials that arrive before they are needed can create as much inconvenience as materials that arrive too late. The materials flow pattern also affects requirements for costly storage space. Thus, the objectives of the department can be summarized as (1) moving materials at the proper time and in the proper quantity and (2) doing so in a manner that will minimize inventory costs and storage costs.

FACILITIES AND EQUIPMENT

The first two questions ask whether facilities and equipment are adequate Obviously this depends on the number of employees and the nature of the product being inspected. In all cases, however, the entire area should be kept in a neat and orderly fashion. Order and neatness are probably more important in the quality control department than in any other production area. Without order, there would be a risk of mixing up rejected and good products.

Questions 48 through 50 are concerned with the testing and periodic calibration of gauges and testing equipment. Inaccurate equipment will result in errors in the rejection/acceptance decision.

The final question asks whether out-of-service tools and gauges are tagged to avoid their inadvertent use. This question applies not only to the gauges and test instruments in the quality control department, but also to defective production machinery. A simple "out of order" sign could prevent a very costly mistake.

SUMMARY

The activities of a quality control department include monitoring and evaluating the end-products of the production process. The need for a quality control program arises from the fact that it is (1) impossible to consistently produce perfect products or (2) the most economical production function in terms of total unit cost factors in a few unacceptable products for the sake of speed. Although a quality control program is costly on paper, it is less costly in the long run than permitting inferior products to be shipped to customers.

The contribution of the operational auditor here takes the form of suggestions for operating the department more efficiently and effectively. The ideal quality control program would prevent mistakes before they occur rather than catch them later. In the final analysis, prevention is cheaper than rejecting finished products after inspection. The operational auditor can help the company maintain an overall quality control program.

There are four basic functions performed by materials handling personnel. These functions are (1) receiving, (2) warehousing, (3) in-process handling, and (4) distribution of the finished product. The receiving activity is the first step in the materials handling location (although, strictly speaking, sometimes materials handling personnel have to fetch materials that are not delivered by the seller or a common carrier). The receiving personnel are responsible for unloading the materials, inspecting them for weight and quality, and then disposing of the items for the next step. The warehousing function involves storage of materials, order picking, order assembly, packing, and distribution. Materials may be stored at the main warehouse or sent to remote storage facilities.

The in-process handling function consists of moving raw materials, parts, and finished products between departments and individual workplaces. This may be by means of forklift, hand truck, conveyor belt, or by hand. Some studies have shown that materials may be moved as many as 50 times before emerging as finished product. All of this movement costs money; thus the operational auditor should look for ways to minimize materials movement.

The final function of the materials handling department involves the distribution of the finished product. This final step may include labeling and packaging, as well as moving the finished goods.

There are at least three ways an inefficient materials handling department can waste company money. First, department employees are usually paid by the hour. Therefore, if they are taking too long to deliver materials, they are aggravating labor costs. Second, an inefficient employee can damage breakable parts. Third, when a delivery is late, the machine operator has to wait. For example, suppose a materials handling employee trips over an obstacle in his path and spills a box of parts. The company incurs unnecessary costs while he picks up the spilled parts. If some of the parts were broken, the company has to replace the damaged items. Finally, the machine operator is waiting for the parts, so the company has the costs of his idle time. The whole problem could have been avoided by removing the obstacle in the laborer's path (or by hiring an employee who does not trip so easily).

The receiving and materials handling department is strictly a service function, but it affects most departments in the organization. Because of the continuing nature of most activities performed by the department, a small inefficiency can significantly aggravate costs over an extended period of time. Therefore, the operational auditor can perform a real service even if he uncovers only minor problems in the department.

There are five guidelines the operational auditor should bear in mind when reviewing the receiving and materials handling department. The auditor should search for ways to (1) boost productivity, (2) reduce waste, (3) improve working conditions in the department, (4) improve distribution, and (5) reduce costs by better utilization of space.

The first objective—increasing productivity—can be accomplished by smoothing out the workflow. This can result in greater productivity per manhour and increase machine efficiency by reducing downtime. As illustrations, the workflow can be improved by placing the receiving dock near the warehouse portion of the building and by using the proper equipment (such as a forklift) to move items.

Waste can be reduced by keeping spoilage at a minimum. Spoilage and damage can occur through improper handling and improper storage. Department employees should look also for ways to reduce scrap losses.

The third objective is to improve working conditions. Although this objective refers primarily to materials handling employees, it can apply also to employees in other departments which are serviced by the materials handling department. Such conditions as employee health and safety should be considered. Methods of reducing employee fatigue and cutting plant accidents also fall in this category. Studies have shown that employees are more productive when they are comfortable, so the auditor should look for foam rubber mats for example, for employees who have to stand for long periods on a concrete floor.

The operational auditor's fourth objective is to look for ways of improving the distribution of materials. Here, the most cost-effective system may not always be the fastest system. Consideration must be given to the possibility of breakage when materials are moved too rapidly. The auditor should consider not only the distribution of raw materials and parts, but also of the finished products. Again, the distribution to the customer should take into consideration more than just the visible cost and the speed of delivery. Packaging and the reliability of the carrier must also be examined.

The auditor's final objective is to look for methods of reducing costs by better utilizing space. Storage space must be kept to a minimum, but still be large enough to permit proper inventory control, provide an efficient handling system, and prevent pilferage and spoilage. In essence, the question is, "How can space be utilized to the maximum advantage?"

Materials handling equipment can be anything from handcarts to wheelbarrows to computer-controlled robots. Choosing the proper equipment in terms of size, sophistication, and cost is often difficult, but can lead to greater efficiencies in the department. There are almost as many types of equipment as there are products to be handled. Naturally, the nature of the company's product will determine its choice of equipment.

Since the choice of the proper equipment can result in tremendous efficiencies in handling materials, the auditor should try to familiarize himself with the various options available. Much of this knowledge will have to be gained through experience, but the following six guidelines will be helpful:

1 **Mechanical equipment saves time.** The use of materials handling equipment, whether it be a wheelbarrow, conveyor belt, monorail system, or robot, can cut labor costs, reduce fatigue, promote safety, increase production, and speed flow of materials. Thus, the first guideline for the auditor is to recommend the use of equipment whenever possible.

2 **Compute the cost/benefit ratio of equipment.** The main reason the auditor recommends equipment is to reduce costs, increase productivity, and improve working conditions for employees. However, all equipment costs money, and some pieces of equipment cost more than others. Thus the equipment purchase decision should be based on facts. The decision should be based also on potential savings, as well as initial cost of the equipment. Regular capital budgeting methods should be utilized before any major equipment is purchased.

3 **Select standard equipment.** The standardization of handling equipment simplifies the training of operators, requires fewer stocked replacement parts, and permits interchangeability of equipment. Specialized equipment should be considered only when the conditions warrant the higher price.

4 **Substitutes should be available.** No matter what type of equipment is purchased, some consideration should be given to alternate handling methods that can be used when the equipment is out of service. An equipment breakdown can be costly if there are no backup facilities available.

5 **Check building limitations.** Some materials handling equipment need concrete floors to run on. Others need special clearances (in both width and height). All possible limitations including doors, elevators, and ramps) should be considered before equipment is purchased.

6 **Consider maintenance costs.** Maintenance costs run higher for some types of equipment than for others. This is particularly true for highly complex pieces of equipment. Therefore, maintenance costs should be considered when the capital budgeting decision is being made.

The operational audit questionnaire for this department will provide insight into most companies. Although no two companies have the same materials handling requirements, some general principles apply to all situations. These general principles are incorporated in the questionnaire (Exhibit 15-1). However, when making recommendations regarding problem areas, the auditor should remember that all organizations are different. Thus although one questionnaire can serve to find inefficiencies in many organizations, the means of solving the problems will vary among companies. Therefore, the auditor will have to use his or her creativity in order to make suitable recommendations.

The questionnaire for use in the area of receiving and materials handling is divided into five sections:

General

Procedures

Department personnel

Physical facilities

Forms and reports

GENERAL

The General section begins by inquiring whether there is a receiving department and whether it is properly used. If some goods that come into the organization bypass the receiving department, there are probably unnecessary costs incurred in tracking down a given delivery. Good internal controls require that merchandise not be paid for until a receiving report is on file. If a shipment is delivered directly to the user, that receiving report is not prepared.

Questions 3 and 18 and Questions 23 through 25 relate to communication with other departments. Because receiving and materials handling is strictly a service department, to be useful, it must remain responsive to user needs.

Questions 4 through 7 pertain to the accessibility of goods kept in the storeroom. A system designed to store supplies facilitates finding a requested item. Convenience is considered also in Question 8. It is impractical to have shipments unloaded at one location and then pay someone to carry the items to the other end of the building.

The subject of inventory control is examined in Questions 9 through 13. An important ingredient in proper materials handling is the realization that carrying inventory is costly. Sound management requires that inventory be kept at the lowest level subject to the constraint that out-of-stock situations do not occur.

EXHIBIT 15-1   Receiving and Materials Handling Questionnaire

General

1. Is there a centralized receiving function?

2. Do all received goods come through the Receiving department?

3. Is the department responsive to user demands for products?

4. Is the department space kept in neat order at all times?

5. Are all materials easily accessible when needed?

6. Are shelf items arranged in a systematic, efficient, and workable manner?

7. Can it be said that there is a place for everything and everything is always in its place?

8. Are the storerooms conveniently close to the receiving dock?

9. Has inventory turnover remained constant or increased over the past few years?

10. How often do out-of-stock situations occur?

11. How often do you receive complaints from departments served?

12. What percentage of inventory is obsolete or no longer used?

13. Do you try to minimize the time between the arrival of a shipment and the delivery to the proper department?

14. Do you know your cost per receiving report processed?

15. Do you know your cost per materials requisition processed?

16. Is the annual physical count of inventory performed by someone other than those responsible for keeping perpetual records?

17. Is a reconciliation prepared between the perpetual inventory records and the year-end inventory physical count?

18. Is there an open line of communication with all departments?

19. Is there written approval by a responsible employee of adjustments made to perpetual records based on physical inventory counts?

20. How much was the last adjustment to perpetual inventory resulting from a physical inventory?

21. Are physical inventories taken in cycles (perhaps $1/12$ counted each month)?

22. Are all inventories insured?

EXHIBIT 15-1 (Continued)

23. Is there close coordination with the purchasing agent?

24. Is there close coordination with the Accounting department?

25. Is a monthly expense report prepared and sent to each department to keep them aware of costs they incurred?

Procedures

26. Is there a written set of established receiving procedures?

27. Are the formal procedures always followed?

28. Do you feel that all set procedures are necessary?

29. Are all items counted as they are unloaded?

30. Are rejected items returned to vendors promptly?

31. Are deliveries checked for damages?

32. Are early or over-shipments returned to vendors?

33. Do you inspect goods against specifications and for quality?

34. Is a perpetual inventory system used?

35. Is a requisition required before materials are given out?

36. Do you have a company catalog with a catalog number for every item in the warehouse?

37. Are only department heads (or other designated persons) permitted to requisition materials?

38. Are files ever purged of old unneeded documents?

39. Is there a system for reacquiring reusable supplies from user areas within the organization?

40. Has an efficient timetable been established for routine ordering of supplies by various departments so that the work of filling orders can be distributed throughout the week?

41. Has a system for automatic floor stocking been established?

42. Do you use an efficient method to rotate stock, so that the oldest items go out first?

43. Are packages date-stamped upon receipt in order to determine the time lapse between receipt and delivery to the user?

44. Is there any type of follow-up procedure on back-ordered items?

45. Are items that are radioactive, perishable, or require controlled temperatures always delivered immediately to the user?

EXHIBIT 15-1 (Continued)

Yes / No / DNA

46. Does your filing system provide for easy retrieval of forms upon receipt of merchandise?

47. Do you try to keep the more frequently called-for items at the most easily accessible points in the department?

48. Have economical order quantities been determined?

49. Are estimated warehousing costs of large-volume purchases ever compared with savings obtainable through quantity discounts?

50. Is there a code system on purchase orders to signal receiving personnel where to deliver received goods—direct to a user department or into inventory?

51. Are reorder points and economical order quantities ever recalculated?

52. Are lists of slow-moving materials ever prepared?

53. Are obsolete or unused items disposed of periodically?

Department Personnel

54. Is the department adequately staffed?

55. Are new employees properly trained?

56. Is there a written job description for each position in the department?

57. Do department employees have a good attitude about their job and the organization?

58. Do all employees in the department have an adequate knowledge of the materials being handled?

59. Is there a level of intelligence and training present that can improvise when no precedent or policy is available?

60. Are employees urged to join professional associations and subscribe to professional magazines?

61. Is access to the storeroom restricted to certain employees?

62. Are department employees bonded?

63. What is the employee turnover rate?

64. What is the employee absence rate?

Physical Facilities

65. Are the physical facilities adequate?

Yes	No	DNA	

EXHIBIT 15-1 (Continued)

66. Is there sufficient equipment in the department?

67. Is storage space adequate?

68. Are aisles wide enough?

69. Is there an item location file that permits quick and easy location of any item?

70. Is there an adequate supply of fire extinguishers?

71. Is a burglar alarm system used?

72. Are storage areas well lighted?

73. Are all materials unloaded and moved mechanically or with machine assistance?

74. If scales are used to verify weights, are the scales inspected periodically?

75. Are prepacked cartons used for simplifying counts and deliveries of small items?

Forms and Reports

76. Are receiving reports sent to Purchasing and to Accounting immediately after the goods are received?

77. Do receiving reports and materials requisition forms have adequate space for all information that should be recorded?

78. Are all forms the proper size for easy filing?

79. Are receiving reports prenumbered and accounted for?

80. Are receiving reports signed by the individual who received the shipment?

81. Are shortages and rejections immediately reported to Accounting and to Purchasing?

Question 12 regarding obsolete items is a problem in many organizations. People are reluctant to dispose of items that were once valuable even though the materials will not be used again. The importance of the sunk cost concept is difficult to apply in practice. However, considering the high cost of storage space and the inconvenience of moving unused items, anything that can no longer be used or returned to the vendor should be either sold as scrap or destroyed. This author witnessed an extreme example of this during the early 1970s. During an annual inventory count, a hidden inventory tag from the previous year turned out to show the same quantity as the current year's tag. Asked whether the items were ever used, the materials manager explained that the items were last used during World War II. The company manufactured auto tires and the obsolete materials were used as an emergency substitute for rubber. The firm had been storing about 1,000 cubic feet of this obsolete material for over 25 years. Just the cost of employees' detouring around the mass of obsolete materials all those years probably exceeded the initial outlay.

Questions 14 and 15 inquire whether the department head is familiar with operating costs. If the receiving department is not provided with cost figures, there is no way the department head can determine whether problems exist.

Questions 16 and 17 and Questions 19 through 21 relate to the accuracy of the perpetual inventory system. Most companies check the accuracy of the perpetual system with a physical count at least once a year. Cycle counts each month may be even more efficient. Any reconciliation with the perpetual inventory should be small, unless the perpetual system is not serving the purposes for which it was designed and therefore should be either eliminated or run better. It should be analyzed to determine why differences exist.

Insuring inventories is the topic of Question 22. If a large amount of assets are kept in one location, the company should at least explore the possibility of insuring the items.

PROCEDURES

The Procedures section begins with questions inquiring whether a formal set of written procedures has been set down, and whether these procedures are followed regularly. Questions 29 through 33 pertain primarily to relations with vendors and freight lines. It is important that the receiving employees check quantity and quality before accepting delivery. Otherwise, the company may find that it has been shorted, or that damaged merchandise has been accepted.

The subject of whether materials requisitions are required is explored in Question 35. The use of requisitions is important not only for charging costs to the proper user department, but also as an internal control device in that a requisition must match any decrease in inventory. Question 37 examines the topic of authorizing only certain individuals to submit requisitions.

Question 36 explores the question of whether catalog numbers have been assigned to products stocked. If so, requisitions of materials can be accurately accounted for. Such catalogs should be kept up to date.

In asking Question 39, the auditor may be able to determine exactly what happens to supplies after they leave the storeroom. There should be some provision for immediate return to the storeroom of those items that are not going to be used by the original requisitioning department.

Questions 40 through 43 and Question 45 discuss relations with user departments. It is usually much more practical to schedule the delivery days for each department than to deliver to every department every day. Supplies that are used regularly can be scheduled for delivery at certain intervals.

Questions 44 and 46 merely require a value judgment about how satisfactory the filing system is. There should be some system to enable the company to check on the status of backordered items. The auditor may have the opportunity to observe the answer to these questions.

The remainder of the questions in the Procedures section pertain to inventory carrying costs. Employees are often reluctant to dispose of obsolete supplies, because the supplies were formerly valuable. As mentioned previously, the accounting concept of sunk costs is often difficult to grasp, but obsolete inventories are a perfect example. They should be disposed of at the earliest possible date. Questions 48 through 50, dealing with economical order quantities, require some degree of sophistication on the part of the company. These are areas where the auditor can sometimes provide a valuable service.

DEPARTMENTAL PERSONNEL

This section is much like its counterpart in previous questionnaires. The first two questions ask whether the department is adequately staffed and employees properly trained. There should also be a written job description for each position, as implied by Question 56.

Question 57 asks about employee attitudes toward the job and the organization. This question is perhaps more important in the area of receiving and materials handling than it is in some other departments, because of the routine nature of the work. Also, the employees are often less well educated than those in some of the other departments. Consequently, the manager has to devote extra effort to the cultivation of employee morale.

The employees need to have a thorough knowledge of all materials that are handled (Question 58). This factor is especially important in companies where a degree of danger is connected with the products. To enhance employee safety and product security, there should be a thorough indoctrination of all employees concerning all aspects of materials handled.

Question 59 inquires whether the staff has enough expertise to permit improvisation when no precedent or policy exists. A brand-new situation can sometimes be a problem, if the department head is the only one who can provide leadership.

Question 60 is concerned with employee professionalism. The company should encourage employees to join professional societies such as the International Material Management Society (214 Huron Towers, 2220 Fuller Road, Ann Arbor, MI 48105) and to subscribe to professional journals such as *Distribution Manager* (Chestnut and 56th Streets, Philadelphia, PA 19139) or *Modern Material Handling* (221 Columbus Avenue, Boston, MA 02116). Professional receiving and materials handling employees can provide a great return for an organization willing to make a very small investment.

Questions 61 and 62 are concerned with internal control. The storeroom should be accessible only to department employees, not to everyone in the organization. Also, all employees should be bonded so that any theft loss can be recovered. The final two questions in the Personnel section deal with turnover rate and absence rate. High ratios can be costly for an organization.

PHYSICAL FACILITIES

The physical facilities questions are particularly important for the receiving department, especially the questions relating to the size of the department. "No" answers to the questions on storage space (Question 67) and width of aisles (Question 68) could mean that the department employees have difficulty in handling inventory to their satisfaction. Questions 70 and 71 relating to fire extinguishers and burglar alarms are important from the point of view of protecting most of the assets in the department. Question 72 dealing with proper lighting also relates to security. In addition, lighting can be important for worker efficiency.

Questions 73, 74, and 75 concern the proper use of equipment. Materials handling can be a backbreaking task unless machines, conveyors, and other equipment are used as much as possible. For smaller items, the use of scales and prepackaged cartons or standard-size bins helps to reduce the work load.

It must be remembered that offering physical space is one of the primary services of the Receiving and Materials Handling department. Thus, physical facilities should be the keynote of the operational audit.

FORMS AND REPORTS

The final section examines the topic of receiving reports and requisition forms. If the forms are too small, employees will waste time trying to cramp the information onto the forms (Question 77). Additionally, there is less chance of error if the forms contain a full description of the materials being requested.

Questions 79 and 80 are basically concerned with internal control. Reports should be prenumbered and periodically accounted for. They should be signed by the employee who received the goods. This fixes the responsibility for receiving the materials.

Finally, Questions 76 and 81 deal with the Receiving department's communication channels with Purchasing and Accounting. Both Accounting and Purchasing need to be notified when goods are received—and when they are not received because of rejections or shortages.

SUMMARY

Many companies can save a great deal of money by improving their procedures for receiving, managing, and supplying inventories. Receiving and materials management need not be a headache. By following the questionnaire analysis outlined in this chapter, the operational auditor can help a department become more efficient and effective.

As materials management has become more computerized, management's understanding of inventory problems has decreased. Therefore, managers may spend less time tackling the problems of materials management than before. Basically, receiving and management of inventories require the proper coordination of storage space, equipment, and people. These three factors are linked by receiving reports and materials requisitions. It is the responsibility of the department manager to see that the three factors of space, equipment, and people combine to get the most work done. It is the responsibility of the operational auditor to help by pointing out ways these three critical factors can be utilized more efficiently and effectively.

Storage space is often a fixed quantity, but the quantity and quality of equipment and people can be changed. To this end, an operational auditor may wish to obtain specialized knowledge concerning materials handling equipment: catalogs are available from the suppliers. Too many companies lack adequate equipment. This creates more physical work for employees, which in turn results in more injuries and greater morale problems.

To make matters worse for the materials handling department, there can be a difference of opinion between the department foreman and top management about what constitutes a problem. For example, top management may think the company has a problem of excessive inventories or, say, inventory shortages. For the materials handling employees, excessive inventories (or shortages) are not problems but rather symptoms of problems. In other words, to the extent that top management gives any consideration to department problems, they will state the problem as excessive inventory (or shortage). This does not help the department foreman solve the problem; he will still have to conduct an investigation to diagnose the underlying problem. Unfortunately, the foreman normally does not have the time to locate the cause of inventory problems—this is the job of the operational auditor.

Fortunately (for the auditor), the same problems arise in most Receiving and materials handling departments. Therefore, the standardized questionnaire in this chapter (Exhibit 15-1) can be applied almost anywhere. In general, the underlying problems are often the result of inadequate facilities, poor internal control, inadequate communication, inaccurate perpetual records or product data, unskilled or undereducated workers, or poor morale. These areas can be identified by the operational auditor. The solutions to the problems may not come quickly, owing to the many interrelationships involved, but the sooner problems are identified, the earlier solutions can be implemented.

sixteen

THE TREASURY FUNCTION

The responsibilities assumed by the company treasurer vary widely among companies. In some companies, many financial functions are performed outside the treasurer's office. In many other organizations, the treasurer performs a broad range of functions. In other situations, one function may be performed at a level higher—or lower—than that of the treasurer. Nevertheless, there is a basic core of financial practices that can be identified as the treasurer's responsibility in the majority of organizations. These basic functions include the receipt, disbursement, protection, and custody of cash and securities; supervision of bond issues; preparation of confidential payrolls; management of real estate tax problems; and negotiating and placing insurance.

There may be some question of where the duties of the controller end and those of the treasurer begin. Actually, there should be a close relationship between the two. The treasurer usually selects the banks and other financial intermediaries used by an organization. The handling of cash is usually done by the treasurer, or someone on the treasurer's staff (usually the cashier). The controller's department, on the other hand, is responsible for keeping a record of all assets maintained, but does not have access to those assets.

The duties of the treasurer generally include most or all of the following:

Maintains custody of all company monies and funds

Endorses checks, notes, and bonds

Opens company accounts at banks or other depositories designated by the president or board of directors

Signs stock certificates (sometimes this function is performed by the secretary)

Maintains custody of investment securities

Arranges for insurance coverage

Serves as a member of the board of directors and on the finance committee

Verifies property tax assessments

Forecasts funds flows

Procures needed financing

Invests surplus funds

Oversees the extension of credit

Prepares confidential payrolls

Disburses money for interest and dividends

Oversees activities of the corporate registrar and transfer agent

The treasurer is appointed by the board of directors and, in the absence of a financial vice president, reports directly to the board. If a company has a financial vice president, the treasurer is generally responsible to that individual. The treasurer is normally equal in rank to the corporate secretary and the controller.

Unlike the questionnaires appearing in previous chapters, the treasury questionnaire (Exhibit 16-1) is concerned primarily with effectiveness, placing less emphasis on efficiency. This is because the treasurer's department, if operating effectively, is not a high-cost operation. Also, the many variations in activities from one enterprise to the next make it difficult to generalize about ways of increasing efficiency in a given department. The Treasury questionnaire is much shorter than those for other departments, containing only four sections:

General

Custodianship

Insurance

Financing

GENERAL

The General section begins by asking about the existence of a procedures manual which delineates the functions, responsibilities, and authority of the treasurer. The manual should explain questions of obligations or authority. Conflicts over jurisdiction should be immediately solved by reference to the manual. The manual should also help prepare employees

EXHIBIT 16-1   Treasury Questionnaire

General

1. Is there a procedures manual which delineates the functions, responsibilities, and authority of the treasurer?

2. Does the treasurer supervise the preparation of cash budgets?

3. Does the treasurer oversee the activities of the registrar and the transfer agent?

4. Is there a specific policy regarding investment of excess funds?

5. Does the treasurer supervise the preparation and maintenance of the confidential payroll for key employees?

6. Does the treasurer supervise the discharge of property tax liabilities?

7. Are relations with tax authorities handled effectively?

8. Are purchases of securities from, or sales to, officers and directors prohibited?

9. Are two signatures required for any purchase or sale of securities?

10. Are marketable securities registered in the name of the company?

11. Are records of security transactions made (at least) in duplicate so that both the treasurer and controller will have a copy?

Custodianship

12. Is the custodian function separate from the record-keeping function?

13. Does the treasurer maintain custody of securities and deeds?

14. Do you supervise the extension of credit and the collection of receivables?

15. Do you utilize every possible legal means of accelerating payments from customers?

16. Do you utilize a bank's lock-box service for customer checks?

17. Does the treasurer arrange banking relationships?

18. Are endorsement signature stamps stored in a vault?

19. Are securities and deeds kept either in a bank or in a fireproof burglar-resistant safe or vault?

20. Is the presence of at least two people from different offices required when vaults are visited?

EXHIBIT 16-1 (Continued)

21. Are periodic surprise inventories made of securities held in vaults?

22. Are records of serial numbers maintained for securities owned?

23. Is the treasurer responsible for the reconciliation of cash balances?

Insurance

24. Are the treasurer and all members of the treasurer's department bonded?

25. Does the treasurer negotiate with more than one company when arranging insurance coverage?

26. Are all tangible assets, including buildings, equipment, and inventories, fully insured?

27. Are risk reduction possibilities made known to management?

28. Are claims handled quickly and efficiently?

29. Has the company considered self-insurance?

30. Are you aware of coinsurance clauses in your policies?

31. Do you have professional liability insurance to cover any misdeeds of your employees and directors?

Financing

32. Does the treasurer arrange for loans from financial institutions?

33. Does the treasurer work closely with the underwriters when considering a stock issue?

34. Is the treasurer notified of cash needs far enough in advance to enable him to carry out his duties most effectively?

35. Does he bargain for lower interest rates?

36. Has the department considered factoring as a source of financing?

37. Does the department maintain good investor relations?

38. Are good relations maintained with securities analysts?

39. Has the possibility of a dividend reinvestment plan been investigated?

40. If the company is involved in foreign currency transactions, are hedging operations used, or have they been considered?

41. Are loan restrictions monitored under the department's scrutiny?

for greater responsibility by providing a certain amount of training for higher-level positions.

The second question asks whether the treasurer's department assists in the preparation of cash budgets. Since cash receipts, disbursements, custody, and procurement all fall within the realm of the treasurer, it makes sense to have the treasurer participate also in the preparation of cash forecasts.

Question 3 asks whether the treasurer oversees the activities of the registrar and the transfer agent. Stock registration and transfer have historically been included in the duties of the treasurer and they still are in smaller corporations. In large corporations, however, the job is usually done by outside agents. In these cases, the treasurer is still responsible, but no longer performs the related detail work.

The subject of Question 4 is whether the company has a specific policy covering investment of excess funds. For example, are investments to be made whenever idle cash reaches a certain level? Such a policy simplifies the treasurer's work. This author has often received a negative response to this question from small clients, but the lack of a policy reflected lack of excess cash—this is a problem they would gladly face.

Questions 5, 6, and 7 ask about special duties usually performed by the treasurer. One of these is the preparation of a confidential payroll for high-paid officials. Relations with property tax authorities is another important area. The treasurer's department should make sure that property is properly assessed and taxes paid on time. Studies should be made to determine whether assessments made on the company are comparable to those made on other local enterprises. The treasurer should also consider ways in which property taxes can be reduced, for example, by leasing of equipment, obtaining inventories on consignment, or moving—to the suburbs, perhaps.

Question 8 asks whether there are any prohibitions on securities transactions with officers and directors of the company. This is simply a question of independence. There may be absolutely nothing wrong with the transaction, but someday someone is likely to accuse the treasurer of profiting from a transaction that was not conducted at arms length. To avoid any taint of unfavorable publicity, it is best to avoid investment transactions with insiders.

The final three questions in the General section are related to internal control. Requiring two signatures on investment transactions is examined by Question 9. Such a policy helps protect a company against a treasurer who would sell the securities and then abscond with the money. Question 10 is similarly concerned with controls in asking whether securities are registered in the organization's name (not in the treasurer's name). The last question checks to be sure that securities records are prepared in duplicate so that both the treasurer and the controller can have a copy.

CUSTODIANSHIP

The first question under Custodianship is also related to the concept of separation of duties. All accountants know that the custody of assets should be separate from the records supporting these assets. Question 13 goes a step further and asks whether the treasurer is responsible for the custody of securities and deeds. Inasmuch as this is one of the major roles of the treasurer, the question will rarely elicit a negative response. However, the auditor may occasionally get the impression—either from the respondent or through observation—that a few deeds or securities are not under the treasurer's control. The operational auditor should then investigate the reasons for such exceptions.

Another of the treasurer's custodianship responsibilities relates to receivables. Question 14 asks whether the treasurer exercises control over extending credit and collecting receivables. Such functions as changing credit terms, placing bad debts with collection agencies, and authorizing bad debt write-offs are ultimately the responsibility of the treasurer. However, in some companies, these duties are handled by a credit department which is closely allied with the sales staff. In these cases, the influence of the treasurer in credit decisions becomes negligible. Questions 15 and 16 pursue the subject of receivables. Both these questions ask whether specific efforts are made to accelerate collections from customers. Such efforts might include offering cash discounts for prompt payment or free freight for prepaid orders. One of the easiest ways to accelerate cash inflows is to have customers mail their checks to bank lock-boxes in various parts of the country. The use of lock-boxes can speed up cash flows by a couple of days, and lock-boxes also serve as an effective internal control device.

Question 17 asks whether it is the treasurer who arranges banking relationships. No other employee should have the authority to open an account in the company's name (although sometimes the treasurer will be told by the president or board of directors which banks to use).

Questions 18 and 19 ask whether signature stamps, securities, and deeds are kept in a vault. This is obviously an important internal control procedure. Whenever securities are examined or taken from the vault for any reason, there should be two people involved from different departments (Question 20), usually the treasurer and the controller. Question 21 inquires whether periodic inventories are made of vault holdings; these inventory counts should be made on a surprise basis. During a physical inventory, securities should be checked not only for quantity (the proper number of shares, for example) but also for serial numbers. Checking serial numbers reduces the risk of "borrowing" securities (perhaps for personal-loan collateral), which are later replaced with a similar security. Question 22 asks whether a record of serial numbers is maintained to permit a detailed audit.

The last question in the Custodianship section asks whether the treasurer is responsible for the reconciliation of bank accounts. This function can sometimes properly be performed by an internal auditor. The purpose of the question, however, is to be sure that reconciliations are not being performed in the controller's department. Because the controller's department writes the checks, another department should do the reconciliations.

INSURANCE

Placing insurance coverage is a duty that normally belongs in the treasurer's realm. The first question in the Insurance section relates to insurance for employees' misappropriations. Are treasury employees bonded? Good internal control requires that all employees who have access to cash or securities be bonded: in the event of a defalcation, the company would be reimbursed by the insurer. Also, the possibility of legal action by the bonding company will help motivate employees to be more honest.

Question 25 asks whether the company negotiates with more than one insurance company when arranging coverage. In fact, a company should seek as much advice as possible from a broker, and then ask the broker to offer an array of possible coverages. Most companies are surprised at the wide variety of policy premiums that are available to the treasurer who shops around.

Insurance activity relates in some way to almost every aspect of a business. Therefore, Question 26 is important, because it asks whether all assets are covered. Some companies, of course, may not wish full coverage, but there should be good reasons for the partial coverage. Excessively high premiums would represent a good reason in many cases. Few companies have complete coverage, in that they have a deductible clause in their policy. However, the auditor should not equate the deductible clause with less-than-full coverage. Such clauses save substantially on premiums and should be interpreted as a sign of a good cost-conscious management.

If a company does not in fact have complete coverage, the auditor should place special emphasis on Question 30, which asks whether the treasurer is aware of the coinsurance clause in policies. Most policies try to encourage policy holders to maintain full coverage. The coinsurance clause will stipulate that, if a company does not have full coverage or close to it (80% is typical), then the company is a coinsurer along with the insurance company. This means the policy holder has to share the burden of any loss along with the insurance company. As an example, assume that a company holds a $40,000 policy on a $100,000 building. If a company suffered a $40,000 fire loss, the insurance company would probably pay off $20,000 or less. The owner of the building (the policyholder) would bear the remainder of the loss. The auditor should explain the coinsurance clause to the client because it is not always understood by people who have never suffered a loss.

Question 27 is concerned with whether management is aware of a variety of risk reduction possibilities. A few simple, low-cost changes can sometimes produce substantial savings in insurance premiums. One policyholder, for example, recently installed a dozen additional fire extinguishers and reduced his insurance premiums several thousand dollars a year. Prohibiting open fires near an insured building or prohibiting smoking can also reduce premiums for some companies.

The treasurer's department is responsible for handling claims on insurance policies. Question 28 asks whether claims are handled quickly and efficiently. Claims must be filed within a specified time and be supported by proper documentation.

Question 29 asks whether the company has considered self-insurance coverage. "Self-insurance" really means no insurance. Self-insurance obviates the payment of premiums, but subjects the company to large losses in the event of a catastrophe. Generally, a company should not consider self-insurance unless it is quite large and is geographically spread out. Wide dispersion of company assets reduces the chances of one catastrophe that would put the organization out of business.

The final question in the Insurance section asks whether the company maintains liability insurance to cover misdeeds of employees and directors. In the past, most companies did not consider liability coverage necessary, but in today's litigous world such coverage is practically mandatory.

FINANCING

Arranging financing is a major responsibility of the treasurer. The first two questions in the Financing section ask whether the treasurer fulfills these responsibilities with respect to banks and underwriters.

Question 34 asks whether the treasurer is notified of cash needs far enough in advance to arrange good terms. It is obviously preferable to acquire cash for future needs than for immediate needs. Immediate needs shorten the time available to bargain with lenders and makes lenders more reluctant to do business with the treasurer. Bargaining for lower interest rates is covered also in Question 35. Saving just a quarter of a percentage point, for example, can make a big difference on a large loan or on a long-term loan.

This author learned about the benefits of bargaining while serving as consultant to an industrial outfit. The company was experiencing dire cash flow problems and faced bankruptcy if it could not obtain a $500,000 loan within a week. Fortunately, a small local bank offered the needed funds at two points above prime, which was better than management had hoped. On the day of the signing, the company's attorney sat in on the meeting with the bankers. When the attorney heard the interest rate, he shouted that he could not permit the company to sign the note: the rate was too high; the money could be obtained for a point less at a competing bank in town. The entire board of directors argued with the attorney that the rate was fair. The board knew that the company had been turned down at every other bank in town. Just as the disgusted officers were about to throw the attorney out, he requested a private conversation with his clients. After the bankers had closed the door, the attorney explained that he was bluffing the bankers. He knew the company had been turned down by the other banks, but the bankers did not. Sure enough, the bluff worked. When the bankers re-entered the room, they said they had just talked to their offices; it seemed that conditions in the economy had changed and they could make the loan at a half-point lower than they had previously offered. Such bargaining is dramatic, but much less nerve-racking when the funds are not needed immediately.

The question of whether the treasurer has considered factoring as a source of funds is asked not so much because factoring is valuable in itself, but because too many financial managers overlook factoring of receivables. Factoring has historically been a last-gasp type of financing. It was known as a high-cost source of funds that was used only as a last resort (except in the textile industry, which has used factoring for decades). Today, however, the image of factoring has changed. New banking laws and the introduction of the computer have made factoring a very competitive industry. Most companies can now factor their receivables at a rate only slightly higher than prime. At the same time, the company can abolish its credit department and its Accounts Receivables department; these services are provided by the factor.

Questions 37, 38, and 39 are concerned with investor relations. This includes sending magazines to stockholders, giving personal responses to stockholder questions, and speaking before groups of securities analysts. One of the newest investor relations tools is the dividend reinvestment plan. These plans permit stockholders to reinvest dividends in company stock at a very low cost. In fact, many corporations now pay all costs of administering dividend reinvestment plans.

Question 40 asks whether the treasurer performs hedging operations with respect to foreign currencies. Some companies may wish to "play the market" with respect to foreign currency translations, because there is often just as much chance for gain as for loss. However, most companies would rather hedge if foreign currency transactions are large. Hedging means the company will have neither gain nor loss because of foreign currency fluctuations.

The final question asks whether the treasurer closely monitors loan restrictions. Because the treasurer arranges for loans, it is also his responsibility to see that the company does not violate any attached restrictions. This is a very important task because a minor violation could mean that the borrower is technically in default on the loan.

SUMMARY

The treasurer basically performs functions associated with capital funds. The job begins with the recognition of cash needs, extends to obtaining and allocating funds, and ends with the return of funds to investors and creditors. Along the way, the treasurer builds relationships with financial institutions, investors, underwriters, and securities analysts. The treasurer also has custody of cash and securities, arranges insurance coverage, and monitors foreign currencies.

Although the activities of the treasurer differ from one organization to the next, and some of the duties may occasionally be performed by the controller or the corporate secretary, this chapter has highlighted the activities typically handled by the treasurer.

INDEX

263